OUR MOTHER
SAINT PAUL

OUR MOTHER SAINT PAUL

Beverly Roberts Gaventa

Westminster John Knox Press
LOUISVILLE • LONDON

Scripture quotations from the New Revised Standard Version of the Bible are copyright © 1989 by the Division of Christian Education of the National Council of the Churches of Christ in the U.S.A. and are used by permission.

The following material by Beverly Roberts Gaventa has been previously published and is now slightly revised for republication in this volume: "The Maternity of Paul: An Exegetical Study of Galatians 4:19" in *The Conversation Continues: Studies in Paul and John in Honor of J. Louis Martyn* (Nashville, TN: Abingdon Press, 1990); reprinted with permission of Abingdon Press. "Mother's Milk and Ministry in 1 Corinthians 3" in *Theology and Ethics in Paul and His Interpreters: Essays in Honor of Victor Paul Furnish* (Nashville, TN: Abingdon Press, 1996); reprinted with permission of Abingdon Press. "Is Galatians Just a 'Guy Thing'?" *Interpretation: A Journal of Bible and Theology* (2000); reprinted with permission of Union Theological Seminary and Presbyterian School of Christian Education. "The Singularity of the Gospel: A Reading of Galatians," originally published in *Pauline Theology,* volume 1, *Thessalonians, Philippians, Galatians, Philemon* (ed. Jouette M. Bassler; SBLSym; Atlanta: Society of Biblical Literature, 2002), 147–50, © Society of Biblical Literature; reprinted by permission. "God Handed Them Over: Reading Romans 1:18–32 Apocalyptically," *Australian Biblical Review* 53; reprinted by permission of the publisher. "The Cosmic Power of Sin in Paul's Letter to the Romans: Toward a Widescreen Edition," *Interpretation: A Journal of Bible and Theology* (2004); reprinted with permission of Union Theological Seminary and Presbyterian School of Christian Education. "The God Who Will Not Be 'Taken-for-Granted'" in *The Ending of Mark and the Ends of God: Essays in Memory of Donald Harrisville Juel* (Louisville, KY: Westminster John Knox Press, 2005); reprinted with permission of Westminster John Knox Press. "Galatians 1 and 2: Autobiography as Paradigm" in *Novum Testamentum* 28 (1986); reprinted with permission of the publisher. "Our Mother Saint Paul: Toward a Recovery of a Neglected Theme" in *The Princeton Seminary Bulletin* (1996); reprinted with permission of the publisher.

Book design by Drew Stevens
Cover design by Lisa Buckley
Cover art by Jay Mulford

First edition
Published by Westminster John Knox Press
Louisville, Kentucky

This book is printed on acid-free paper that meets the American National Standards Institute Z39.48 standard. ♾

07 08 09 10 11 12 13 14 15 16 — 10 9 8 7 6 5 4 3 2 1

Library of Congress Cataloging-in-Publication Data

Gaventa, Beverly Roberts.
  Our mother Saint Paul / Beverly Roberts Gaventa.
     p. cm.
  Includes index.
  ISBN 978-0-664-23149-1 (alk. paper)
  1. Bible. N.T. Epistles of Paul—Theology. 2. Bible. N.T. Epistles of Paul—Language, style. 3. Metaphor in the Bible. 4. Motherhood in the Bible. I. Title.
  BS2651.G38 2007
  225.9'2—dc22
                                2007003348

For
Susan Deborah King
and
James C. Gertmenian

Contents

Introduction

Some years ago, in response to a stray comment made by a visiting lecturer about the near absence of feminine imagery in the New Testament in general and in the letters of Paul in particular, I happened to think about Gal 4:19, where Paul refers to himself with the language of a woman in labor. I turned to the Greek text, noting for the first time the twists and turns of logic that I discuss below in chapter 2. Then I turned to the commentaries on my shelves in search of some simple explanation. Finding none that satisfied and some that actually irritated me, I went back to the text, curiosity thoroughly awakened. A day passed without my even noticing: the text had me in its grasp and would not let me go.

Over the years that have elapsed since that first day of studying maternal imagery in Paul, I have realized that I was retrieving Gal 4:19 and related texts not just for myself but for many other readers as well. Implicit conventions that govern our reading of Paul suggest that the texts that pertain to women are to be found in Gal 3:28, 1 Cor 7, 1 Cor 11:2–16, and perhaps 1 Cor 14:33b–36. Even Rom 16:1–16 has escaped attention until recently. Texts that employ maternal imagery have been overlooked almost entirely. So, in part 1 I take up four passages in which Paul uses maternal imagery. In three of those passages Paul is speaking of himself and in the fourth of all creation in language that is unmistakably associated with childbirth and nursing.

But I am doing more in this book than reclaiming texts that have been neglected for generations. This work is also a study in Pauline theology, and two underlying perspectives on Paul's theology characterize these chapters. The first perspective is that Paul's urgent need to announce and interpret what God has done in Jesus Christ pervades everything he writes, so that the investigation of Paul's theology cannot be limited to discrete portions of his letters. In Galatians, for example, theology is pervasive; it is not confined to his remarks about faith and law in chapters 3–4. The autobiographical account in Gal 1–2 is neither memoir nor personal defense but is instead deeply connected with the account of God's action in freeing "us from the present evil age" (Gal 1:4). Galatians 4:19 is not, as commonly understood, an emotional outburst peripheral to the real "meat" of the letter; it reflects Paul's convictions about the christocentric character of the gospel.

The claim that Paul's theology saturates the letters as a whole, that they are not to be divided into sections that are "theological" and other sections that are "personal" or "practical" or "ethical," runs against the scholarly grain. I refer not simply to those scholarly approaches that eschew the notion of Paul as theologian, but also to those that limit themselves to passages that fit easily within the traditional loci of Protestant theology (e.g., revelation, Christology, soteriology), implicitly seeking to disentangle Paul's theological assertions from their epistolary homes, as if God's action in Jesus Christ were a single, removable aspect of Paul's work rather than the decisive event from which all else follows.

The second perspective is that Paul's theology requires a much larger framework than has usually been thought to be the case. Recent decades have witnessed an important shift away from interpreting Paul as addressing the individual human being; from many quarters the insistence has rightly come that Paul is concerned not simply about the individual but especially about the community of faith. More specifically, Paul is concerned about the reconciliation of Jew and Gentile. I argue in part 2 that this extension has not yet gone far enough. It is not sufficient to observe that Paul is concerned for the community as distinct from the individual, whether that community be described as the church, Israel, or the entirety of humankind. Paul's theological horizon is nothing less than the cosmos itself which is in need of deliverance, not merely from human misdeeds but also from the grasp of powers that are aligned against God.

These two perspectives seem to move in different directions, one focusing on the theological interpretation of Paul's own experience, the other on the infinitely larger canvas of the cosmos. Yet the two conclusions are complementary. As I show in part 2, Paul's comments about himself and his leadership are part and parcel of perceiving and interpreting God's apocalyptic act, invading the territory held captive to cosmic powers (such as Sin and Death), cosmic opponents of God. Conventional thinking about human leadership has no place in the cross and resurrection of Jesus Christ.

Ernst Käsemann once wrote that God claims the entirety of human life because God "is no longer leaving the world to itself" (see p. 159 below). The chapters that follow offer evidence of the rightness of Käsemann's words. The title, *Our Mother Saint Paul*, refers to the startling language Paul applies to himself, language of a woman in labor, language of a mother nursing her child. It extends, however, to refer to Paul's role as a nurturer of communities who know themselves to be in the hands of the God who will not leave the world alone, who reclaims the world for God alone.

A number of these chapters were published earlier. Collecting them in this book has allowed me the opportunity to clarify some points, to indicate changes in my own thinking, and especially to show their interconnectedness. I have taken into account at least some subsequent developments in the scholarly literature, although I have not attempted to engage all the recent publications on any text or topic. Some chapters were originally written for a scholarly audience and others for pastors. Where Greek is required for the argument, I have offered translation in order to make the argument accessible. Translations are my own unless otherwise indicated.

Because this book has undergone a long period of gestation (to borrow a metaphor), my debts to colleagues at Princeton and elsewhere, to many students, and to a number of research assistants, are beyond recalling or recounting. In the final stage of writing and revising, I have been helped in various ways by Shane Berg, Charles B. Cousar, Cleo M. Kearns, Jacqueline Lapsley, J. Louis Martyn, Carey Newman, Kate Skrebutenas, J. Ross Wagner, and Patrick J. Willson. The support and encouragement of Stephanie Egnotovich have been invaluable. And I would be irresponsible indeed not to record my appreciation for my graduate assistants Carla Works and Brittany Wilson, who assisted in preparation of the manuscript. My friend Jay Mulford has offered her own stunning interpretation of Paul for the cover, and I am deeply grateful for her artistic gifts and her generosity.

Publication offers the welcome opportunity of acknowledging debts of other kinds as well. My family and I have long rejoiced in the friendship of Susan ("Sam") Deborah King and James C. Gertmenian, both in and out of season. This book is dedicated to Jim and Sam with gratitude, on the occasion of their thirty-fifth wedding anniversary.

PART 1

Maternal Imagery in the Letters of Paul

Maternal Imagery in the Letters of Paul

Long before Paul's letters were the object of scholarly investigation, they were read aloud to gatherings of Christians in cities scattered across the Roman Empire. In 1 Thessalonians he sharply admonishes that the letter be read in the presence of the community (5:27). At the conclusion of Romans, he commends the deacon Phoebe, who evidently delivers the letter and almost certainly reads it to house churches across the residential areas of Trastevere and the Appian lowlands (16:1–2).[1] As interpreters we strain to catch a glimpse of those gatherings: How many people are present? What is their ethnic identity? From what social classes do they come? What is the ratio of male to female participants?

We might also wonder about the sounds and smells of these gatherings. We know that the cities of the first Christian century were teeming with people, which means that they were also dense with the sounds and smells of food and disease and death.[2] The early gatherings of Christians must also have been filled with birth and new life. In some gathering, a midwife was called out to attend a delivery. In another, she returned—with joyous news or somber? In other gatherings, wet nurses brought their charges, whose fussing and cooing sprinkled the reading of Paul's letter. However removed the Roman notion of children and childhood might be from that of the contemporary West, the sights and smells and sounds of infants could not be alien to these assemblies.[3]

Although it has seldom been recognized, the real business of birth and infancy comes to expression in Paul's letters also:

> But we became infants in your midst, as if a nurse taking care of her own children. (1 Thess 2:7)[4]

> Then sudden destruction will come upon them as labor pangs upon a pregnant woman. (1 Thess 5:3)

> God set me apart from the womb of my mother and called me through his grace. (Gal 1:15)

> My children, with whom I am in labor again until Christ is formed in you . . . (Gal 4:19)

> But, brothers and sisters, I could not speak with you as spiritual persons but only as fleshly persons, as infants in Christ. I gave you milk to drink, not solid food, for you could not take solid food, and even now you cannot. (1 Cor 3:1–2)

> Now last of all, as to something monstrously born, he appeared also to me. (1 Cor 15:8)

> For we know that all creation groans together and is in labor together until now. (Rom 8:22)

As we strain for a glimpse of these early gatherings, we may ask how such texts played in the imaginations of their earliest auditors.

In the next four chapters I will explore the most significant of these passages,[5] but first it is important to introduce maternal imagery, asking whether it is something that can rightly be called a "topic" or a "thread" in the Pauline letters, or whether it is simply a handful of disparate images. Four considerations prompt me to regard it as a topic.

First, most of these passages involve complex metaphorical movements, movements I have come to think of as "metaphors squared." When Paul says in 1 Cor 4:15 that he begat the Corinthians, he speaks metaphorically. He transfers the fathering act of which he is presumably capable from the begetting of a physical child to the begetting of a spiritual child. Similarly, when he describes himself as a "skilled master builder" (3:10) or a farmer who plants a field (3:6), he employs metaphors that are relatively simple and direct.

All that changes when he writes, "I gave you milk to drink, not solid food." While it is within the realm of possibility to imagine Paul as "a skilled master builder" who laid a foundation, or as a farmer who planted a field, or as a father to children, he could never be a nursing mother. That metaphor involves a kind of double switch that I intend by the expression "a metaphor squared." First, he metaphorizes (with apologies for the barbarism) the gospel as milk, then he "squares" that image by metaphorizing himself as the mother whose body supplies the milk.

An extrabiblical example helps to clarify this point. Among my dearest friends is a male colleague who is several years younger than myself. I have actually introduced him on occasion as my "little brother." Had I introduced him as my "little sister," I would have been squaring the metaphor—taking a friendship, metaphorizing it by means of an appropriate familial relationship, and then metaphorizing the metaphor.

More complex than 1 Cor 3:2 is 1 Thess 2:7: "But we became infants in your midst, as if a nurse taking care of her own children."[6] First Paul speaks of himself and his colleagues as "infants," then he abruptly takes up the nurse metaphor. When Paul identifies himself as a nurse caring for her own children, he again speaks metaphorically about his relationship with the Thessalonians. As in all metaphors, the relationship is figurative, but here also the figure has been squared: first, Paul metaphorizes the relationship between himself and the Thessalonians as that between family members; then he metaphorizes himself into the role of the nurse-mother.

The most complex of these passages, metaphorically speaking, is Gal 4:19: "My children, with whom I am in labor again until Christ is formed in you . . ." As in other passages, Paul is the mother. Here he is in the process of giving birth *again*. (How exactly it is possible to give birth a second time we will not pause to consider at present.) Paul remains in labor, not until the child is born, but until Christ is born in the child. Anyone who does not perceive the difficulty this verse involves should attempt to sketch its dynamics.

The point is simply that, time and again, these passages involve complex metaphorical moves.[7]

A second consideration that leads me to connect these texts with one another is that they cannot be dismissed as mere variations on the larger theme of paternal imagery. That would seem to be obvious, since mothers and fathers are not customarily confused with one another, but apparently it is not obvious. Commentaries on these passages regularly say things such as: "Paul often refers to himself as the father of believers; see also 1 Cor 4:15." The two sets of texts are understood as being part and parcel of the same phenomenon, and in one sense they are, because both employ metaphors of family to speak of the Christian community.

The distinction between them is important, however. At one level, it is important because we have too long neglected any sort of references to women or imagery involving women. Just as we failed to ask about the apostle Junia and the household of Chloe, we failed to notice these astonishing references to the maternity of a male apostle. As one conversation partner, not incidentally a woman, commented in response to my initial work on this problem, "I have been reading the Bible my entire life, and I never even noticed these texts."

Beyond this first-level task of retrieval, however, these passages convey something quite distinctive from what is conveyed with paternal imagery. Maternal imagery appears in contexts referring to the ongoing nature of the relationship between Paul and the congregations he founded; paternal imagery, by contrast, regularly refers to the initial stage of Christian preaching and conversion.[8]

English translations sometimes render this distinction obscure. The NRSV of Philemon 10 says that Paul became the father of Onesimus, a translation that might suggest a protracted period of care and concern. The Greek, however, is more concise; Paul says he begat Onesimus, and the context makes it clear that he refers to the fact that he is the one who introduced Onesimus to the Christian faith. Similarly, in 1 Cor 4:15, Paul refers to his role in the initial formation of the church at Corinth as an act of begetting and appeals to that role to persuade the Corinthians to continue to listen to him. The biological act of fathering takes place in a single instant, and Paul's references to begetting believers are metaphorically congruent with that biological fact: he refers to a single event in past time.[9]

Apart from these two passages in Philemon and in 1 Corinthians, only two others refer unmistakably to Paul's paternity. In Phil 2:22 he compares the relationship between himself and Timothy with that between father and son. Since he is referring to a specific working relationship rather than to his relationship to believers in general, that text seems to fall outside our purview. In 1 Thess 2:11–12 (just following the use of maternal imagery in 2:7), he speaks of the apostles as dealing with the Thessalonians "as a father with his own children, urging and encouraging you and insisting that you lead a life worthy of God. . . ." Here paternity does involve a process of maturation, of course; however, in 1 Thess 2, Paul is contrasting his mission with those who would flatter and seek praise and make demands (2:5–7), so that he may have a particular reason for drawing attention to "urging and encouraging" in this context. That is, Paul distances himself from the Sophist who manipulates his disciples for his own ends.

Incidentally, these four texts are the only ones I can identify in which Paul uses paternal imagery, apart of course from his references to God as father.[10] Statistically, that means that Paul uses maternal imagery more often than he does paternal imagery, a feature that is impressive, especially when we consider its virtual absence from most discussions of the Pauline letters.

I have left out of consideration the occasions when Paul addresses believers as his children without clearly depicting himself either as father or as mother. In 2 Cor 6:13, he writes, "I speak as to children—open wide your hearts also." And in 2 Cor 12:14 he defends his decision not to be a burden to the Corinthians by analogy with parental responsibilities: "For children ought not to lay up for their parents but parents for their children" (NRSV). Other than perpetuating the familial relationship between apostle and congregation, these texts add little to our understanding of Paul as either father or mother.

To return to the question of the difference between Paul's use of paternal and maternal metaphors, it is striking that none of the instances in which Paul uses maternal imagery can be read as referring to a single event that occurred at one moment in the past. Quite the contrary, when Paul uses maternal language, the image always requires the elapse of some extended period of time: a woman who is pregnant, after all, is pregnant for a period of time and does not control when her labor will begin; the process of labor itself generally extends over a period of time; the physical nurture of feeding an infant is seemingly endless; the care of a nurse-mother lasts until the child is able to perform certain tasks independently. Later, parents may feel as if infancy lasts only moments, but for a nursing mother, a 3:00 a.m. feeding can be a glimpse of eternity.

Whether or not Paul is conscious of the choices he makes, the biological and, to a certain extent, cultural differences between mothering and fathering shape the differences between these two sets of texts. However much the paternal metaphors and the maternal metaphors have in common, they are not simply interchangeable with one another. To take a particularly telling example, it is hard to imagine recasting the laboring image of Gal 4:19 in the language of fathering.

A third factor that connects these texts is that in them Paul describes the apostolic office; he is not referring to himself in general terms but to his vocation. Given that most of Paul's statements of self-reference have to do with his apostolic role, that claim is almost tautological, but the distinction is nevertheless important. These metaphors do not serve merely to decorate Paul's text or to illustrate a point; instead, they are a vital part of communicating what the apostolic task involves.

The connection between maternal imagery and apostolic task is easy to see in 1 Thess 2:7, where not only the verse but the passage as a whole describes the work of an apostle. And in Gal 4:19 Paul explicitly applies the image of a woman's birthing labor to his work as apostle in sustaining Christians in the Galatian churches. Even in 1 Cor 3:2, however, where he speaks of feeding with milk rather than with solid food, he is concerned both with the maturity (or the lack of maturity) of the Corinthians *and* with his own task as apostle, as the remainder of the chapter and chapter 4 make clear. And in the strange case of 1 Cor 15:8, where he speaks of himself as a "monstrous birth," he is referring to his calling as an apostle and makes that connection explicit in the very next sentence. Something in Paul's understanding of the apostolic task causes him to turn to this language of maternity.

A fourth feature that connects several of these texts is their association with apocalyptic contexts. Obviously that is the case with 1 Thess 5:3, where the topic under discussion is the "day of the Lord." Similarly, Rom 8:22 depicts the longing of creation for its future redemption. Although 1 Cor 15:8 ("something monstrously born") does not directly concern the apocalyptic future, certainly the larger discussion of the resurrection and the final triumph of God does concern apocalyptic.

In connection with apocalyptic, Gal 4:19 is the text that proves most interesting. Paul's comparison of himself to a woman in labor may well derive from the literary convention of using the birthpangs of a woman to refer to the suddenness of the end time or its unpredictability. By applying that conventional metaphor to himself, to his own work, Paul associates his own apostolic vocation with the anguish anticipated in an apocalyptic era and recalls for the Galatians their crucifixion with Christ. As such, Gal 4:19 employs a conventional metaphor, that of the anguish of a woman in labor, to identify Paul's apostolic work with the apocalyptic expectation of the whole created order.

By virtue of their unusual metaphoric structure, their distinctiveness from paternal imagery, their association with Paul's apostolic vocation, and their location in apocalyptic contexts, then, these texts merit our attention under the general rubric of maternal imagery.

QUESTIONS

Of the many approaches that are helpful in understanding Paul's use of maternal imagery, three seem essential: history of traditions, sociocultural context, and gender construction. First, attention to the history of traditions within these passages will help us to see where Paul may have acquired some of these expressions and how he has employed them.

Most obvious here is the way in which Gal 4:19 replays maternal imagery in texts such as Jer 6:24:

> We have heard news of them, our hands fall helpless; anguish has taken hold of us, pain as of a woman in labor. (NRSV)[11]

And Paul's depiction of himself as a nursing mother in 1 Thess 2:7 recalls Moses' frustrated complaint to God:

> Did I conceive all this people? Did I give birth to them, that you should say to me, "Carry them in your bosom, as a nurse carries a sucking child"? (Num 11:12 NRSV)

Somewhat less aggrieved, in the Hodayoth of Qumran the Teacher of Righteousness rejoices:

> You have appointed me as a father to the children of mercy
> and as guardian to men of portent.
> They open their mouth wide like a nursing ch[ild],
> and as a child delights in the embrace of its guardian.
>
> *(1QH^a 15.20–22)*[12]

The maternal imagery in these and other texts promises to enhance our sense of ways in which biblical and other Jewish traditions (consciously or unconsciously) shape Paul's language, but the history of traditions must be supplemented by attention to the sociocultural context of Paul's usage. What cultural codes are enforced or violated when Paul images himself as a woman in labor or a nurse caring for her own children? Do other men use such imagery and, if so, how?

These questions are exceedingly complex, both because of the vast literature that might be regarded as relevant and also because of the difficulty of deciding what constitutes a parallel. To take but one example, commentators often adduce a passage from Epictetus as a parallel to 1 Cor 3:2. Epictetus asks his audience: "Are you not even yet willing, like little children, to be weaned and to grasp more solid food, and not to cry for mothers and wet nurses—the wailings of old women?" (*Discourses* 2.16.39). Epictetus does make use of the distinction between milk and solid food, although his usage differs dramatically from Paul's. Paul places himself in the middle of the analogy (he is the mother who feeds), but Epictetus stands at arm's length from those who must be weaned. Epictetus also scorns the very role of "mothers and wet nurses," a role Paul claims for himself.

This last observation moves from the issue of parallels to the even more elusive question of how Paul's contemporaries might have heard his use of maternal imagery. The emerging literature on gender-construction in the Greco-Roman world offers some important clues.[13] One of the prominent themes in that discussion is gender hierarchy and the severe loss of pride experienced by a male who was suspected of "going AWOL from [his] assigned place in the gender hierarchy."[14] One could go AWOL by wearing women's clothing, by engaging in certain sexual practices, or simply by not being sufficiently "manly." It is not difficult to imagine that some would hear Paul's use of maternal imagery as an abandoning of his assigned role.

These three approaches are important, but they risk dismantling the metaphors into parts that can be traced and analyzed without looking directly at the metaphors themselves and what they accomplish in their contexts. Here I think recent work in metaphor theory is instructive. First, much discussion of metaphor, beginning with a pivotal essay by Max Black in 1954, attends to the *cognitive character* of metaphor. Precisely how metaphor influences cognition is hotly debated and is not significant for my purposes at present. What is important is to recognize *that* metaphor does not merely decorate or illustrate; it provokes reflection and even insight. Metaphors ask us to change our minds.[15]

Samuel Levin notes that when we encounter a metaphor, especially one that is either novel or still lively, typically we react by noticing what's wrong with it. We reject it out of hand.[16] An example may illustrate my point. An advertising agency was devising a campaign that required some way of identifying the Society of Biblical Literature that would catch the attention of the general public (and I happened to be the contact person for the Society in those negotiations). One draft of a brochure the agency proposed read: "The SBL is the NFL of biblical scholarship." Although the advertising people had my great sympathy for a difficult task, I did reject that particular metaphor out of hand. (And I have not revised my view.)

If a metaphor does work its way with us, however, it forces us to consider things differently. It alters our perspective. Let me offer a somewhat more successful example. During my son's freshman year in high school, the Northeast Corridor experienced an especially fierce winter season. Since his English class was studying metaphor, a teacher who knew how to capitalize on current events asked the students to compose metaphors for snow. One metaphor that emerged was, "Snow is the underside of hell."

That metaphor makes no literal sense. We reject it, seeing initially only the absurd differences between snow and hell. Or we recall other expressions in which snow and hell are treated as opposites, such as, "a snowball's chance in hell." By thinking through the new metaphor, however, especially by recalling the frigid days in the Northeast, we may think differently about both snow and hell. We may see points of similarity. We may change our judgment. We have gained a new perspective.

Eva Fedder Kittay, speaking metaphorically about this aspect of metaphor, says that a metaphor rearranges the furniture of the mind.[17] Take the living room as an example. If I move the sofa across the room and add a chair on the opposite wall and place the coffee table between them, something happens to the room. The room may seem larger, or smaller. It becomes more hospitable or perhaps colder. The changes force us to take a new path through the room. Metaphorically speaking, metaphors do all these things also.

Similarly, when Paul says, "I am in labor [with you] again until Christ is formed in you," he invites the Galatians to contemplate their relationship with him, to consider how he can be their mother, how he can be giving birth a second time, and how Christ can be formed in them. Rather than dismissing this assertion as some sort of odd mistake or unimportant misstatement, we are provoked to look more closely at exactly what he is saying.

To a certain extent, at least, this vivid use of language requires a decision on the part of the hearer or reader. As Wayne Booth puts it, "To *understand* a metaphor is by its very nature to *decide* whether to join the metaphorist or reject him [or her], and that is simultaneously to decide either to be shaped in the shape [the] metaphor requires or to resist."[18]

Here Booth touches on a second feature of metaphor theory that proves helpful for reading the maternal imagery in Paul, namely, the relationship between metaphor and intimacy. Ted Cohen has proposed that a metaphor is an invitation to intimacy.[19] That insight is helpful *if* we realize that the invitation may be quite unconscious on the part of the speaker or writer. If I say to you, "Snow is the underside of hell," I am implicitly inviting you to join in my assessment of snow. You may respond negatively (but only if you sat out that grim winter in some southern territory) with something like "Snow is a white cotton blanket." Or you may concur, "Snow is a curse from the heavens." If we find that we agree, a certain relationship has been created, however transient and even silly in this instance.

The relationship between metaphor and intimacy is particularly appropriate when we think about the way Paul employs maternal imagery. That is easy enough to see in texts such as 1 Thess 2:7, where he is recalling his close relationship with the Thessalonians, or in Gal 4:19, where he seeks to reestablish a relationship that now seems jeopardized. But even in 1 Cor

15:8, where he refers to himself as "monstrously born," he creates a connection between himself and his correspondents. Had he said, "Even though I did not deserve it, Christ appeared to me," the letter might have been clearer (*if* that is what he means). For the Corinthians, however, the figure of the "monstrous birth" serves as an invitation to puzzle through Paul's meaning and to draw their own conclusions.

To associate metaphor with intimacy is not to say, of course, that all metaphoric intimacy is of the happy, collegial sort. Just as jokes can be told with hostile intent, metaphors also can be invitations to hostility. If metaphor creates boundaries around a community, it also creates barriers against outsiders, against those who "just don't get it."

The third development in metaphor study concerns a specific category of metaphor, namely, kinship metaphors. Here I am drawing particularly on Mark Turner's book, *Death Is the Mother of Beauty*.[20] Turner analyzes the ways in which a vast number of kinship metaphors work. Behind these metaphors he detects ten basic metaphoric inference patterns about kinship. One of the inference patterns Turner identifies is that "what springs from something is its offspring," as in "A proverb is the child of experience."[21] Or to return to snow metaphors, we might say "Snow is the mother of boredom." Another of Turner's inference patterns is that "members of a natural group are siblings," as in "Death is the brother of sleep" or "Accuracy is the twin of honesty."[22] It is this inference pattern that prompts me to refer to my colleague as my "little brother" because we are members of a "natural" group.

By definition, Paul's use of maternal imagery belongs in Turner's category of kinship metaphors. What is helpful about Turner's work is that he demonstrates the overwhelming prominence of metaphors involving mothers and sisters within the vast realm of kinship metaphors. And he finds that biological and social expectations drive the creation of these kinship metaphors. To no one's surprise, then, metaphors having to do with nurture are almost exclusively associated with mothers.[23] Turner's work appears to corroborate two points I made earlier: mother-talk relates to nurture over a period of time, and Paul's uses of maternal imagery and paternal imagery are not interchangeable.

THE CHAPTERS THAT FOLLOW

In part 1, I want to retrieve these texts from their place in the footnotes of Pauline studies. Even those passages that have received attention have not been examined in connection with the topic of maternal imagery as such.

But I am doing more than retrieving these texts, for this work has implications for the continuing discussion of how to identify and understand Paul's theology and theologizing.[24] Here I am helped by Steven J. Kraftchick's work on metaphor theory as a way into thinking about Paul's theology in general. Kraftchick works with generative metaphors, those implicit metaphors that may structure large aspects of thought, such as "War on Poverty." In 2 Corinthians, for example, Kraftchick argues that Paul uses the death and resurrection of Jesus as a metaphor that structures his understanding of his own task and challenges his readers to restructure their understandings.[25] What these two approaches have in common is that each of us is moving away from the notion that Paul's theology is to be found and described only in his use of propositional statements. Paul speaks theologically when he says, "All have sinned and fall short of the glory of God." He *also* speaks theologically when he says, "I am in labor until Christ is formed in you."[26]

The study of maternal imagery should also enhance our understanding of the social functions of Paul's language. Wayne Meeks has helped us to see ways in which Paul's use of familial terminology creates and maintains internal cohesion.[27] I suspect that is particularly true when the language is maternal, precisely because references to the anguish of labor, to childbirth, and to nursing assume a profound intimacy between parties.

Finally, a study of Paul's use of maternal imagery may have implications for the interrelated and complex sets of questions regarding Paul's understanding of leadership and his attitudes toward women. One reading strategy that has become conventional in recent decades involves dissecting Paul's letters into texts labeled "hierarchical" and other texts labeled "egalitarian." With that dualistic approach to Paul, the texts in which Paul refers to himself as "father" fall neatly into the hierarchical pile, and those in which he refers to believers as "brothers" fall neatly into the egalitarian pile.[28] The result is a conflict between the "bad" hierarchical Paul and the "good" egalitarian Paul.

What happens when we take seriously the use of maternal imagery for the apostolic office? Maternal imagery scarcely belongs in the egalitarian pile, for mothers do not treat their children as their equals (as my son would be the first to insist that I acknowledge). We might conclude that maternal imagery belongs in the hierarchical pile, but that designation also will not fit. Mothers in Paul's world do not have the authority of fathers. More important, when Paul presents himself as a mother, he voluntarily hands over the authority of a patriarch in favor of a role that will bring him shame, the shame of a female-identified male. Still, maternal imagery becomes effective precisely because it plays on hierarchical expectations: Paul presents himself as the authority who does not conform to standard norms of authority.

Taking seriously the presence of maternal imagery in fact subverts the reductionistic dichotomy between hierarchical and egalitarian texts. It nudges us to seek some other lens through which to view the matter of leadership in the Pauline letters. In my judgment, the lens that lies ready to hand is that of apocalyptic theology, to which we turn in the second part of the book. With its strong emphasis on God's unilaterial action of intervention in the cross and resurrection of Jesus Christ, apocalyptic theology has no room for conventional thinking about human leadership. The same cross that reveals the criminal as Son of God and the bankruptcy of human wisdom also calls forth leaders who can risk identifying themselves as slaves of Christ Jesus (Rom 1:1), as the "refuse of the cosmos" (1 Cor 4:13), and even as women in labor for the second time with the same child.

THE AFTERLIFE OF PAULINE MATERNITY

As we turn to the texts themselves, we recall that, however recent generations of readers have neglected them, earlier generations of Christians read these passages closely and drew upon them when they spoke of Paul. Evidence for this assertion comes as early as the Acts of Paul, a second-century text that culminates in an account of Paul's execution. When struck by the executioner's sword, so the story goes, Paul's body yielded up not blood, but milk:

> But when the executioner struck off his head, milk spurted upon the soldier's clothing. And when they saw it, the soldier and all who stood by were amazed, and glorified God who had given Paul such glory.[29]

Origen draws on 1 Cor 3:1–2 and Gal 4:19 when referring to the "maternal affection" Paul had for his churches,[30] and Methodius identifies the "glorious Paul" as "mother," citing Gal 4:19.[31] In his discussion of the Song of Songs, Gregory of Nyssa refers to Paul as a "breast for infants" who "nourishes the newly born of the Church with milk" and provides food for the church's children.[32] This association between Paul and the nursing mother comes to startling expression in a sermon by the twelfth-century Cistercian, Guerric of Igny. Commenting on the tradition that milk rather than blood flowed from Paul's body at his execution,[33] Guerric proclaims that Paul's conversion changed him from torturer to mother, from executioner to nurse:

> Truly there was no element of blood but the whole was of milk
> in him. . . . He abounded with such a wealth of loving kindness
> that he yearned not only to impart the milk of his spirit in its
> totality to his children but also to give them his body.[34]

In what is perhaps the most extended play on these texts, Anselm of Canterbury prays to Paul as "our greatest mother":

> O St. Paul, where is he that was called
>   the nurse of the faithful, caressing his sons?
> Who is that affectionate mother who declares everywhere
>   that she is in labor for her sons?
> Sweet nurse, sweet mother,
> who are the sons you are in labor with, and nurse,
> but those whom by teaching the faith of Christ
>   you bear and instruct?
> Or who is a Christian after your teaching
>   who is not born into the faith and established in it by you?
> And if in that blessed faith we are born and nursed by other
>   apostles also,
> it is most of all by you,
> for you have labored and done more than them all in this;
> so if they are our mothers, you are our greatest mother.[35]

CHAPTER ONE

Apostles as Infants and Nurses

> But we became infants in your midst, as if a nurse taking care of her own children.
>
> *1 Thessalonians 2:7*

In Paul's earliest letter, he employs unusual and even provocative imagery to describe his work as an apostle. In this chapter, I argue that in 1 Thessalonians Paul is bringing his understanding of apostleship to expression. If 1 Thessalonians is Paul's first letter to a Christian community, it is "an experiment in Christian writing,"[1] and we must keep the experimental character of this letter in the foreground as we read and interpret it. As part of Paul's experiment, he must explain what an apostle is and, to do so, he uses several images of the apostles, not only as fathers of believers (2:11), but also as infants and as nurses. These terms are not merely part of a conventional description of the philosopher but also indicate something essential to Paul's understanding of what he and his coworkers do.

Among the many questions that arise from this verse, I want to address the following: First, what is the best text of this verse, and how should we translate it?

Second, what is the origin of this imagery, with which an adult male speaks of himself as a nurse and, as I shall argue, even as a child? What other sources employ this metaphor of the nurse? What can we learn about the status and function of nurses in the ancient world, and how might that knowledge illumine Paul's words?

Third, what shall we make of Paul's use of metaphor here? Technically, of course, this is a simile, since he writes "as if a nurse" (ὡς ἐάν, *hōs ean*). But the distinction is grammatical rather than substantive, and most discussions of metaphor and its usage consider both types of figures. Beyond the place of metaphor in this verse, we also want to know what function the verse plays in this part of the letter, where Paul seeks to consolidate and enhance the relationship between himself and the Thessalonians. Related to that question is the larger matter of the connection between this section of the letter, with its imagery of nurture, and the apocalyptic concerns that dominate 1 Thess 4 and 5.

TEXT AND TRANSLATION OF 1 THESSALONIANS 2:7

First Thessalonians 2:7 contains a significant text-critical problem. The NRSV translates the verse: "But we were gentle among you, like a nurse tenderly caring for her own children." Nevertheless, the NRSV also contains a footnote indicating that some ancient authorities read "infants" rather than "gentle."[2] The NRSV translates according to one set of Greek manuscripts, in which the reading is, "We were gentle [ἤπιοι, *ēpioi*] among you, like a nurse taking care of her children." Another set of manuscripts, reflected in the footnote, reads, "We were infants [νήπιοι; *nēpioi*] among you, like a nurse taking care of her children."

The external evidence is clear. Both the 27th edition of Nestle-Aland and the 4th edition of the United Bible Society read νήπιοι (infants). Although ἤπιοι (gentle) appears in several of the major uncial manuscripts (including Sinaiticus, Alexandrinus, Ephraemi, Bezae), in all these manuscripts except Alexandrinus this reading comes from the hand of a corrector. Νήπιοι (infants) appears in P[65] and Vaticanus, and it is the original reading in Sinaiticus, Ephraemi, and Bezae. If we considered only the external evidence, there would be little doubt that 2:7 reads νήπιοι or infants, rather than ἤπιοι or gentle. The explanation of the reading ἤπιοι (gentle) would be that later scribes altered νήπιοι to ἤπιοι, omitting one letter to produce a less difficult or awkward reading.

Many objections to this reading of 2:7 have been lodged, however, and they include at least the following.

1. The reading νήπιοι (infants) could easily have resulted from the simple scribal error of dittography. That is, the ν at the end of the preceding word, ἐγενήθημεν (*egenēthēmen*, we became) was accidentally doubled with the result that ἤπιοι (gentle) became νήπιοι (infants).[3]

2. Paul elsewhere employs the word νήπιος (infant) when describing the immaturity of his converts, as in 1 Cor 3:1: "And so, brothers and sisters, I could not address you as spiritual people, but rather as people of the flesh, as infants in Christ" (NRSV). He would scarcely use that same word with reference to himself and his coworkers.[4]

3. Since Paul immediately follows this word with the image of the nurse, only ἤπιοι (gentle) fits the context. While Paul does occasionally use a mixed metaphor, it would be quite awkward to write, "We became infants among you, like a nurse. . . ."[5]

These arguments form a scholarly judgment sufficiently strong that Helmut Koester can refer to the preference for νήπιοι (infants) in the 26th edition of Nestle-Aland as "clearly wrong."[6] Yet the weight of the external evidence should prevent us from coming to a hasty conclusion that Paul "must" have meant something other than what the earliest and best manuscripts read. There are also good reasons, indeed better reasons, for concluding that Paul did in fact write νήπιοι (infants). Among them I note five:

1. The scribal error posited by the consensus view could easily have resulted from haplography rather than dittography. That is, a scribe wrote one ν where there should have been two, resulting in the omission of the ν in νήπιοι (infants); hence, ἤπιοι (gentle).

2. Although it is true that Paul elsewhere employs νήπιος (infant) for converts who are still new in their understanding, that usage is not uniform in the letters. He actually uses the word in only five verses outside our passage in 1 Thessalonians. In addition to 1 Cor 3:1, which was noted earlier and will be discussed in chapter 3, νήπιος (infant) also appears three times in 1 Cor 13:11 ("when I was a child"). In Gal 4:1, 3 it is used of the heir who has not yet inherited. Finally, in Rom 2:20 Paul employs it to refer to those who call themselves teachers of children but who are instead hypocrites. While none of these instances could be said to have positive connotations, neither is the term clearly negative nor is it always associated with recent converts.[7]

On the other hand, in 1 Cor 14:20 Paul does use the related verb νηπιάζειν (*nēpiazein*) in an admonition: "Brethren, do not be children [παῖς, *pais*] in your thinking; rather, be infants [νηπιάζειν] in evil" (cf. Rom 16:19). Moreover, in some passages in the Septuagint (e.g., Pss19:7 [18:8 LXX]; 119:130 [118:130 LXX]; Wis 10:21) and in Matt 11:25, νήπιος does refer to those who are simple or guileless.[8] This connotation of the term would offer an excellent contrast to the characteristics Paul has just insisted do not pertain to himself and his coworkers (error, guile, flattery, greed, seeking glory, etc.).[9]

3. Certainly reading νήπιοι (infants) with the better manuscripts results in a mixed metaphor, but those are by no means uncommon in the letters of Paul. In the next chapter, we take up Gal 4:19, which

employs another mixed metaphor, again a metaphor focusing on maternal imagery. Others are found in the marriage analogy in Rom 7:1–3 and the reference to the veil of Moses in 2 Cor 3. I suspect that these mixed metaphors often result, not from some defect in Paul's imagination,[10] but from his struggle to articulate all that needs to be said. (I shall return to this issue again below.)

4. While the context of this verse may make νήπιοι (infants) difficult, the syntax does not. Paul often uses γίνομαι (*ginomai*, become) with a noun; indeed, he does so even in this section of 1 Thessalonians (1:5b; 1:6; 1:7; 2:14).[11] More important, the phrase stands parallel to ἀπό-στολοι Χριστοῦ in 1 Thess 2:7a: "we might have made demands as apostles of Christ, but we became . . ." This parallel anticipates a noun following ἐγενήθημεν (we became).[12]

5. Finally, the revered text-critical rule that the more difficult reading is usually earlier and preferable should incline us to regard νήπιοι (infants) as the earlier reading, since there can be no doubt that it is more difficult than ἤπιοι (gentle). It is easy to imagine why a scribe would find the mixed metaphor confusing and respond by altering νήπιοι to ἤπιοι. A deliberate or conscious change from ἤπιοι to νήπιοι is unthinkable.

Taken together, these considerations point to infants, or νήπιοι, as the preferred reading. This, of course, does not in itself make 1 Thess 2:7 clearer; indeed, the verse is now more rather than less confusing.[13]

With this text-critical judgment in place, the question of punctuation and translation becomes urgent. Those who read νήπιοι (infants) sometimes suggest that this reading requires a full stop between the expressions "We became infants in your midst" and "as a nurse taking care of her children."[14] This punctuation would provide a slight separation between the two metaphors and would result in the following translation: "But we became infants in your midst. As a nurse taking care of her children, thus we were desirous of you." The difficulty with inserting a full stop is that the ἀλλά (*alla*, but) in v. 7b runs parallel to the ἀλλά in v. 4. In other words, vv. 4–7a state the characteristics of the apostles in a negative way—all the things they are not. The ἀλλά of v. 7b then introduces the positive claims made about them, which must also be taken together. I think we must translate: "But we became infants among you, as if a nurse taking care of her own children." Somehow these two statements belong together. They are amplified in v. 8, where Paul turns from metaphorical speech to more direct assertion: "We were pleased to share with you not only the gospel but also our selves."

BACKGROUND OF THE METAPHOR OF THE NURSE

Having established a workable text and translation of this verse, we turn to Paul's reference to himself and others as nurses. The most influential discussion of this reference is that of Abraham Malherbe, whose work on this text has found wide acceptance. Among Malherbe's early contributions to the study of 1 Thessalonians is "Gentle as a Nurse," in which he argues that in 1 Thess 2:1–12 Paul employs a conventional topos concerning the work of the philosopher.[15] As a result of the number of disreputable figures among the Cynics who were presenting themselves as public speakers, it had become advisable to distinguish oneself as a true philosopher by contrasting oneself to false philosophers by means of antithetical comparisons. Malherbe takes as a prominent example the comments of Dio Chrysostom, who contrasts the true philosopher to the charlatan. Significantly, Dio's remarks do not presuppose that he personally has been attacked, which leads Malherbe to conclude that Paul's use of a similar self-description does not require us to think that he is engaged in a personal defense against charges.[16]

Pertinent to our consideration of the metaphor of the nurse in 2:7 is Malherbe's identification of that metaphor as part of a conventional topos regarding the behavior of the ideal philosopher. Just as the ideal philosopher speaks with "boldness" and acts without deceit or error, the true philosopher also should be prepared to be as gentle as a nurse. As evidence for this use of the metaphor of the nurse, Malherbe cites a number of texts (primarily from Dio Chrysostom, Epictetus, Plutarch, and Pseudo-Diogenes). For example, Dio Chrysostom, while describing a conversation between Diogenes and Alexander, explains that Diogenes knows that he has been harsh with Alexander and so he tells Alexander a story, just as nurses tell a story to comfort a child after a whipping (*Oration* 4.74). Elsewhere Dio refers to the custom of nurses to sweeten an unpleasant drink by smearing honey on the cup (*Oration* 33.10). More negative is Dio's contrast between proper instruction in knowledge and truth and the nurse who feeds her children with milk and wine and various foods (*Oration* 4 [*Kingship* 4] 41).

As Malherbe points out, Epictetus's references to nurses are largely negative. Individuals ought to be content with what they have, not crying after things they want as children cry after their nurses (*Discourses* 2.16.28). Some people are never willing to take solid food, but cling to their nurses (2.16.39; cf. 2.16.44). Here the nurse's charge symbolizes the immaturity of one who has not yet reached Epictetus's ideal. Similarly, Pseudo-Diogenes assaults those who, due to their own corruption, need radical surgery but instead opt for the gentle attentions of a nurse (*Epistle* 29).

Plutarch also employs the nurse as an example. In his essay, "How to Tell a Flatterer from a Friend," Plutarch employs the nurse to illustrate the need to speak gently in time of misfortune. When children fall down, their nurses do not rush up to them and berate them. Instead, they pick them up, wash them, and straighten their clothes—then they berate them (69C). When writing about the education of children, Plutarch urges that rebuke and praise should be used alternately and again mentions the practice of nurses, who cause babies to cry and then offer them nourishment ("The Education of Children," 3C–F).

Some of these texts admittedly use the imagery of a nurse's care to illustrate (either positively or negatively) aspects of the philosopher's relationship to his students. Whether there is enough consistency here to call this an established topos is, in my judgment, an open question. Quite apart from that question, however, it is problematic to connect this usage to that of Paul in 1 Thess 2:7, for at least three reasons:

1. In the texts Malherbe cites, Dio and others employ the nurse as an example. The relationship between the nurse and the speaker is actually quite remote. Not only is the nurse sometimes viewed negatively (that is, she is too soft and accommodating), but the speaker uses the nurse as an example to illustrate the point rather than as a metaphor to describe himself. For example, Dio does not say that he himself is like or unlike a nurse; he speaks of Diogenes, who in turn refers to a nurse's behavior. The difference is comparable to the difference between telling a parable and illustrating a sermon with an anecdote.

2. In Dio's sustained descriptions of philosophers of varying types, the image of the nurse does not appear. For example, *Oration 32* (*To the People of Alexandria*), which Malherbe uses extensively to show the way in which Dio describes philosophers, makes no mention of the activity of a nurse. Instead, as noted above, the image of the nurse appears in a limited number of illustrations (e.g., *Oration 4* [*Kingship 4*] 73; *Oration 33* [*First Tarsic Discourse*] 10). If there is a topos concerning the ideal philosopher, it is not clear that the topos includes the reference to the nurse.

3. Most puzzling is the fact that the word τροφός (*trophos*, nurse) does not appear in the texts to which Malherbe points. Uniformly, these texts employ the term τίτθη (*titthē*, wet nurse) for the individual described.[17] It is not immediately obvious what significance we should attach to this observation. One study of the nurse in Greek life concludes that these terms are not distinguished sharply from one another. The noun τροφός,

however, appears as early as Homer and refers in a general way to one who nurtures; τίτθη appears in the literature only later and with reference more narrowly to the role of the wet nurse.[18] Pseudo-Ammonius confirms this distinction and refers to the nurture of the τροφός after a child is weaned.[19] While the two terms are clearly related to one another, they do not seem to be used interchangeably.

Given this range of problems, we may conclude that, while Malherbe has identified a topos which contrasts the ideal philosopher to the charlatan, it is far from clear that the behavior of the nurse has a fixed place in that topos.[20] A more helpful approach to the nurse image is one that asks how the nurse was perceived and what role she played in the social context. Early Greek literature usually portrays the nurse as a slave (e.g., Homer, *Odyssey* 7.9; *Iliad* 389; Euripides, *Medea* 65), although by the fourth century BCE there are already references to free women taking on the role of the nurse as a result of dire poverty (Demosthenes, *Oration 57* [*Against Eubulides*] 35, 42). Within the household, the nurse not only had responsibility for the care of infants and small children, but often also continued as the attendant for a young woman and remained in the affection of young men who were her former charges. In addition to caring for children, the nurse is portrayed as a general assistant in domestic affairs—supervising the work of others, acting as steward of the household, performing an array of household tasks. In some texts she appears to exercise a role of authority over others in the household, giving them directions and supervision. From Homer onward, writers portray the nurse as a generous and kind figure, and there are few references to neglect or maltreatment.[21] Nor is the evidence exclusively literary, as Pliny the Younger resolved to provide a farm for the care of his nurse in her old age (*Epistle 6* 3).[22] All of this suggests that Paul's metaphorical use of the nurse would conjure up in the minds of his audience an important and beloved figure. Whatever the social status of the Thessalonian Christians, they could understand this reference to an important social relationship, one proximate to kinship itself.[23]

Before leaving this discussion of the nurse, we need to consider briefly two important texts, one from the Septuagint and the other from the Dead Sea Scrolls. These texts are important for our understanding of 1 Thess 2:7 because of the way a male figure attaches to himself the language of nursing.

The first text comes from Num 11 and is part of the traditions about Israel's wandering in the wilderness.[24] In this particular text, the people have grown weary of eating only manna and cry out for the meat, fruit, and vegetables of Egypt. Moses turns to God in anger and frustration with the people and cries out, "Did I conceive all this people? Did I give birth to them, that you should say to me, 'Carry them in your bosom,' as a nurse carries a sucking child?" (Num 11:12 NRSV). Of course, we cannot simply leap from this passage to 1 Thess 2:7. The word τροφός (nurse) does not appear in the LXX; we have no verbal connection between the two texts. Moreover, unlike Paul, Moses is complaining here; this is a role which God has thrust upon him, and he would be happy to be relieved of it.

There are, however, some tantalizing connections between the two passages. Both apply the role of nurse to a male; and in both instances it is the male in question who identifies himself with the role. Moses, like Paul, nurtured the people. While Moses insists that he did not assume this role for himself, it is nevertheless the role he continues to play in relation to Israel. In the same way, Paul continues to nurture his congregations. Paul does not explicitly link himself to the role of Moses, but he does elsewhere apply to himself language found in the prophetic call passages (Gal 1:15). I suggest that Num 11:12 may well have exerted an influence on Paul's reflection about his own role.

The second example of the use of the image of the nurse comes from the community at Qumran. There, in the Hodayoth, the Teacher of Righteousness describes himself as the father of the pious:

> and You have appointed me as a father to the children of mercy
> and as guardian to men of portent.
> They open their mouth wide like a nursing ch[ild],
> and as a child delights in the embrace of its guardian.
> *(1QHᵃ 15.20–22)*[25]

As with Num 11:12, the text regarding Moses, we must not overstate the similarities between this passage and 1 Thess 2:7. The imagery here is largely paternal rather than maternal. It is intriguing, however, to find another instance of maternal imagery, and again here it is the speaker who identifies himself in language that is maternal.

This discussion about the τροφός (nurse) has ranged rather widely, and it will therefore be useful to summarize the major points before we ask specifically what place the term has in Paul's letter. I have argued that Paul's usage of τροφός (nurse) does not derive from the topos of the philosopher and his gentleness. Instead, Paul draws upon a well-known figure in the ancient world, one identified not only with the nurture of infants but also with continued affection for her charges well into adulthood. Moreover, Paul's reference to himself (and others) as nurses bears an interesting resemblance to passages in Numbers and the Hodayoth where Moses and the Teacher of Righteousness, respectively, identify themselves with nursing roles.

THE METAPHOR(S) IN CONTEXT

The answers offered to the first two questions identified at the beginning of this chapter confront us with what appears to be a significant contradiction. By arguing that the earliest reading is νήπιοι (infants), I conclude that Paul applies to himself and his coworkers the metaphor of infants. By arguing that the reference to the τροφός (nurse) does not simply derive from the topos of the ideal philosopher, I insist that the metaphor of the nurse is something more than conventional. It is part and parcel of what Paul wishes to say here about his work. That means that we are looking at what we usually call a mixed metaphor, although in this case the mixture is odd enough that we might term it inverted.

Before addressing the inverted or mixed character of this particular metaphor, we may profitably recall our discussion of metaphor in the introduction. A metaphor is "a device which speaks of one thing (tenor) in terms which are appropriate to another (vehicle), with the vehicle serving as the source of traits to be transferred to the tenor."[26] But this distinction between tenor and vehicle should not lead us to draw a very firm line between the two parts of a metaphor. Indeed, as noted in the introduction to part 1, discussions of metaphor often comment on the way a metaphor changes or enhances meaning by juxtaposing tenor and vehicle. I. A. Richards argues that a metaphor combines "two thoughts of different things active together and supported by a single word, or phrase, whose meaning is a resultant of their interaction."[27] The two parts of a metaphor create new meaning by their interplay.[28] Philip Wheelwright has termed this interplay a kind of metamorphosis, in which the imagination reaches out and combines things that are different.[29] Wayne Booth speaks of the expansive character of metaphor; that is to say, metaphor is a process in which meanings are added or multiplied rather than subtracted.[30] Metaphor does not merely decorate or illustrate; it broadens our understandings. Indeed, to the degree that language is inherently metaphorical, one might even say that metaphor creates understandings as well as amplifies them.

In the text under consideration the difficulty is that Paul uses not one metaphor but two. He compares himself with infants and then immediately with the one who cares for those infants—the nurse. That dramatic change of metaphors has given rise to the usual comments on Paul's inability to complete an analogy. But when Shakespeare uses metaphors that might be called mixed, critics speak of "rapidly shifting figures" and say that his thoughts flow faster than his speech.[31] I suggest that something similar happens to Paul in 1 Thess 2:7. Having introduced the expression "apostles of Christ," he searches for ways of explaining what those apostles are. In this section he employs two metaphors, infants and nurses, and in v. 12 he will use the less jarring metaphor, fathers.[32]

According to many reconstructions, 1 Thessalonians is Paul's first letter to a community of believers, and this letter does not begin with "Paul an apostle," or even "Paul a slave of Christ Jesus." In fact, alone among the Pauline letters, 1 Thessalonians begins with the unadorned itemization of the names of the coworkers. Therefore, the mention of "apostles of Christ" in v. 7 is the first such reference in Paul's letters. Having used the term, he must explain what it means. In vv. 4–6, leading up to the phrase "apostles of Christ," Paul describes himself and his coworkers negatively. That is, he contrasts them with the charges sometimes made against wandering philosophers. Paul and his associates are not abusive, greedy, seeking for glory. Instead, they are apostles of Christ.

In v. 7 Paul turns to a positive description of the apostles. They are infants among the Thessalonians. Notice that it is "among you" or "in your midst" that the apostles became infants. They were innocent characters, lacking the guile and deceit of a charlatan. In 2 Cor 10–13 we see Paul making a similar kind of claim about his work among the Corinthians, again contrasting himself to those who act abusively and who seek only their own glorification, who pervert Paul's own apostolic understanding (11:13).

But "apostles of Christ" are also nurses who care for their children. The intensity of the metaphor here is striking. It is not enough to assert that the apostles are nurses. Paul adds the verb θάλπειν (*thalpein*), to warm, cherish, comfort. The nurse cares for, literally, "her own children." At this point we encounter a certain lack of clarity. The word ἑαυτῆς (*heautēs*, her own) may mean that the nurse is caring, not for someone else's children in this instance, but for her own. However, the pronoun does not require that translation, and the way in which nurses are described in the literature makes it difficult to think of a nurse with children that were, in fact, her own biological children.[33] As I explained earlier, however, the affection between a nurse and the children for whom she cared was axiomatic. So, whether Paul has in mind the nurse and her own children or the nurse and her charges, the reference to the children again intensifies the metaphor, as does the reflexive pronoun ἑαυτῆς (her own).[34] Verse 8 extends the comparison by speaking about the sharing not only of the gospel but also of the "selves" of the apostles.

Here Paul does use a mixed metaphor, perhaps even an inverted one, but for good reason. He is struggling to identify two aspects of the apostolic role. The apostle is childlike, in contrast to the charlatan who constantly works to see how much benefit he can derive from his audience. The apostle is also the responsible adult, in the first instance the nurse who tends her charges with care and affection.

Yet the juxtaposition of these two metaphors, infants and nurses, is itself significant, and separating them as I have done diminishes the connotations of the text. For what the text suggests is that the apostles of Christ are not to be understood in an ordinary way. To understand them, just as to understand the gospel itself, one must employ categories that seem outrageous outside the context of Pauline paradox. To apply the language of children and nurses to grown men is to create a jarring image, one that challenges and expands understanding. In later letters, this same conviction comes to expression via irony; as, for example, when Paul speaks of the apostles as the "offscouring of all things" in 1 Cor 4:13. In 1 Thess 2 the imagery is that of the nursery, but it is no less shocking.[35]

Although I am referring to the theological functions of this language, the metaphors have important social and paraenetic functions as well, and these various functions work together. To apply metaphors of family life (infants, nurses, fathers) to the apostles and their relationship to believers is to suggest that those believers constitute a family. As Wayne Meeks's work on the social world of the Pauline churches reveals, this kind of language serves to create a new family for those who are being disenfranchised from their families of origin and invites Christians to reconceive conventional roles in startling ways.[36] The paraenetic function of these metaphors goes hand in hand with their social function. By invoking the language of family, Paul implicitly exhorts believers to continue in those relationships. Indeed, throughout the first half of the letter, the philophronetic elements set the stage for the more explicitly paraenetic material in chapters 4 and 5.

At the end of this "experiment in Christian writing," Paul demands that the Thessalonians read his letter in their assembly, an act that Raymond Collins identifies as the very beginning of the New Testament itself.[37]

When those women and men gathered to hear this letter read, probably in the context of worship, fellowship, and mutual encouragement, it seems likely that there were also nurses tending to hungry, fussing babies. As the reader came to the passage we know as 1 Thess 2:7, I imagine that at least some among the listeners smiled in recognition.

CHAPTER TWO

The Maternity of Paul

My children, with whom I am again in labor until Christ is formed in
you . . .

Galatians 4:19

$\mathbf{I}$f some among the Thessalonians managed a gentle smile when they
heard Paul declaring himself to be both infant and nurse, it seems less
likely that the Galatians heard Paul's letter with sympathy. Whatever
their disposition as they listened to this letter for the first time, they most
probably were familiar with the sounds of women in labor. Unlike contemporary Westerners, for whom birth is largely an event confined to the
birthing suites of hospitals, in the first century birth was not hidden
away or compartmentalized. It is safe to assume that most people were
familiar with the cries of labor and delivery, but it seems unlikely that the
Galatians were grateful for this particular reference to childbirth.[1] The
word Paul employs in Gal 4:19, ὠδίνειν (*ōdinein*), refers to the physical
labor, even pain, that accompanies human birth. Paul's claim to be doing
something that is manifestly impossible—giving birth (again!)—immediately attracts attention.

Although Paul is the one who is in labor, and in labor with the Galatians, the second half of Gal 4:19 seems to contradict the first. It is not
the Galatians who are being born but Christ: "until Christ is formed in
you." How is it that Paul is giving birth, but it is Christ who is formed
rather than the Galatians? If we draw a picture corresponding to Paul's
words in this verse, we would have Paul concentrating in labor. Inside his
"womb" we would find the Galatians, and the object of the labor is
Christ who is coming to birth among the Galatians. The portrait is, to
say the least, complicated.

No less troubling than these strange statements within the verse is the
context in which the verse occurs. In v. 12a Paul appeals to the Galatians

to imitate him.[2] He then recalls the way in which they received him, despite his bodily affliction (vv. 12b–14). He reminds them of their ardent desire to help him and asks whether he has become their enemy. Referring to the Teachers[3] who have entered their churches and have proclaimed a different gospel according to which Gentiles must obey the Mosaic Law, Paul accuses them of making much of the Galatians merely to lead them astray. Then he says this:

> It is always good to be made much of in a good way, and *not only* when I am present with you. My children, with whom I am again in labor until Christ is formed in you! I could wish to be present with you now and to change my tone, for I am perplexed about you. (4:18–19)

Grammatically, v. 19 follows closely on v. 18 and seems to be in apposition to the *hymas* at the end of that verse.[4] The transition at the end of v. 19 is awkward, however. In fact, if v. 19 were removed, the whole section would read more easily; that observation again raises the question of the function of v. 19 in its context.

When this text and its accompanying problems first began to provoke me, I cast a casual eye on the commentaries to see what help they might offer. Surprised to find little attention given to the verse, I looked further into the secondary literature. I found only one article on the second part of v. 19 and a few brief remarks in the commentaries and monographs.[5] It fascinates me to find so little written about a text in which there are so many interesting problems. We could find perhaps dozens of articles about an issue like the nature of Paul's thorn in the flesh, but this passage with all its complexities has attracted relatively little attention.

The reason that first comes to mind for the strange silence about Gal 4:19 is that, until recently, few women have been involved in the scholarly exegesis of biblical texts. Perhaps Gal 4:19 is simply one of the texts in which the anomalies strike women with particular force. I suspect that the more decisive factor in the silence about Gal 4:19 arises from its location in what is usually regarded as Paul's personal appeal. This portion of the letter, 4:12–20, concerns Paul's relationship with the Galatians and is thought to have little to do with the important theological matters of the letter itself.[6] In fact, what most commentaries suggest about our text is that Paul is here overcome with emotion and that he plays on the relationship he has had with this community. This line of interpretation goes back at least to Chrysostom, who wrote regarding Gal 4:19: "Behold his paternal tenderness, behold this despondency worthy of an Apostle. The cry which he utters is far more piercing than of a woman in travail."[7] H. D. Betz attempts to move beyond this reading of 4:12–20 with the suggestion that all of 4:12–20 employs the friendship topos in order to rectify the relationship between Paul and the Galatians.[8] Betz also suggests, although tentatively, that 4:19 may draw upon regeneration or rebirth motifs such as are widespread in the ancient world.

In what follows, I argue that Gal 4:19 is not merely an emotional outburst or a typical rhetorical device. Galatians 4:19 associates Paul's apostolic vocation with the anguish anticipated in an apocalyptic era and recalls to the Galatians their own crucifixion with Christ. As such, Gal 4:19 employs a conventional metaphor, that of the anguish of a woman in labor, to identify Paul's apostolic work with the apocalyptic expectation of the whole created order.[9] The goal of Paul's anguish, in this instance, is that Christ be formed within the communities of believers in Galatia. This reading of 4:19 suggests that it is not an emotional outburst but an important theological link between this section of personal appeal and the remainder of the letter.

GALATIANS 4:19A

What can it mean for Paul to say that he is in labor with the Galatians? Because Paul prefaces this statement with the affectionate address "my children,"[10] commentators normally identify this text with passages in which Paul describes himself as the father of believers. For example, in 1 Cor 4:14–15 we find:

> I am not writing this to make you ashamed, but to admonish you as my beloved children. For though you might have ten thousand guardians in Christ, you do not have many fathers. Indeed, in Christ Jesus I became your father through the gospel. (NRSV)

Similarly, Paul compares his role with that of a father in 1 Thess 2:11: "As you know, we dealt with each one of you like a father with his children, urging and encouraging you and pleading that you lead a life worthy of God, who calls you into his own kingdom and glory"[11] (NRSV). Placing Gal 4:19 within the context of these statements about Paul's relationship to believers supports the contention that what Paul presents in this verse is an emotional personal appeal based on the relationship he had earlier established with Galatian Christians. While there are perhaps connections between Gal 4:19 and Paul's sense of being the father of believers in his congregations, to beget a child is not the same thing as to give it birth, and we should not hastily equate the two.[12]

The commentary of H. D. Betz presents one extended attempt at taking this image seriously. Although Betz refers to the "somewhat pathetic" character of this verse and draws the customary comparison to Paul's use of the father imagery elsewhere, he does acknowledge the unusual character of the verse and attempts to understand it, first, as part of a conventional topos of friendship and, second, as part of the larger complex of rebirth imagery. Betz initially comments on the imagery of maternal relationship as a part of the friendship topos, but the texts he cites refer in a most general fashion to the nature of family relationships and have little in common with Gal 4:19.[13] In addition, Betz himself recognizes that Paul wants to accomplish more here than "merely *compare* himself to a mother."[14]

As I indicated above, Betz does go on to suggest that *ōdinein* may be associated with the language of spiritual rebirth that appears in many religious traditions.[15] He points to a text in the Nag Hammadi corpus in which the figure Hermes explains rebirth to his spiritual son. The son asks whether those who are so reborn have mothers as well as fathers and receives the response: "My son, they are spiritual [mothers]. For they are potencies; they let the souls grow. Therefore I say, they are immortal."[16] Also in the Hermetic literature, Betz points to the conversation between Hermes and his son regarding the soul's rebirth through special knowledge. But these discussions of the hows and wherefores of the soul's passage to knowledge of its divine origins seem far removed from Paul, and Paul himself does not use the language of rebirth or regeneration.

For insight into Paul's strange claim to be in labor with the Galatians, we need to look more closely at the use of the word *ōdinein*. *Ōdinein* appears as early as the *Iliad*, which compares the pain of Agamemnon with the "throes a writhing woman suffers in hard labor" (11.268–272). In his treatise on biology, Aristotle employs *ōdinein* to refer to the actual pain of a woman in the process of giving birth (*Historia animalium* 7.9[586b, 27–29]). Thus the term appears both in discussions of physical travail and in metaphors that compare various forms of pain to that of a woman giving birth.

For closer parallels to Paul's use of *ōdinein*, we must look to the Septuagint, where *ōdinein* often appears in metaphors having to do with situations of agony or pain. In fact, the Septuagint reserves the word and the related noun *ōdin* almost entirely for such metaphors. The verb *tik-*

tein, to give birth, occurs in the multitudinous references to the fact of a human birth (see Gen 3:16; 4:1, 2; Exod 1:16; 1 Sam 1:20). *Ōdinein,* however, never refers to the mere *fact* of a birth, but always to the accompanying anguish (see Deut 2:25; 1 Sam 4:19; Sir 19:11; Jer 4:31). Further, *ōdinein* usually appears in contexts having to do with the situation of the people collectively, rather than with the situation of an individual.

This use of *ōdinein* and *ōdin* is especially clear in the case of the prophetic passages that speak about the day of the Lord:

> Writhe [*ōdinein*] and be strong and draw near, O daughter of Zion, like a woman giving birth; for now you will go forth from the city and dwell in the open country; you will go to Babylon. (Mic 4:10 Lxx)

> Wail, for the day of the Lord is near; as destruction from the Almighty it will come. . . . Travail [*ōdin*] will seize them like a woman giving birth. (Isa 13:6, 8 Lxx)

> We have heard their report, our hands fall helpless; anguish has taken hold of us, pangs [*ōdin*] as of a woman giving birth. (Jer 6:24 Lxx)

This association between travail and tribulation also occurs in a variety of places outside the Septuagint. For example, *1 En.* 62:4 speaks of the pain that will come, at the last judgment, upon the rulers of this age as on a woman in childbirth (see also *2 Bar.* 56:6, *4 Ezra* 4:42). In the library of the community at Qumran, a famous passage describes what appear to be the birth pangs of the new community:

> They set [my] soul as a boat in the [d]epths of the sea,
> and as a fortified city before her enemy.
> I am in distress, as a woman about to give birth to her firstborn.
> For her pangs come over her,
> and she has excruciating pain in her birth canal,
> writhing in the womb of the pregnant one.
> *(1QHª 11.6–8)*[17]

In these texts we find an established association between apocalyptic expectation and the anguish of childbirth. That association appears in the New Testament most explicitly in Mark and in Revelation. Mark 13:8 warns that "nation will rise against nation, and kingdom against kingdom; there will be earthquakes in various places, there will be famines; that is but the beginning of the birth pangs [*ōdin*]" (see also Matt 24:8).

Revelation 12:2, in its description of the woman whose child is to rule all the nations, refers to her cries in "her birth pangs [ōdinein]."[18]

Paul uses this word group only three times outside of Gal 4:19. Just after our text, in his treatment of the story of Sarah and Hagar, he quotes Isa 54:1: "Rejoice, you barren one, who does not give birth; break forth and shout, you who are not in labor pains [ōdinein]" (Gal 4:27).[19] When Paul discusses the Parousia in 1 Thess 5:3, he warns against those who proclaim peace and security, for "sudden destruction will come upon them, as labor pains [ōdin] come upon a pregnant woman, and they will by no means escape." In Rom 8:22, he speaks of the whole creation's "groaning in labor [synōdinein] together until now."

From this variety of evidence we may conclude that, by the first century, it was customary to speak of a coming cataclysm, however interpreted, as being accompanied by anguish like that of a woman giving birth.[20] It is widely recognized that Paul himself employs that theme in Romans 8 and in 1 Thessalonians 5. In my judgment, the best explanation of Gal 4:19 is that the same association is at work here as well.[21] Paul's anguish, his travail, is not simply a personal matter or a literary convention having to do with friendship or rebirth but reflects the anguish of the whole created order as it awaits the fulfillment of God's action in Jesus Christ.

This leaves us with the question of how Paul, an individual, can claim to be giving birth in this apocalyptically construed manner. That question can best be answered by turning to the second half of the verse: "until Christ is formed in you."

GALATIANS 4:19B

Earlier we noted the puzzling nature of this half of the verse. While Paul is in labor with the *Galatians*, it is *Christ* who is formed, and not the Galatians. Before dismissing this verse as another of Paul's incomplete analogies, we need to examine the expression "until Christ is formed in you."

What does it mean to say that Christ is formed? Commentators have posed a variety of answers to this question, but the answers do not adequately reflect the context of this expression in Galatians. For example, E. D. Burton argues that the formation of Christ refers to the spiritual maturation of the Galatians, "the full development of the Christ begotten in them."[22] Aside from the absence of this motif elsewhere in Paul, which Burton himself acknowledges, the difficulty with this interpretation is that the present context does not suggest that Paul views this formation as a natural progression toward spiritual maturity.[23] Instead of spiritual formation, Lietzmann suggests that Paul has in view here moral formation, so that the invisible Christ would be made visible in each believer.[24] But the language here is not moral language, at least not in the sense that Paul refers to the behavior of individual Christians as reflecting the behavior of Christ.[25] Hermann and Mussner regard the "formation of Christ" as the formation of the right image or understanding of Christ. The phrase then signals the need for the Galatians to return to right doctrine regarding Christ.[26] However, while Paul surely wants the Galatians to return to the gospel he has preached among them (1:6–7), there is little indication that 4:19 refers narrowly to a correct Christology.

To move beyond these suggestions, we need to examine Paul's reference to the formation of Christ within a larger context. Paul uses *morphousthai* (μορφοῦσθαι) only here, but he does employ some closely related verbs. For example, in 2 Cor 3:18, he speaks of the transformation (μεταμορφοῦσθαι; *metamorphousthai*) of believers into the likeness of the Lord. In Phil 3:10, he refers to his hope of being conformed to the death of Christ (συμμορφοῦσθαι; *symmorphousthai*). And in Rom 12:2, he urges Christians at Rome to be transformed (*metamorphousthai*) by the renewal of their minds. While none of these texts refers specifically to the formation *of Christ*, each reflects the conviction that the Christ event issues in a profound shaping and reshaping of human perceptions.[27]

With this constellation of usage in mind, we return to Galatians and notice several passages that may shed light on the formation to which Paul refers in 4:19. First is 2:19b–20, which commentators frequently associate with our text:

> I have been crucified with Christ; and it is no longer I who live,
> but it is Christ who lives in me; and the life I now live in the flesh
> I live by faith in the Son of God, who loved me and gave himself
> for me. (NRSV)

Paul experienced crucifixion with Christ, and now Christ lives in Paul. What comes to expression here is Paul's conviction that Christ has overtaken him. Everything that preceded, even his status among his Jewish peers, to which he refers in 1:13–14, counts for nothing. The gospel has eclipsed Paul's life. (On this point, see chapter 6 below.)

That this crucifixion with Christ is not a characteristic only of Paul or only of Paul and his apostolic colleagues becomes clear in 3:27–28. Because of the prominence of this text in contemporary Christian discussions regarding pressing issues of justice and equity, we may overlook the repetitious references to Christ here: "You were baptized into Christ"; "You have put on Christ"; "You are all one in Christ Jesus." Whatever Paul says about the nullification of divisions among human beings he says because and only because of the prior claim that all believers are in Christ and, by implication, nowhere else. The Christ who overtook Paul overtakes all believers.[28]

That this change goes beyond even the corporate life of the believing community becomes clear in 6:15, where the cosmic implications of this claim are made: There is neither circumcision nor uncircumcision, but new creation. As J. Louis Martyn has shown, what is at stake in this letter is the apocalyptic antinomy between cosmos on the one hand (which includes both law and "unlaw") and the new creation ushered in by Jesus Christ on the other.[29]

If we look at the words in 4:19b again in this larger context, we see that they begin to take on a different meaning. For Christ to be formed in the Galatians is not simply for them to develop spiritually or morally or christologically. The formation of Christ among the Galatians is simultaneously their crucifixion with Christ.[30] It means that the eclipse of the old occurs among them. The letter reflects Paul's conviction that the Galatians were called, that they had heard the gospel, and that they responded in faith. But he also believes that they are in danger of turning again, of converting back to their earlier views. For that reason he speaks of his own labor with them and the need for Christ to be formed.[31]

The phrase μέχρις οὗ (mechris hou, until) gives us pause. It is unclear whether Paul regards this formation as one that will have a completion date in the near future or whether the formation is continuous. In his letters we find both the expectation that the believer is actually changed by the gospel (Rom 6:1–4) and the awareness that such change is ongoing (1 Cor 3:1–4). Here those two expectations seem to be held in tension. What creates Paul's dilemma in this letter, after all, is that believers are in danger of being led away from that birth (he is in labor again!); but these people have been called (Gal 1:6), have received the spirit (3:2), and have been baptized into Christ (3:27). It is difficult for him to imagine such a development. On the other hand, the apocalyptic setting of the first part of Gal 4:19 indicates that the formation of Christ continues until the fulfillment of the Christ event in God's final triumph (see also Rom 8:29 and 1 Cor 15:49).[32]

The formation of Christ is ἐν ὑμῖν (en hymin, in you), and the plural pronoun requires comment. Formation does not belong to individual believers, as a personal or private possession only. Instead, formation refers to the community of those who are called to faith, what Paul elsewhere refers to as the body of Christ.[33]

Now we may ask again how the two parts of this verse work together: "My children, with whom I am again in labor until Christ is formed in you . . ." The first part of the verse invokes not only Paul's apostolic role, but also the apocalyptic stage on which that role is played. At stake here are not the birth pangs of an individual apostle, but the birth pangs of the cosmos itself. Paul's labor is that of an individual who knows that the world has been invaded by a new reality: a crucified Lord who confronts and overturns the world.

The flaw that appears in the second part of Paul's analogy occurs, not because his imagination is defective, but because he does not wish to carry the analogy through to its logical conclusion. It is not believers who are born. That reflects the attitude of the philosophical schools of Paul's day, in which a premium was placed on the full development of the individual. Paul's point, by contrast, is that it is Christ who is formed, and the apocalyptic maternity is completed only when Christ is formed.

Still the analogy seems flawed, for we might expect Paul to say, "until *I bring forth* Christ in you." But that is not to be said for two reasons. First, God and God alone brings forth Christ. God is the one who sends Christ (Gal 1:4); it is not Christ who authorizes himself. Second, neither Paul nor any other believer wills Christ into existence or forms Christ within oneself. Paul's use of *morphousthai* here and related verbs elsewhere is consistently in the passive voice. The formation of Christ occurs as a gift, not as an achievement.

So the analogy is flawed, but for a specific set of reasons. It is not that Paul is unable to make the analogy work, but that he is unwilling to do so.

Now we return to the larger context of v. 19 in Gal 4:12–20. At the outset I noted the awkward way our text stands in relation to the larger passage. Galatians 4:19 seems, at first glance, to be an aside in a passage that appeals primarily to the earlier warm personal relationship Paul has established with the Galatians. We have discovered that 4:19 is not simply an appeal based on the friendship Paul and the Galatians have established, however. It is, instead, a theological claim that Paul's work as an apostle occurs within an apocalyptic framework that is created by God's revelation of Jesus Christ and that looks forward to the full incorporation of all believers—indeed, of the cosmos itself—into Christ. This theological claim provides the grounding for the personal appeal of earlier lines, not merely in the person of Paul but also in the action of God.

AFTERWORD

When an earlier version of this chapter appeared as an article in 1990, as I note at the outset, relatively little had been written about Gal 4:19 (at least in modern exegesis; as the introduction to part 1 of this book shows, earlier generations of interpreters were more familiar with this passage and other of Paul's maternal metaphors). Since its initial publication, the reading of Gal 4:19 offered in this chapter has been taken up in an extended and serious way both by J. Louis Martyn and by Susan Eastman.

In his magisterial commentary on Galatians, Martyn argues that Isa 45:9–11 played a shaping role in Paul's formulation of Gal 4:19.[34] In particular, Martyn takes note of Isa 45:10, with its use of both paternal and maternal imagery:

> Woe to anyone who says to a father, "What are you begetting?"
> or to a woman, "With what are you in labor?"
>
> (NRSV)

Although Paul was well aware of this text and of the convention of referring to a teacher as the "father" of his students, here he uses only the maternal metaphor.[35] Martyn posits that he does so because he cannot speak confidently, as he does in 1 Cor 4:14–15, of the birth of the Galatian congregations as a *punctiliar event.* The incursion of the Teachers among the Galatians has "reversed the birth process, . . . throwing Paul back into anxious labor."[36] Paul understands this suffering and the Teachers' activity that gives rise to it as "an instance of the last-ditch effort by which God's enemies hope to thwart the eschatological redemption of the elect."[37] I am not as confident as Martyn is that we should read Isa 45:10 as having primary textual influence on Gal 4:19, but his suggestions about the apocalyptic location of Paul's birth pains are persuasive.[38]

The most recent and by far the most extensive treatment of Gal 4:19 appears in Susan Eastman's study of Paul's "mother tongue," which is a significant attempt to press Martyn's apocalyptic reading of Galatians forward to understand how the invasive ("punctiliar") gospel can produce transformed human lives and communities.[39] Eastman takes up Ursula Le Guin's suggestive distinction between "father tongue" and "mother tongue," that is, between language that seeks objectivity, that speaks in a single direction (from above or outside to a passive subject) in an effort to exert power, and "mother tongue," in which language is not simply communication but also relationship, language that binds and unites rather than distancing.[40] In Gal 4:12–5:1 Eastman finds an instance of Paul's own use of "mother tongue"; that is, here Paul draws on familial language, and especially on his own suffering, to provide the Galatians with "the motivation and power necessary to move them from their wavering *sic et non* to a faith that 'stands fast' in its allegiance to Christ alone as the source of their unity and life together."[41]

Eastman welcomes an apocalyptic reading of this text, but she probes for a more concrete identification of Paul's labor pains, turning back to Paul's statement about his "fleshly weakness" in 4:13. Drawing on earlier exegesis, both ancient and modern, she argues that this "weakness" refers to the wounds, even scarring, Paul endured as a result of persecution. It is this very scarring of his own body that Paul refers to when he recalls for the Galatians the public exhibition of the crucifixion (3:1; see also 6:17), and these scars distinguish Paul from the Teachers (6:12–17).[42] Paul's "labor," on this reading, is "his embodied, cruciform proclamation of the gospel."[43] This labor Eastman goes on to contrast with the "Jerusalem above" of Gal 4:27 (Isa 54:1), which brings children to birth *without pain.*[44]

While I concede that my own earlier argument that Paul here identifies himself with the anguish of all creation may be unsatisfying,[45] I am somewhat skeptical about such a close rendering of Paul's labor in terms of his physical suffering from persecution. This connection relies on identifying a highly particular historical context for several elusive details in Galatians (3:1; 4:13; and 4:19).[46] It further involves the near dissection of the metaphor of 4:19, so that it becomes less metaphor than allegory. These disagreements about fine details in no way undermine the contributions made here, however. Susan Eastman has considerably advanced the discussion by bringing together what are usually referred to as the "personal" and the "theological" dimensions of Paul's argument. Eastman rightly insists that Paul does not claim to be or wish to be "objective" here or anywhere else in this letter, in which he appeals intensely to God's intervention in his own life and in that of the Galatians.[47]

CHAPTER THREE

Mother's Milk and Ministry

> But, brothers and sisters, I could not speak with you as spiritual persons but only as fleshly persons, as infants in Christ. I gave you milk to drink, not solid food, for you could not take solid food, and even now you cannot, since you are still fleshly persons.
>
> *1 Corinthians 3:1–3a*

Because the texts we have explored in chapters 1 and 2 present Paul as a nurse (1 Thess 2:7) and as a woman in labor (Gal 4:19), it may not come as a surprise to find him writing about the Corinthians and their readiness (or the lack thereof) to move from baby food to something more substantial. The passage nevertheless raises a number of questions. How can "people of the flesh" be simultaneously "infants in Christ," since those who are in Christ are supposed to have put away living according to the flesh? Does Paul understand there to be varying kinds or degrees of Christian instruction, corresponding to milk and solid food? Is the proclamation of "Jesus Christ, and him crucified" (2:2) to be equated with infant's milk? If so, then what constitutes the "solid food" of those who are more mature in faith?

These are the questions that arise most often in scholarly discussion of this passage, but in keeping with the approach of the previous chapters, I want to press the importance of yet another question: What is the significance of Paul's referring to himself as the nursing mother of the Corinthians? In this chapter I argue that we cannot understand the drama presupposed in 1 Cor 3:1–2 until we take into consideration both of the characters, not only the child who may or may not be ready to begin eating solid food, but also the mother who has thus far nursed the child with milk. That is, Paul's presentation of himself as a nursing mother suggests that 1 Cor 3:1–2 illumines Paul's understanding of the nature of the apostolic task.[1] When Paul employs the image of a nursing mother in self-reference here, he accomplishes several things. First, the use of maternal imagery reinforces the imagery of family that appears throughout 1 Corinthians, language that serves to build up the Corinthian community. Second, the use of this image undermines the culturally approved masculine role and hence renders Paul susceptible to attack as weak and ineffective. Third, this metaphor of the nursing mother introduces the later series of metaphors in which apostles are compared with farmers and builders, and prepares the way for further remarks about the character of apostolic labor.

As noted above, most scholarly discussion of this passage has focused on questions about the diet of the Christian community at Corinth. Many interpreters, taking their cues from the reference in 2:6 to speaking wisdom among the "mature," identify milk with Paul's initial instruction in the gospel and solid food with his more extensive instruction in wisdom.[2] Other interpreters have rightly pointed to the difficulties inherent in this two-tiered system of Christian diet. For Paul there is only one Christian gospel, that of the cross, and this gospel itself contains all the wisdom needed (1:18, 24; 2:1). As Morna Hooker nicely puts it, "The fundamental contrast in Paul's mind is . . . between the true food of the Gospel with which he has fed them (whether milk or meat) and the synthetic substitutes which the Corinthians have preferred."[3] At most, the solid food Paul refers to may be a more profound understanding of the gospel rather than some mystery tradition.[4] In addition, some interpreters appeal to 14:20 as evidence that the Corinthians have not made sufficient progress in their faith.

These views of 3:1–2 share a focus on the Corinthians and their wisdom or maturity (or the lack thereof). The majority of scholars agree that Paul is saying something like this: "*You* are not mature enough for the special wisdom [or the more mature forms of the kerygma] that we dispense among a few. It is time now for *you* to grow up and grasp the gospel as mature adults."

What I find intriguing is that none of these interpretations of the passage attends to the fact that Paul casts his remarks in the first person. At most, the occasional commentator suggests that the "and I" (κἀγώ, *kagō*) in v. 1 implicitly contrasts Paul with other Christian teachers. But Paul speaks here in first person of himself as the nursing mother of the Corinthians: "I could not speak with you. . . . I gave you milk to drink, not solid food." Indeed, the "milk and solid food" analogy would work better as a reprimand if Paul had omitted the reference to himself at the beginning of v. 2 and substituted something like "You are still drinking milk when you should at least be ready for cereal." In other words, using the first person actually confuses things, or at least it does *if* Paul's primary concern is the maturity of the Corinthians or their readiness for advanced instruction. The oddness and intrusiveness of Paul's "I gave you milk to drink" suggests that we need to attend a little more closely to the use of first person in this passage.

MILK AND SOLID FOOD ELSEWHERE

Support for my claim that we need to pay attention to the use of first person in this passage comes from a surprising source. The food imagery in this text is not unique to Paul, of course. Virtually every interpreter of this passage, regardless of the position taken on "milk, not solid food," makes reference to other Hellenistic texts that employ the contrast between milk and solid food. To the best of my knowledge, however, no one has recognized the most significant difference between the texts adduced and 1 Cor 3:1–2: unlike the parallels, Paul speaks of himself as the one supplying the milk.

It will be instructive to review some of the passages cited most often so that the differences from 1 Cor 3 will be apparent. In Heb 5:12–14 the author complains:

> For though by this time you ought to be teachers, you need some-one to teach you again the basic elements of the oracles of God. You need milk, not solid food; for everyone who lives on milk, being still an infant, is unskilled in the word of righteousness. But solid food is for the mature, for those whose faculties have been trained by practice to distinguish good from evil. (NRSV)

And the author of 1 Peter admonishes:

> Like newborn infants, long for the pure, spiritual milk, so that by it you may grow into salvation. (1 Pet 2:2 NRSV)

These two early Christian instances of the milk and solid food metaphor are customarily read alongside several texts from Philo and Epictetus:

> Philo, *That Every Good Person Is Free* 160 (LCL): But souls which have as yet got nothing of either kind, neither that which enslaves, nor that which establishes freedom, souls still naked like those of mere infants, must be tended and nursed by instill-ing first, in place of milk [γάλα, *gala*], the soft food of instruction given in the school subjects, later, the harder, stronger meat [τροφή, *trophē*], which philosophy produces.

Philo, *On the Preliminary Studies* 19 (LCL): Observe too that our body is not nourished in the earlier stages with solid [τροφή] and costly foods. The simple and milky [γαλακτώδης, *galaktōdēs*] foods of infancy come first. Just so you may consider that the school subjects and the lore which belongs to each of them stand ready to nourish the childhood of the soul, while the virtues are grown-up food, suited for those who are really men.

Philo, *On Agriculture* 9 (LCL): But who else could the man that is in each of us be save the mind, whose place it is to reap the benefits derived from all that has been sown or planted? But seeing that for babes milk [γάλα] is food, but for grown men wheaten bread, there must also be soul-nourishment, such as is milk–like suited to the time of childhood, in the shape of the preliminary stages of school–learning, and such as is adapted to grown men in the shape of instructions leading the way through wisdom and temperance and all virtue.

Philo, *On the Migration of Abraham* 29 (LCL): In this country there awaiteth thee the nature which is its own pupil, its own teacher, that needs not be fed on milk [γαλακτώδης] as children are fed, that has been stayed by a Divine oracle from going down to Egypt and from meeting with the ensnaring pleasures of the flesh.

Philo, *On Dreams* 2.10 (LCL): The noble company is led by Isaac who learns from no teacher but himself, for Moses represents him as weaned, absolutely disdaining to make any use of soft and milky food [γαλακτώδης] suited to infants and little children, and using only strong nourishment fit for grown men, seeing that from a babe he was naturally stalwart, and was ever attaining fresh vigour and renewing his youth.

Epictetus, *Discourses* 2.16.39 (LCL): Are you not willing, at this late date, like children, to be weaned and to partake of more solid food [τροφή], and not to cry for [mothers] and nurses—old wives' lamentations?

Epictetus, *Discourses* 3.24.9 (LCL): Shall we not wean [ἀπογαλακ-τίζειν, *apogalaktizein*] ourselves at last, and call to mind what we have heard from the philosophers?

First Corinthians 3:1–2 shares with these passages the image of milk and solid food. As should be clear from my earlier summary of the discussion, commentators debate the adequacy of these ostensible parallels, particularly on the question whether Paul thinks there are two tiers of Christian instruction.[5] What the discussion of these parallels neglects is the fact that Paul is himself the nurturer, a feature that appears in none of the examples adduced. Paul does not speak with Philo's detachment about what food the soul requires or about the "shape of instruction." Neither does Paul cajole the Corinthians to cease their crying "for mothers and nurses." Instead, he images himself as the mother who nurtures, the one who knows what food is appropriate for her children. In other words, even though the image of milk and meat was current, Paul does something distinctive with it: he presents himself as the mother of the Corinthians.

Attending to the use of first person in 3:1–2 alters the way we read this passage. It is no longer about the single issue of what the Corinthians eat; it also concerns the one who feeds them. And the language is unequivocal: Paul is the nursing mother of the church.

That point would seem to be obvious from the phrase "I gave you milk to drink" (γάλα ὑμᾶς ἐπότισα, *gala hymas epotisa*). Before the advent of infant formula and baby bottles, it is the mother or the wet nurse who feeds milk to an infant. Commentators overlook or at least underinterpret this point, preferring to focus instead on the paternal imagery at the end of chapter 4. Some even connect this use of maternal imagery with the later passage, as if the nursing mother were somehow a father.[6] Paul does not use the two kinds of images interchangeably, however. In 3:1–2, as elsewhere, he uses maternal imagery to refer to the ongoing process of nurturing Christian faith. Paternal imagery, as in 4:15–16, he employs for the initial act of missionary preaching.[7]

PAUL AS MALE NURSE?

Before exploring the implications of this use of maternal imagery, one possible objection requires attention. In his study on parents and children in the letters of Paul, O. Larry Yarbrough contends that the figure of a male nurse (*nutritor*), rather than a nursing mother or wet nurse, stands in the background of 1 Cor 3:1–2. The male nurse might have fed his charges with a mixture of goat's milk and honey (presumably in the absence of an available wet nurse).[8] Inscriptional evidence suggests that male nurses were often fondly remembered by their charges, so that Paul's imagery in this passage suggests the intimate connection between himself and the Corinthians.[9]

Yarbrough's identification of 1 Cor 3:2 with male nurses depends on Keith R. Bradley's study of male involvement in child care at Rome.[10] Bradley examines both literary and inscriptional evidence for the figures of the *paedagogus,* the *educator,* and the *nutritor* or male nurse. Only in the single case of C. Mussius Chrysonicus is someone identified as *nutritor lactaneus* (or male nurse who feeds milk to his charges).[11] Bradley himself observes that *nutritores* were sometimes foster fathers. More often they appear to have been figures who assisted wet nurses with very young children, perhaps because the *nutritor* and *nutrix* (wet nurse) were themselves married.[12] Bradley also speculates that the *nutritor's* role involved watching over children who were no longer confined to the women's quarter with the *nutrix.*[13] Bradley himself makes no claim that the *nutritor* offered babies a substitute for breast milk.[14] In other words, the Roman male nurse as Bradley reconstructs him seems quite removed from the direct acts of feeding an infant that are involved in the metaphor of 1 Cor 3:2.

It appears that Yarbrough has either misunderstood Bradley or exaggerated the importance of one small sample in Bradley's study. In addition, Yarbrough does not take into account those other instances in which Paul speaks of himself in unambiguously maternal terms (e.g., Gal 4:19; 1 Thess 2:7).

PAUL AS NURSING MOTHER

The preceding remarks might be dismissed as a serious case of overkill, an elaborate attempt to persuade readers of 1 Cor 3:1–2 to take seriously two small Greek words: κἀγώ (*kagō*, and I) and ποτίζειν (*potizein*, cause to drink). What warrants such extended attention to such minute details?

In the first place, we have already seen that Paul employs maternal imagery. As students of Paul continue to explore his remarks about women, the roles of women in the Pauline churches, and the implications of Paul's letters for women, this cluster of passages merits consideration in its own right. Beyond that initial task of retrieval, the image of the nursing mother in 1 Cor 3:1–2 contributes in specific ways to the case Paul develops in this letter. To begin with, there is in this letter an extensive network of family imagery, language that serves to reinforce Paul's urgent appeal for unity in Corinth. The letter opens by invoking "God our Father" (1:3) and "his Son, Jesus Christ" (1:9). It discusses relationships between husbands and wives (7:1–16; 11:2–16),[15] it refers to meals eaten at home (11:22), and it refers to believers in households (1:16; 16:15; and probably 1:11).[16] One extraordinary passage recalls "our ancestors" (literally, "all our fathers," 10:1) who wandered in the wilderness, boldly claiming for an assorted group of Corinthian Gentiles the ancestors of Israel.

Most prominent in this network of family language in 1 Corinthians is Paul's use of "brother," rendered "brother and sister" in the NRSV (ἀδελφός, *adelphos*).[17] This is a regular feature of Paul's letters, of course, but the term occurs thirty-nine times in this letter, as compared with nineteen times in Romans and twelve times in 2 Corinthians. From the opening of the letter (1:1, 10, 11) through to the very end (16:11, 12, 15, 20), Paul speaks to and about his siblings in the faith.[18]

Paul's references to himself as the nursing mother and begetting father of the Corinthians are also part of this network of family language.[19] It seems unlikely that this extensive network is merely accidental. Instead, it serves to reinforce Paul's concerns about factions in the Corinthian church.[20] If believers in Corinth accept Paul's designation of themselves as "brothers and sisters," if they understand themselves to have Paul as their begetting father and their nurturing mother, if they affirm their connection with Israel's ancestors and, most important, if they agree that God is the father of them all—then it should prove far more difficult for them to maintain their divisiveness.

Even within this impressive array of family language, however, Paul's self-designation as the nursing mother of the Corinthians is particularly striking. To state what is manifestly obvious: Paul may have been a biological father, but he surely did not nurse an infant (his own or anyone else's). The very incongruity of the imagery presses the question of how the Corinthians might have heard it. What would they make of a male speaking of himself in what are unmistakably female tones?

Answers to this question will need to be couched in exceedingly cautious terms. If we have difficulty identifying Paul's "intentions," how much more complicated is it to construct the responses of the Corinthians, from whom we have not a single scrap of evidence on this matter? Some tantalizing clues appear, nevertheless, in the burgeoning literature on gender-construction in the Greco-Roman world. Thomas Laquer has identified a "one-sex" model of sexuality that dominated the ancient world, a model in which women are understood to be "inverted" males. On this view, "the standard of the human body and its representations is the male body."[21]

For the purposes of this study of 1 Cor 3, what is important about this one-sex model is the way it dominates not only understandings of physiology but every aspect of appearance and behavior.[22] For example, the *Physiognomonics* attributed to Aristotle identifies an amazing array of physical characteristics associated with persons of varying dispositions (including men who are shameless, orderly, insensitive, morbid, and so forth). In this elaborate scheme, a "real man" (σκληρὸς ἀνῆρ, *sklēros anēr*) possesses such identifiable traits as stiff hair, erect carriage, a strong neck, and a fleshy broad chest. One who is less manly (μαλακός, *malakos*) may be identified by his soft hair, sedentary habits, weak eyes, and small legs (*Physiognomonics* 807a–b). Seneca claims that men who dress like women and attempt to look young and boyish behave contrary to nature (*Moral Epistles* 122.7). Quintilian complains that when a speaker's style and content are inconsistent with one another, "It is as if men deformed themselves by wearing necklaces, pearls, and long flowing robes, which are feminine adornments" (*Institutes* 11.1.3 [LCL]).[23] Dio Chrysostom purports to be able to identify males of bad character and disposition from such features as "voice, glance, posture, . . . style of haircut, mode of walking, elevation of the eye, inclination of the neck, the trick of conversing with upturned palms" (*Oration 33* [*First Tarsic*] *Discourse* 52 [LCL]).

Later physiognomists such as the second-century Polemo pride themselves on their ability to identify those males who were not "real men," no matter how much such persons labored to conceal their identity. In her study of Polemo and Favorinus, Maud W. Gleason concludes that the polarized gender distinctions they used "purported to characterize the gulf between men and women, but actually served to divide the male sex into legitimate and illegitimate members."[24]

John J. Winkler has characterized these concerns as reflecting the belief that "male life is warfare, that masculinity is a duty and a hard-won achievement, and that the temptation to desert one's side is very great."[25] In this view, the female is not only an inverted male but also a threat to masculine identity. A male who transgresses the boundaries in dress, behavior, deportment, even in physical features may be accused of "going AWOL from [his] assigned place in the gender hierarchy."[26]

Given this environment, I find it reasonable to imagine that "I fed you with milk" (that is, "I was your mother or wet nurse") would cause the attentive among the Corinthians to suspect that Paul himself was not a "real male." By actively taking upon himself a role that could only be played by a woman, he effectively concedes the culturally predisposed battle for his masculinity.[27] This environment may help to explain why Philo and Epictetus do not speak in first person when they invoke the milk and meat image, lest their own masculinity likewise be called into question.

Why would Paul risk such a perception while dealing with the Corinthians? We can best assess the function of the maternal imagery here by looking ahead to Paul's comments about the apostolic role later in this chapter and in chapter 4. Paul introduces the topic in 1 Cor 3:5 with the question "What then is Apollos? What is Paul? Servants [διάκονοι, *diakonoi*] through whom you came to believe, as the Lord assigned to each" (NRSV). He promptly elaborates on this notion of servanthood through the analogies of planting and building (vv. 5–16), but the discussion as a whole needs to be read over against the question of v. 4: "For when one says, 'I belong to Paul' and another, 'I belong to Apollos,' are you not merely human?" (NRSV). The Corinthians belong, not to Paul or Apollos, but to Christ, as becomes clear in v. 23: "You belong to Christ" (NRSV). Over against any perception that Paul and Apollos are, even figuratively, owners of the Corinthians, Paul responds, "But we are *mere* servants."[28]

That Paul and Apollos are mere servants may seem to be contradicted by the imagery that follows. When Paul identifies himself as the planter or the architect and the Corinthians as the field or building, he places himself in a role that appears active and authoritative over against the Corinthians who are mere recipients. Elizabeth A. Castelli finds in the passage

> a clear hierarchical separation between the apostles on the one hand and the community on the other. . . . While Apollos and Paul are the fellow workers of God, the community is characterized as the passive object of that apostolic work. Also, while there is no equality being expressed here, neither is there any expression of reciprocity: the community is the recipient of the apostles' work.[29]

Another reading is possible, however, and even preferable. Paul does not say that the Corinthians are his field or Apollos' building; they are "God's field, God's building" (v. 9). Indeed, vv. 16–17 raise the volume of the metaphor, making the Corinthians into God's own holy temple. Anyone who destroys that temple will be destroyed. Paul is not the authoritative ruler, then, but the servant commissioned by the proprietor, a servant who stands under the threat of destructive judgment should that possession be violated. The issue at stake in this passage is not who is active and who is passive, but to whom the Corinthians belong and to whom Paul and Apollos are accountable. Dale Martin gets it right:

> In 3:5–17 he relativizes the position of apostles: they are only workmen, planters or waterers, whereas the Corinthians are God's field, the object of his care. . . . Paul portrays the Corinthian church as God's temple and himself and other teachers as mere architects or builders.[30]

The ironic remarks of 4:8–13 confirm this reading of the apostolic task as found in 3:5–17. Apostles are not identified with those people and things normally perceived as wealthy, strong, and honorable. In fact, the apostles are the polar opposite: "last of all, as though sentenced to death, . . . a spectacle to the world, to angels and to mortals" (4:9). It seems appropriate that Paul introduces this view of apostolic ministry in the language of the nursing mother. The metaphor expresses the bond of affection and care that characterizes the relationship and simultaneously places Paul at the margins of what is perceived to be "genuine" manhood.

Conventional interpretations of 3:1–2 read backward: they take their cues primarily from the discussion of wisdom in chapter 2 and see in 3:1–2 the sharp expression of Paul's concern for the Corinthians' maturity. I have argued that the passage *also* needs to be read forward, since it contributes to Paul's immediate argument about what constitutes authentic apostolic ministry.[31] By speaking in first person, Paul anticipates his comments about his own work as servant (διάκονος). By speaking in first person as a nursing mother, Paul compromises his own standing as a "real man," anticipating the loss of standing that later emerges as he depicts his ministry as that of a planter of someone else's field, a servant of someone else's builder, the "dregs of all things" (4:13). If we are to read 3:1–2 backward, then we need to read back as far as 1:18, for the images of apostolic ministry Paul employs in chapter 3 have their origin in his proclamation of the crucified Jesus, who is no more a "real man" by the world's standards than is a nursing Paul.[32]

CHAPTER FOUR

The Birthing of Creation

For we know that all creation groans together and is in labor together
until now.

Romans 8:22

In the preceding chapters I explore texts in which Paul speaks of himself in maternal terms. He compares himself and his colleagues with a
wet nurse who cares for her own children (1 Thess 2:7). He is in the labor
of childbirth with the Galatians (4:19). He complains that he must continue to feed the Corinthians with milk, as they are not yet ready to take
solid food (1 Cor 3:2). The Pauline corpus offers other instances of
maternal language as well. In Gal 1:15, Paul writes that God set him aside
for apostleship "from the womb of my mother" (NRSV: "before I was
born"). Later in the same letter, he refers to Jesus Christ as having been
"born of a woman" (Gal 4:4), and to the children—both physical and
allegorical—of Sarah and Hagar.[1] In Rom 4 Paul makes a brief reference
to "Sarah's womb" (v. 19), and 9:9–10 similarly refers in passing to the
children of Sarah and Rebecca. Unlike the passages we have examined in
earlier chapters, however, these passages refer to actual flesh-and-blood
mothers or draw upon those actual mothers metaphorically.[2]

In Rom 8, however, there is an additional instance of birth imagery,
referring neither to a physical mother nor to Paul's apostolic endeavors:

> For I hold that the sufferings of the present time are not worth
> comparing with the glory that is to be apocalyptically revealed[3]
> to us. For the eager expectation of creation yearns for the apoc-
> alypse of God's children [υἱοί, *huoi*; lit., sons]. For creation was
> subjected to futility, not freely but by the one who subjected it
> in hope, since creation itself will be freed from slavery to decay
> for the freedom of the glory of God's children [τέκνοι, *teknoi*].

51

> For we know that *all creation* [πᾶσα ἡ κτίσις, *pasa hē ktisis*]
> *groans together* [συστενάζει, *systenazei*] *and is in labor together*
> [συνωδίνει, *synōdinei*] until now. Not only that, but we—we
> who already have the firstfruit of the Spirit—*we indeed groan*
> [στενάζομεν, *stenazomen*] as we long for adoption, the redemp-
> tion of our body. (8:18–23)

In this passage neither Paul nor a biological mother is in labor; instead, the one who labors to bring to birth is creation itself.

Debate about the precise connotations of this passage is ancient,[4] but in recent decades a near consensus has formed that Paul refers to all of creation *except* human beings ("subhuman" creation is the term often employed).[5] Following from that consensus, three additional points frequently attend the discussion of this passage. First, what creation longs for is the public disclosure of the identity of God's children. J. D. G. Dunn imagines creation as the audience

> of a play in which the final curtain is drawn back to reveal the
> various actors transformed (back) into their real characters. . . .
> Only some of the actors ("the sons of God") will take part in the
> final curtain call, and . . . the audience's eagerness is to see who
> these are and what is this transformation they have undergone.[6]

Second, once these children of God are revealed, they have a role to play in the redemption of creation itself. Following the lead of Ernest Best, Sylvia Keesmaat contends that the "glory" to be revealed is "the wise rule of the children of God over creation," based on the responsibility given humanity in Gen 1:28 and 2:15.[7] Similarly, N. T. Wright speaks of the role of humanity in rescuing "the whole created order" and bringing "the wise, healing restorative divine justice to the whole created order."[8]

Third, at least some scholars conclude that what is envisioned in this passage is not an apocalyptic inbreaking into the present but a gradual movement toward transformation. Edward Adams characterizes creation as "part of a productive process which will result in a positive and joyous outcome," and avers that the glory that is to come grows out of the present time of suffering.[9] Similarly, Philip Esler writes of the revealing of God's children as something that is "organically evolving out of present experience but not yet visible."[10]

For a variety of reasons, not least of which is the current environmental crisis, this reading of Rom 8 generates considerable sympathy. Before endorsing this interpretation, however, it is important to linger over some details in the passage, beginning with the logic of vv. 22–23. Having initially commented on the eagerness of creation itself, Paul affirms:

> All creation groans together and is *in labor together*.

He *then* adds:

> We also groan together . . .
> *while we wait for adoption, the redemption of our body.*

The highlighted wording reveals the difficulty: *the labor of giving birth that is introduced in v. 22 never comes to completion*. What is awaited is not a birth but an adoption, not a baby but redemption. As with Gal 4 and 1 Thess 2, the text takes an unexpected twist. We are led to imagine that creation will give birth to something new, perhaps to its own renewal or to new life. And "we" may be in anguish for something to be delivered as part of this new creation. What happens instead is that Paul returns to the language of adoption introduced earlier in the chapter (v. 15). He then explains adoption in the language of redemption introduced in 3:24.

This is not simply a failure of Paul's imagination or his mental powers. What seems at first glance to be a logical mistake actually offers a clue to what is going on in this text, which anticipates neither creation's giving birth nor humanity's rescue of creation (attractive as both those notions might be), but God's deliverance of all that God has made from the powers of Sin and Death. Establishing this apocalyptic reading of Rom 8 requires locating the text in the larger argument of the letter, but first we must attend to the terms "creation" and "God's children."

WHAT CONSTITUTES "ALL CREATION"?

Paul's language in Rom 8:18–25 draws attention to creation. Creation's own eagerness is the subject of the verb in v. 19, and creation itself the subject of the verbs in vv. 20–21. This rhetoric is heightened in v. 22, which draws the audience's attention with the introduction "We know" and the emphatic expression "all creation." What exactly does Paul mean by "creation"?[11] As previously noted, there is widespread agreement that "creation" refers to creation *apart from human beings*, based on several considerations. First, v. 20 describes the subjection of creation as "not of its own will" (NRSV), which many take to mean that the subjection of creation takes place because of Adam's fall. Genesis 3:17 ("Cursed is the ground because of you" [NRSV]) often comes into the discussion as evidence that, while humanity is subjected by its own actions, nonhuman creation is subjected because of Adam. Second, the fact that creation is waiting for the apocalypse of the children of God and that v. 24 refers to the groaning of "we" suggests to many that Paul is making a distinction between creation and believers.[12] Third, some scholars draw upon the usage of "creation" (κτίσις, ktisis) elsewhere to confirm the notion that 8:19–22 has to do with nonhuman creation (e.g., Wis Sol 2:6; 5:17; 16:24; 19:6).[13]

On closer examination, none of these arguments is as persuasive as is often assumed, and both this text and the larger context suggest that creation does include *all of humanity* along with *the remainder of creation*. To begin with, too much stress has been placed on the phrase in v. 20 which the NRSV translates as "not of its own will." This Greek phrase (οὐκ ἑκοῦσα, *ouk hekousa*) often appears paired with its opposite (ἄκων, *akōn*), as in 1 Cor 9:17, to draw attention to a contrast between doing something freely and doing it under compulsion.[14] That pattern suggests that reading the phrase in v. 20 as a comment about the "will" of creation may be an overinterpretation; instead of drawing attention to the disposition of creation, the phrase draws attention to the one who *subjects* creation, namely, God.[15] What v. 20 does, then, is to describe the subjection and to reinforce the notion that creation was *acted upon* by God: "creation was subjected—not freely—but by the one who subjected it."

Second, the eagerness with which creation longs for the apocalypse of God's children does not preclude those children themselves from being part of the eager expectation. Indeed, far from saying that the children are *not* part of creation's longing, v. 23 highlights that longing. Even the fact that they possess the firstfruit (or perhaps precisely *because* they do), "we" long right along with (and indeed as part of) the rest of creation. If creation is imagined as an orchestra "performing" this work of longing, "we" are a featured section of the orchestra, not a different orchestra or performers of a different composition.

Although other Jewish texts may employ the word "creation" (κτίσις) in ways that distinguish humanity from the remainder of creation, several features of Romans and elsewhere in the Pauline corpus suggest that humanity is understood to be part of creation. To begin with, in Rom 1:18–32 Paul charges humanity with idolatry, asserting that they made images of "a human being, birds, four-footed animals, and reptiles" and exchanged those for the glory of God (v. 23). He subsequently sums up this accusation with the words, "they worshiped and served the *creation* [κτίσις, *ktisis*] rather than the one who created" (1:25), which suggests that human beings are part of the creation itself; indeed, the problem with humanity lies in its refusal to understand itself as made by God. (And it is in this sense that it might be said that creation, humanity included, is subjected "not willingly," i.e., humanity did not wish to be subjected; in fact, humanity rebelled against its rightful place as creature.)

Other passages corroborate this understanding of the joining together of human and nonhuman parts of creation. In the closing doxology of Rom 11:33–36, Paul draws on Scripture to voice the impossibility of understanding God's own wisdom and knowledge, concluding with the words "since from him and through him and for him are *all things.*" Less ambiguous and more to the point are the hymnic lines of 1 Cor 8:6:

> But for us there is one God, the Father,
>   from whom are all things, and we exist for him;
> And one Lord, Jesus Christ,
>   through whom are all things, and we exist through him.

There is here a unity of everything in its createdness and in its relationship to God that is hard to reconcile with the notion that chapter 8 separates humanity from the remainder of creation.[16] Indeed, the "all" ($\pi\acute{\alpha}\varsigma$, *pas*) of v. 22 may be further indication of the inclusive connotation of "creation" in this passage, since the word "all" plays a significant role in this letter in reference to the whole of humanity (see, e.g., 1:5, 7, 8, 16; 2:9–10; 3:9, 12, 19, 23; 5:18; 11:26, 32, 36; 15:11).[17]

THE APOCALYPSE OF GOD'S CHILDREN

If students of Rom 8 feel obliged to give an account of their interpretation of "all creation," most seem to assume that the phrases "the sons of God" or "the children of God" or "we" are self-explanatory.[18] The expression "sons of God" comes into Rom at 8:14, where it refers explicitly to those who are being led by God's spirit, who receive a spirit of adoption and who are God's children and fellow heirs with Christ.[19] Understandably, then, most commentators freely identify the "sons of God" in v. 19 also as believers, without pausing to ask whether the fact that these "sons of God" are to be *apocalyptically revealed* means that this group might be distinguished from the group introduced earlier in the chapter.

In a significant contribution to this discussion, Susan Eastman has asked exactly that question and has argued that "the future apocalypse of the sons of God promises the rectification of all who are called to be God's sons and daughters, including those who are not yet included in the category 'Christian.'"[20] Those "not yet included" means not only those who will come to believe but also all of Israel as well as the Gentiles. Eastman takes note of the fact that the LXX and other Jewish writings frequently characterize Israel as "sons of God" and "children of God." In addition, in Rom 9:4 Paul affirms that the Jews are recipients of "adoption" and "glory."[21] This affirmation is no mere historical relic, a gift pushed aside by Israel in its disbelief, since in 11:29 Paul declares, despite all that has preceded in this tortured section of the letter, that the "gifts and the calling of God" to Israel are "irrevocable." This point becomes even more explicit in 11:32: "God confined all in disobedience, so that God might have mercy on all." For these reasons, Eastman rightly concludes that Israel as a whole must be included among those "children of God" who are apocalyptically revealed in 8:18 and whose adoption is anticipated in 8:23. In other words, 8:23 hints at the full inclusion that comes to explicit expression in 11:32. Elsewhere in Paul this apocalypse is not merely a public disclosure of something that has been kept secret; it is an event in which something happens that so radically disrupts the world as to be called an invasion.[22] This in turn suggests that the "we" who know about the longing of creation and who have the firstfruit of the Spirit are among God's children but are not the only ones to be apocalyptically revealed.[23]

What is it that these children of God do? The notion that they care for creation, which is eloquently expressed by Keesmaat and Wright, is not articulated in the text but can only be inferred on the assumption that Paul anticipates the reversal of Gen 3:17. Yet Rom 8 says nothing about humanity restoring creation or practicing care for creation. To the contrary, humanity's role here is to wait—eagerly, expectantly, hopefully, yes—but to wait. The "freedom of the glory" of God's children lies in the future that God will bring about, but the precise contours of that future are curiously absent from this passage.

BIRTHING, ADOPTION, REDEMPTION

If all of creation, including humanity, waits for the apocalyptic revelation of God's children, Jew and Gentile, then what Paul has in view in this passage is almost unimaginably large. It will be important to return to the question of what Paul means by subjection and liberation, but the path toward understanding that subjection and liberation returns us to our opening observation about creation being in labor pangs. The verbs of Rom 8:22 are unambiguous. As observed in the discussion of Gal 4:19 (see above, chapter 2), the ὠδίνειν (ōdinein) word group is used, both literally and metaphorically, of women in the act of childbirth. Here that explicit reference to childbirth is preceded by the verb συστενάζειν (*systenazein*, to groan). While this verb and its cognates are not usually associated with childbirth, the noun does refer to the groaning of childbirth in Gen 3:16 LXX, and it appears paired with "being in labor" in Jer 4:31 LXX. It is not too much, then, to suggest that both "all creation" and "we" are understood to be in the process of giving birth. Logically, what should follow is *the arrival of an infant.*

So effective is Paul's rhetoric that some interpreters seem to have read the text in just this way. N. T. Wright sees here the continuity "of new life that is at the same time the mother's own life, delighting her, despite the pain of labor, with a fresh fulfillment."[24] Luzia Sutter Rehmann emphasizes the active role of creation in "birthing a new world."[25] Both Wright and Rehmann properly underscore creation's straining for what lies ahead and the hard work involved in the actual process of giving birth. Yet what is it that creation will bring to birth? Exactly nothing, because creation itself is captive to nothingness, to "futility." Creation itself cannot possibly give birth, nor does the participation of humanity make a difference.

In this passage, the birthing metaphor captures creation's active cry for liberation,[26] but the birthing metaphor has its limits: creation does not in fact give birth. As noted at the outset of this chapter, nothing in the text indicates that creation itself—in whole or in part—is the agent of what follows. Instead, there is adoption and redemption, activities that are carried out not by creation but by God. What creation longs for is God's action, not its own. This is consistent with the usage of the birth-pangs metaphor in some Old Testament passages, where the laboring image often has to do with waiting for that which is out of one's control (e.g., Ps 48:6; Isa 13:8; 26:17–18; Jer 13:21; Mic 4:9).[27]

Paul describes the action of God in Rom 8:23: "We indeed groan as we long for adoption, the redemption of our body." The anticipation of adoption recalls 8:15, where Paul affirms that those who are led by the Spirit have received "a spirit of adoption," so that they cry out to God as father (see also Gal 4:6). It seems odd to imagine a woman in labor who cries out with longing for adoption.[28]

Paul then further explains this adoption with the phrase "the redemption of our body." Earlier in the letter, as he expands on his initial comments about God's rectifying power in the gospel (1:16–17), Paul speaks of God's gracious, free rectification "through the redemption in Christ Jesus" (3:24). In the context of Rom 3, humanity is being redeemed from the power of Sin ("all sinned and fall short," "through the passing over of past sins"). Similarly, elsewhere in Romans, Sin is an enslaving power from whose grasp humanity is delivered by Jesus' death (see, e.g., 5:12–14, 17, 21; 6:16–17, 20–23).[29] Although the word "redemption" (ἀπολύτρω-σις, *apolytrōsis*, 8:23) is rare, it is found in contexts having to do with the freeing of slaves or captives (e.g., Philo, *That Every Good Person Is Free* 114; Josephus, *Antiquities* 12.27; Dan 4:34 LXX; *Letter of Aristeas* 12; 33; BDAG, 117); similarly in 8:23, "redemption" is not simply renewal but especially release from captivity.

What is it that requires redemption from slavery? Many contemporary translations of 8:23 read "our bodies" (NAB, NIV, NJB, RSV, NRSV),[30] which commentators often identify as the resurrection of individual believers based on 8:11. Yet the Greek term in 8:23 is not "bodies" plural but "body," singular (as in the KJV). And it does not appear that Paul is inattentive to the difference. Paul's reference to resurrection in 8:11 concerns "your mortal bodies," not "your mortal body." Similarly, 12:1 calls for the presentation of "your bodies," but 12:4–5 address believers as "one body." While 8:23 may well encompass a reference to the resurrection of individual believers, it should not be confined to that, as it surely has to do not just with the rescue of individuals but also with the rescue of the corporate body of humanity.[31]

Having arrived at this cosmic understanding of the adoption and redemption of "our body," we are in a position to return to the language of glory that appears at the opening of the passage with its robust affirmations:

> The sufferings of the present time are not worth comparing with the glory that is to be apocalyptically revealed to us. (8:18)

> Creation itself will be freed from slavery to decay for the freedom of the glory of God's children. (8:21)

The significance of these expressions is reinforced by the statements in 8:17 that "we" will be glorified with Christ and in 8:30 that God glorified those whom he rectified. In Paul's letters (as elsewhere in the canon), glory is overwhelmingly associated with God (e.g., 1 Cor 10:31; 2 Cor 4:6, 15; Phil 1:11; 2:11) or with Jesus Christ (2 Cor 4:4; 8:19; Phil 4:19). In Romans this motif is particularly strong, as humans are indicted for their failure to glorify God (1:21, 23), Abraham is remembered for his rightful glorifying of God (4:20), and chapter 15 anticipates the eschatological act of Jew and Gentile together glorifying God (15:6, 9; see also 15:7). That being the case, the notion that "God's children" will be characterized by glory is a powerful statement about what the future holds for humankind. It is crucial to keep in mind where this glory comes from: like the rectification of God in 1:16–17 and elsewhere, the glory of God's children is a function of their being *God's* children. It is a function of God, not something that comes from them or in any way inheres in them.[32]

While all that God has made is in the veritable pangs of labor awaiting God's glorious apocalypse, there is nothing creation or humanity can do to bring it to completion. Even though believers have already received the first glimpse of what is on the horizon, they cannot make the day come one moment faster. Instead, they wait for what God will do.

THE PASSAGE IN LITERARY AND HISTORICAL CONTEXT

What role does this passage play in the letter as a whole? Commentators often notice that at Rom 8:18 Paul resumes the language that opens chapter 5.[33] Paul W. Meyer characterizes this as a return "to the afflicted and precarious quality of life mentioned in 5:3–4,"[34] drawing attention to the references to suffering in both passages (5:3–4; 8:18). In addition, chapter 8 returns to the language of hope (5:2, 4, 5; 8:20, 24, 25) and glory (5:2; 8:18, 21, 30). The notion of being at peace with God (5:1) and having access to grace (5:2) may be replayed in chapter 8's affirmations about the intervening work of the Spirit (8:26–27; and see 8:6) and the actions of God on behalf of those who are called (8:28–30).

It is easy to understand, therefore, why some students of Paul take chapter 8 as the conclusion of a section of the letter begun in chapter 5.[35] We have already noted, however, that in 8:23 Paul replays the language of redemption in chapter 3 and the concepts, if not the precise terminology, of freedom from slavery in chapters 5–6. Yet 8:18–25 reaches even further back into argument of Romans, all the way back to 1:18–32, as the following lists will indicate:

apocalyptically reveal (ἀποκαλύπτειν,		
ἀποκάλυψις)	1:18	8:18, 19
creation (κτίσις)	1:20, 25	8:19, 20, 21, 22
glory, glorify (δόξα, δοξάζειν)	1:21, 23	8:18, 21
futility, become futile (ματαιοῦν,		
ματαιότης)	1:21	8:20
bodies, body (σῶμα)	1:24	8:23

In addition to these verbal repetitions, the subjection referred to in 8:20 echoes the "handing over" of 1:24, 26, and 28 (see chapter 8 below).[36]

Steve Kraftchick rightly contends that there is a kind of reversal in chapter 8 of the situation depicted in chapter 1:

> In chap. 1 it was the action of God in creation which was to affect humans positively, but it did not. In chap. 8, however, Paul argues that it will be the action of God directed to humans which affects the creation. Further in chap. 1 Paul maintains that humans sought autonomy and so creation was reduced to a state of bondage. Then in chap. 8 he states that the restored human is one who recognizes theonomy.[37]

This point deserves to be pressed even further: the handing over of humanity to the powers of Sin and Death is no mere punishment; it is a concession of the totality of creation to the powers that oppose God ("slavery to decay," 8:21). Paul understands that creation continues to be sold into slavery, despite the resurrection of Jesus Christ and the new life of believers. But God's intervention, God's handing over of his own son (8:32), means that the powers cannot and will not prevail (8:31–39).

Chapters 8 and 9 below return to Paul's treatment of Sin in this letter and the reasons for the discussion.[38] Paul's reasons for writing this particular letter are notoriously difficult to discern and have generated a small library of their own, but among those reasons is Paul's fear that those gathered in house churches in Rome have an understanding of the gospel that is far too small. Largely a disparate group of Gentile immigrants (possibly second or third generation), people who have been attracted to Judaism and who participate in the life of the synagogues, they hear the gospel as an invitation to become part of Israel. In their hearing, it is a social and ethical invitation; they become part of a people, a people noted for their high moral standards and their strong group identification. What Paul hopes is that his journey to Rome will allow him to preach the whole gospel there (1:15). By way of laying the groundwork for that proclamation, Phoebe will read this letter introducing the gospel of God's reclamation of the entire creation out of the powers of Sin and Death.

APOCALYPSE IN THE PRESENT TENSE

Two related questions about the way in which this text is often characterized remain to be considered. Although Rom 8 is routinely spoken of as having to do with the future, Philip Esler astutely observes that "Paul refuses to provide a picture of the glory that is to come. He holds out the prospect of describing the glory in v. 18 and then singularly fails

to do so."[39] Those who are familiar with 1 Thess 4 and 1 Cor 15 anticipate that some such picture will be offered here as well; God will finally
defeat all the enemies, even death itself (1 Cor 15:20–28); the returning
Jesus will grasp his own to be with him forever (1 Thess 4:13–18).
Romans 8 offers no such resolution. To the contrary, 8:35–39 parades for
the audience the identities of those enemies who continue to attempt to
separate "us" from God. Pain and suffering and death are very much
front and center here.

Esler's explanation of this silence is that Paul understands the future
adoption and redemption to be "organically evolving out of present
experience,"[40] but the emphasis on God's own intervention and the
inability of creation to give birth argues against any evolutionary reading
of the passage. It is more likely that Paul does not here celebrate the
future consummation in the detail of 1 Thess 4 and 1 Cor 15 precisely
because of the problem to be taken up in chapters 9–11. It is only at the
end of chapter 11 and again in 15:7–13 that Paul turns to the future culmination of God's work.

A slightly different question emerges when Edward Adams contends
that Rom 8 is not appropriately understood as apocalyptic. Adams rightly
observes that "creation" in Rom 8 is not presented negatively. Unlike
some forms of apocalyptic, in which the natural world is to be destroyed
or pass away, Paul affirms the future redemption of creation itself.[41] In a
similar vein, Leander Keck contrasts this passage with Paul's declaration
in Gal 1:4 that God is rescuing "us" from "the present evil age."[42] Both
these observations neglect the fact that Rom 1 emphasizes the creation
precisely as *creation*, that is, as God's own work. It is God's own work
that is to be redeemed. That does not mean, as Adams concludes, that
there is here no "cosmic battle."[43] To be sure, God is not in conflict with
the natural world, even less "creation," but the end of this chapter relent-
lessly catalogs those powers that are set on separating "us" from the love
of God in Christ Jesus. Unless vv. 31–39 are to be dismissed as meaning-
less rhetorical excess, there is indeed a cosmic conflict at work here.
Adams further observes that Rom 8 does not project a sharp disjuncture
between the "elect" and the "nonelect," the "righteous" and the "unrighteous." These observations, however, similarly overlook the extent to
which Rom 1:18–3:20 insists that there are none who are righteous, or
Rom 11:32, which implies that God has elected "all." The chasms in
Paul's apocalyptic are not chasms between human groups or between an
evil world and its coming replacement; rather, the chasms in Paul's apocalyptic are between those powers who are aligned with God and those

who are aligned against God. Here he posits that the entirety of God's created order is in slavery, human and otherwise.

CONCLUSION

As I noted at the outset, the maternal imagery of Rom 8:22 differs in significant ways from the imagery we examined in previous chapters. Paul does not here employ maternal imagery in self-reference; neither does he use it to describe apostolic labor in general. There are, however, some important connections apart from the birthing language itself. This passage participates in the peculiar logic we have followed in earlier chapters, not this time the "metaphor squared" of a man metaphorizing himself as a nursing mother (as in 1 Cor 3:2) or as a nurse with her own children (1 Thess 2:7). The logic here more closely resembles that of Gal 4:19, where it is Paul who is in labor, but it is not Paul who has given or will give birth. All of creation may be in labor, but creation does not give birth. As it was Christ who is to be formed among the Galatians, here it is God who will redeem "our body." Both texts concern God's deliverance from powers that are set over against God, whether they are identified as "the present evil age" (Gal 1:4) or by the names Paul lists at the end of Rom 8.

In part 2 we return to this question of apocalyptic conflict in a series of studies of Galatians and Romans. Before turning to those studies, however, I want to offer some reflections on Pauline theology and its significance for the lives of women.

CHAPTER FIVE

Is Pauline Theology Just a "Guy Thing"?

In the preceding chapters I have addressed Pauline texts that draw on maternal imagery to refer to Paul's own apostolic labor (1 Thess 2:7; Gal 4:19; 1 Cor 3:1–23) and to the yearning of all creation (Rom 8:22). At a number of junctures I have contended that Paul's theology is to be understood as an apocalyptic theology, and that phrase is the focus of the second half of this book, where I will take up questions of Pauline interpretation having to do with the apocalyptic character of these texts and their contexts in Paul's letters.

Before turning to those issues, however, I want to engage in an important digression. My impression is that, notwithstanding some three decades of feminist studies of biblical texts and the increasing number of women among biblical interpreters, most exegetes and theologians still conduct themselves as if the letters of Paul largely have to do with men. For many readers, there is a sense of danger similar to the concern that prompted Howard Thurman's grandmother to forbid him to read Paul's letters.[1] For others, there is often a sheer lack of traction, a sense that Paul is irrelevant if not offensive. My own conviction is that Paul's letters are of urgent importance for the lives of women, and in this chapter I undertake a brief foray into that question with the letter to the Galatians in the foreground.

Galatians is a particularly apt location for this thought experiment since, despite the fact that Paul's letter to the Galatians contains the famous verse that some have called the "Magna Carta" of Christian feminism (3:28), the letter generally reveals itself as decidedly male in character. It concerns a surgical procedure that pertains only to men, it

63

speaks about male characters, and it speaks to men who will make a decision. Although Paul refers to the law as a whole, the specific commandment that appears to have generated the controversy is the requirement that males be circumcised (5:2–6).[2] Paul refers to Peter and Timothy and James but to no women among the Galatians, their Teachers, or the Jerusalem church. We search in vain for the Chloe of 1 Corinthians, Euodia and Syntyche of Philippians, or Phoebe and Junia of Romans. The only woman whose name appears is Hagar, in whose enslaved motherhood Paul finds an antecedent for the enslaving mission carried out by the Teachers (4:25).[3] Even if we imagine that women are listening to the letter Paul sends the Galatians, they will hear direct address to people who contemplate circumcision, not to themselves (5:2).[4] Brigitte Kahl concludes that Galatians could be perceived as "the most 'phallocentric' document" in the New Testament.[5] To put it in the vernacular, Galatians appears to be nothing more than a "guy thing."

The presence of Gal 3:28 does not overturn that characterization of the letter. However we interpret the verse and its history, and that has become a matter of considerable debate in recent years, Paul clearly introduces it into its present context in order to assure Gentile believers that the gospel does not require them to become Jews.[6] Neither the relationship between slaves and free people nor the relationship between men and women is prominent in chapter 3 or elsewhere in the letter.

What happens if we concede—simply for the purposes of this thought experiment—that Paul does not directly address women in the Galatian churches, that in this conversation the speakers, the audience, and the decision at stake are thoroughly male? Historically, at least some of us will find that conclusion troublesome, even offensive. Does that mean we simply abandon this letter and look elsewhere for conversation partners? I think not. Instead, we need to ask a different sort of question: What understanding of God and the world does this letter articulate or reflect? And what implications might those understandings have for women's lives?

The questions I am raising are both straightforward and, to the best of my knowledge, largely neglected in the discussion of the Pauline letters in relationship to women. Several factors contribute to that silence. First, much of the investigation of the "women texts" in the New Testament, particularly in the Pauline letters, came about in connection with the lengthy ecclesiastical debates regarding the ordination of women. In that context various parties in the discussion looked for historical precedent; they wanted to know whether and how women had acted as leaders in early Christianity. Naturally, they turned to passages that seemed to them most directly pertinent, such as Gal 3:28; 1 Cor 11:2–16; and 14:33b–35, not to mention 1 Tim 2:11–15 and Eph 5:22–24. The assumption that the leadership of the church in the twenty-first century and beyond should resemble that of the church in the first—or at least that there had to be an explanation for a radical change in leadership—dictated the consideration of certain texts and the nature of the questions to be asked.

Resolving the question of ordination, of course, does not resolve the difficulties Paul poses for some readers. One legacy of generations of interpreters drawing attention to texts that silence and subject women (or at least appear to do so) is that many women readers feel little inclination to turn to Paul as a theological resource. It is difficult to offer more than anecdotal evidence for this assertion, but three decades of teaching in Protestant seminaries provide me with considerable such evidence. To put the matter directly: for many seminarians, pastors, and laypeople with whom I have talked, it is simply assumed that women will read Paul with suspicion, even with hostility.[7]

Yet another factor that prevents Christians from asking the larger question about the understanding of God and humankind reflected in this letter lies in the history of the theological disciplines. In much of biblical scholarship, the preoccupation with historical reconstruction or literary analysis has virtually eclipsed questions of a theological nature. Even when scholarly agendas have included the theological perspectives of biblical texts, the classic loci of systematic theology have often functioned as blinders that limit the kinds of questions addressed. Inquiries limited to Paul's "doctrine of God" or Paul's "doctrine of the Spirit" are unlikely to issue forth in fresh reflections on the implications of Paul's gospel for the lives of women.[8]

The inquiry I propose is neither ahistorical nor antihistorical. It simply urges the importance of asking other questions *in addition to* conventional questions about the attitude of the historical Paul to women and their leadership in the Christian community. Those conventional questions inevitably become questions of permission and prohibition: What does Paul's interpretation of the gospel *permit* women to do, and what does the gospel *prohibit* women from doing? That way of putting things has the effect of truncating our reflection and, more important, it bears little resemblance to the dynamic character of Paul's letters, letters that over and over again speak about vocation rather than about permission.[9] These letters, instead, call for the question: What is God doing in the gospel of Jesus Christ, and what does that gospel mean for the lives of women? In what follows, I put that question to Galatians, but with an eye to the other letters as well.

THE SINGULARITY OF THE GOSPEL

When the word "gospel" appears for the first time in Galatians, it does so not in a context of confession or thanksgiving, but in a fierce rebuke. Scarcely has the letter opened when we read the caustic accusation: "I am amazed that you are so quickly turning away from the one who called you in the grace of Christ to another gospel—another gospel that does not exist!" (Gal 1:6–7a). The statements that follow, with their characterization of the Teachers as desiring to turn the Galatians away from the gospel (1:7) and a twice-repeated curse on those who preach differently than Paul, dramatically underscore the rebuke (1:8–9). At least in Paul's judgment, what stands between the Teachers and himself is not a small difference of opinion but a chasm.[10] What the Teachers have spread among the Galatians is so far removed from the gospel that Paul must think of it as a second gospel, even if no such thing exists.

Would the Teachers themselves have characterized their disagreement in such harsh terms? Probably not. Instead, they understand themselves to be completing the work Paul began but left unfinished. They declare that the good news of Jesus Christ means that Gentiles may now become children of Abraham, full members in the people of Israel. Unlike Paul, however, the Teachers insist that such membership in Israel requires the circumcision of male Gentiles and observance of other aspects of the Mosaic torah.

What is it that Paul finds so objectionable in the Teachers' proposal regarding law observance? A conventional Protestant view that Galatians articulates the superiority of grace over legalism does not suffice, both because of its deeply flawed understanding of Judaism and because it transforms this polemical letter into an abstract essay on the virtue of faith.[11] We might, instead, imagine that Paul's objection is simply pragmatic; he sees in the Teachers' view the failure of the Gentile mission because the requirement of torah observance would be so odious that it would severely limit the number of Gentile believers. Yet nothing in the letter hints that Galatian males are *resisting* the Teachers' message because of the anticipated trauma of circumcision; on the contrary, Paul clearly has reason to believe that the Galatians themselves find the Teachers' views compelling.

These observations force the question: Why is it that Paul, who elsewhere reports that he was himself circumcised on the eighth day (Phil 3:5), not only rejects the Teachers' position but also characterizes it as "another gospel," one that cannot exist? At the very least, we may wonder whether Paul would craft a compromise with the Teachers. Paul is not, in principle, opposed to compromise, as is clear in his discussion of the eating of food sacrificed to idols (1 Cor 8–10; cf. Rom 14:1–15:13) and in his advice about the place of dramatic spiritual gifts within worship (1 Cor 12–14). Why not move in the direction of compromise on this occasion as well? What if certain leaders among the Galatian Christians, fearful of a rupture in their congregations, had posed to Paul something like the following alternative?[12]

> We understand that *you* do not regard it as essential that Gentile Christians uphold the Mosaic law, but some of our people have come to believe that this is the right thing for *them* to do. The Teachers have persuaded them of the benefits of torah observance. Now, what harm can it do if some or even all of us *add* torah observance to our lives? Nothing that torah asks of us is bad, is it? It might even help us, since the moral guidance it offers assists us to remain faithful to our calling. What harm can possibly come from keeping God's commandments?

With this imaginary offer of a compromise in mind, we return to the letter itself to find that certain elements stand out in sharp clarity. A moderate and tolerant response to the Teachers might have been to insist that Gentiles are not *obliged* to follow the law, although they may if they find it expedient for their faith. Yet Paul rejects any such position: Gentile Christians *must not* observe the law of Moses (see esp. 3:1–5, 23–25; 5:2–4).

What causes the sharpness of Paul's response? A compelling answer to that question emerges in J. Louis Martyn's work on Galatians.[13] Martyn's penetrating reading unpacks the genuinely apocalyptic character of the gospel Paul proclaimed among the Galatians. In the death and resurrection of Jesus Christ, God has not simply introduced a "new and improved" version of Moses or revealed a means by which human beings can be rescued from the consequences of their own wrongdoing. Instead, in the gospel God has invaded the "present evil age" (1:4) so as to shatter its power and bring about nothing less than "new creation" (6:15).[14]

With this view of the gospel as invading force, then, Paul cannot agree with the Teachers, nor can he imagine a compromise with their position.

The gospel's invasion *necessarily obliterates worlds*, including particularly the world of the law. This conviction comes to expression in a variety of ways in the letter. In Gal 1:13–14 Paul recalls for the Galatians his earlier "way of life," the life characterized by his attempts to destroy the church and his zealous pursuit of patriarchal tradition. That world comes to an end with God's "apocalypse" of God's Son (1:15–17). Paul offers no reassessment of his behavior, no explanation of an independent decision about the gospel. Instead, the gospel and its attendant vocation simply take over Paul's earlier life.[15]

The gospel's invasion, however, extends well beyond the invasion of individual lives and their efforts, as is clear in the discussion of chapters 3–4. Complex exegetical disputes plague almost every syllable in this section of the letter, one of the most contested of which is the metaphor of torah as "pedagogue" in 3:24. All readings of the metaphor, however, must account for the dramatic shift at v. 25: because faith (i.e., the faithful obedience of Jesus Christ) has arrived, "we are no longer under the pedagogue's power." As in 1:11–17, here also the gospel invades and destroys. It is not just life in the world of the law that is obliterated, however, and this is where much reading of Galatians falls short. Other worlds also come to an end:

> There is no Jew nor Greek,
> there is no slave nor free,
> there is no male and female,
> for you are all one in Christ Jesus.

Whatever the history and earlier function of Paul's statement in 3:28, in its Galatian setting it radically extends Paul's claim about the world-obliterating character of the gospel.[16] As the gospel's arrival obliterates the law, it also obliterates those other "places" with which people identify themselves, even the most fundamental places of ethnicity, economic and social standing, and gender. The only location available for those grasped by the gospel is "in Christ."

The anesthetizing familiarity of these lines makes their radical claims difficult to hear. Put directly, the gospel leaves those grasped by it with no other place to be; it moves people from one place to another, from the place of torah observance or slavery or gender into the world of Christ: "You who were baptized into Christ, you put on Christ" (3:27). John Schütz's perceptive phrase "the singularity of the gospel" captures this underlying dynamic of Galatians.[17] In Paul's view, then, it is as impossible for the Galatians to be simultaneously "in" the world of the law and "in" Christ as it is for them to be "in" the world of their former paganism and "in" Christ. This helps to explain why compromise with the Teachers is unimaginable, since any compromise assumes the possibility of shared territory, a possibility Paul cannot fathom.[18]

What takes the place of these obliterated worlds? Paul does not provide a systematic guide to this new location "in Christ," but the letter does depict some of its major landmarks. Just as God is the one who rescues from the "present evil age," God is the one who calls this new location into being, in Jesus Christ creating anew (6:15; and see 2 Cor 5:17). Those in its grasp experience the gifts of the Spirit, which Paul recalls for the Galatians in a way suggesting that those gifts are powerful indeed (3:1–5). The Spirit shows itself in the life of the community in "love, joy, peace, patience, kindness, generosity, faithfulness, gentleness, and self-control" (5:22 NRSV). Importantly, these are not achievements either of the individual or of the community; they are "fruit" of the Spirit. And life "in Christ" means freedom. The freedom so powerfully invoked in 5:1 is not the "freedom-to-do-as-I-please" that so often serves only to license narcissism[19] but freedom that serves others, a freedom that knows it owes its existence to God's invasive act of liberation (1:4).

What has been said here concerns Galatians in particular, but the singularity of the gospel comes to expression in other letters as well. In Phil 3, Paul contrasts his current location in Christ Jesus, a location that was imposed upon him (see 3:12), with his prior location in a world of achievement (see especially 3:6). The appeal to unity in 1 Corinthians arises from the conviction that the cross alone is God's saving power (1:18–25; 2:2). In Romans Paul develops the gospel's singularity over against the charge (whether hypothetical or actual) that his preaching encourages immorality (3:8; 6:1); those who have died with Christ belong to him alone (Rom 6).

PAULINE THEOLOGY AND THE WORLDS OF WOMEN

With this understanding of God and the gospel, how might Paul's letters be reread for women in the present? To put it somewhat differently: What does the singular apocalyptic gospel of Jesus Christ bring to an end and what does it generate in the lives of women? .

Any reflection on "women in the present" or "the lives of women" is doomed from the start as impossibly—even insultingly—vague. Yet my hope here is to demonstrate the possibilities of another way of framing a question about "Paul and women," not to provide an answer that will go unchallenged. Even as a first attempt, however, several qualifications are necessary. First, much of what follows would apply to the lives of men as well as to those of women. Because so few attempts to hear Paul's letters have been written by women or written with women's lives self-consciously in the foreground, however, in what follows I hope to do just that, to listen as a woman and on behalf of women. Second, despite the appalling generality of the phrase "women's lives," I do not advocate an essentialist position that ascribes to all women certain biologically determined characteristics. Third, I understand that "women's lives" diverge from one another in an endless number of ways. Certainly what I offer below speaks from my experience as a white privileged woman in North America. Even with that qualification, my reflections will not hold true for all such women, and I will have neglected important points. My hope is to generate further reflection and conversation, from which other such attempts might emerge.

Returning to the letter, we may begin with the singular invasion in Paul's life in chapters 1–2. When Paul characterizes his earlier life, he uses the language of achievement: "You heard . . . how I advanced in Judaism beyond many of my peers among my people, for I was especially zealous for the patriarchal traditions" (1:14). The pedigree in Phil 3:5–6 expands on this notion: Paul was "circumcised on the eighth day, from the people of Israel, the tribe of Benjamin, a Hebrew from among Hebrews, according to the law a Pharisee, according to zeal a persecutor of the church, according to rectification based on the law, blameless." Although the pedigree begins with characteristics acquired by birth or the actions of others, it moves in the direction of Paul's own achievements. Both passages move abruptly to God's apocalypse that overturns such achievements, with Phil 3:8 offering a new assessment in vivid language. At least one of the things that the gospel invades and exposes is the deep flaw in Paul's assessment of himself, in his system of measurement. Although he speaks of that system in terms of the faith of his ancestors, analogues may extend well beyond the arena of religion.[20]

Paul's flawed system of measurement may find a telling and powerful counterpart in our endless striving after the distorted female images constantly generated by a consumerist society. The media world, with its message that worth—particularly the worth of women—consists largely of our physical attractiveness, extends to us at every possible moment the invitation to use its standards for assessing ourselves. Yet even as we see that manipulation for what it is, we continue to reach after the goal of approval. We recognize the utter corruption of this assessment when our prepubescent daughters begin to worry about being overweight, but it extends even to those of us who have never purchased from Calvin Klein or moisturized with Estée Lauder.[21] Indeed, even when we deliberately flaunt the norms of attractiveness by wearing clothing that is unfashionable and adopting hairstyles conventionally perceived as "mannish," we merely substitute one yardstick for another, replacing the desire for attractiveness with the desire to be more radical in our feminism than our neighbors.

The pursuit of attractiveness may be an especially pervasive system of measurement, but it is by no means the only one we employ. Another way in which we measure ourselves is through our network of relationships both at work and at home, constantly taking their temperature to be certain things are healthy and holding ourselves responsible for every fluctuation in the thermometer.[22] Or we measure our achievements in the arena of work, where we increasingly ask, not what we are *called* to do, but only what rewards us with money and prestige. For many of us, the church itself offers simply another means of assessing ourselves, giving us yet another place to prove our value by meeting every need, whatever the cost to ourselves or our families.

All of these arenas become for us norms of measurement. As such they are also brought to an end by the apocalypse of Jesus Christ. Paul's words of disruption in Gal 1:15, "But when God called me," speak invasively not only to his world of assessment but to our own. His insistence that it is God's invasion alone that has the power to identify us puts an end to these worlds of measurement. This is not a matter merely of replacing one set of "oughts" and "shoulds" and "musts" for another, so that I no longer reach for Madison Avenue's yardstick but for another, a Christian yardstick: "What would Jesus do?" Rather, God's takeover means that we look into a different mirror, one not of our own creation but of God's, and one in which we see, not lines or blemishes or a flawed nose or hair that needs thickening or straightening or curling. We instead see a beautiful creature, one on whose behalf Christ's own faithfulness extended to death (2:20), and who is an instance of God's "new creation" (6:15; see also 2 Cor 5:17).

When Paul introduces his calling in Gal 1:11–17, he writes not only about his assessment of himself but also about tradition, and the disanalogy between Paul's seeking after the law and our seeking after societal norms for acceptance as women requires some attention. There is, to be sure, a categorical difference between torah and the sort of seeking I have just depicted. These worlds that the gospel obliterates are worlds apart from one another. Yet they share an underlying dynamic in that both involve acts of human seeking that have no place in the gospel. Moreover, if the gospel obliterates even the claims of torah itself, how can the world of Madison Avenue stand?

What the gospel invades is more than this world of our individual and collective striving for achievement, as becomes evident when we return to the famous line "You are all one in Christ" (3:28). Paul here insists that those who are "in Christ Jesus" are baptized "into" Christ and even "put on Christ" (3:27; see also 2:19–20), which means that they cannot simultaneously be "in" or "under" the power of the law. One's identity—one's place of residence—is *in* the gospel, because God has made it so. Despite the frequent and commonsense reaction that Paul cannot possibly "really" mean that there is no longer male and female, since manifestly there are men and women in the world, that is exactly what he means: that being "in Christ" brings life in the identity-conferring realm of "male and female" to an end. Like the other pairs in the verse, "male and female" functions as a metonym for places in which we live, the spheres in which we name ourselves and find our identity. Those who are "in Christ" cannot also be in the identity business of being first of all female or male.

On that reading, rendering Gal 3:28 as a declaration of equality is not only too little,[23] it is distinctly beside the point. Those who find themselves "in Christ" also are not "in" the power arena that makes questions of equality necessary. Equality is a concept or principle invoked in order to insist that individuals or groups be treated uniformly, that they have the same access to decision making, that they have the same privilege or status. All those who are "in Christ," however, know that they all have only what has been granted them by the Spirit, and *all* have exactly the same standing in that God rescued all from "the present evil age."[24] To be sure, the pairs reflect not simply spheres of identity but also the privilege assigned to one member of each pair: the Jew, the free person, the male. Yet what Paul declares is not simply that the gospel brings these privileges to an end, but that the pairs no longer exist. The best paraphrase comes in 6:15: "there is neither circumcision nor uncircumcision but new creation."

Although an earlier generation celebrated 3:28 with its "You are all one," more recent practitioners of cultural criticism have charged Paul with abolishing "difference" in favor of "sameness." For Daniel Boyarin, for example, 3:28 prompts the question: "Are the specificities of human identity, the differences of value, or are they only an obstacle in the striving for justice and liberation?"[25] To claim that all are one in Christ Jesus does not require "sameness," however, as Paul's letters elsewhere make clear. Paul understands that spiritual gifts arrive in an array that may prove distressing and that requires ordering (1 Cor 12–14), and he acknowledges differences of conviction regarding dietary practice (Rom 14:1–15:7). Throughout much of Romans he identifies the particular situation of Gentiles in distinction from Jews, and vice versa (see, e.g., 2:14, 17; 3:1; 7:1). Being "in Christ" does not mean that we become part of some bland, overcooked, and underseasoned stew, in which the infinite array of women's gifts (and men's gifts) lose their particularity. Instead, it means that the first and most important thing to be said about us is that we are "in Christ."

At first glance, this aspect of Galatians will appear to be deeply unwelcome for those of us who are eager to understand ourselves and other women as fully human and to rejoice precisely in being women, in that identity that in many quarters remains marginalized. Yet Paul's words challenge us to rethink the way we argue for such understandings, both among ourselves and with others. In an act of new creation, God invades our several worlds of meaning and claims us as part of Christ's own body. Surely that identity is so powerful that it provides the lens through which we interpret and appropriate all our other and lesser assertions about identity.

It is in this sense that the word "freedom" rightly enters the discussion. The freedom Paul celebrates in this letter is freedom made possible by Christ and in the sphere of Christ, as is clear both in Gal 5:1, "Christ freed us," and in 5:13, "You were called in freedom." In a way that utterly collides with the modern West's confusion of freedom with independence, Paul understands that freedom binds; it binds those who are freed both to Christ and to one another. In this Pauline sense, then, freedom does not exist when women mimic the other half of humanity, a half that is also manifestly in bondage. Genuine freedom emerges from, and only from, the secure knowledge that one lives in the sphere of Christ.

In response to a lecture along just these lines, a student posed the inevitable question: "But what good does it do for me to say that my identity is in Christ and that that identity obliterates all others, when the world around me still assesses me by my dress size or my income? What you say sounds good, but it does not *change* anything in the real world where I live."[26]

The question returns us to the letter itself, where we see that Paul understands the gospel to be more than a series of revelations to individuals or groups. The gospel involves the cosmos, as is clear both at the beginning and at the end of the letter. The letter opens with the assertion that in Jesus Christ, God acts to set human beings free "from the present evil age" (1:4), and the letter closes with a joyous evocation of "new creation" (6:15). That cosmic perspective might seem to have little to contribute to a question so pressing and practical as the one my student asked, yet it is fundamental to our interpretation. Our deep attachment to corrupt systems of measurement, our distorted quest for identity, to say nothing of the malformed relationships between men and women— all of these are more than attitudes in need of adjustment. They are symptoms of the persistence of the "present evil age" with which the gospel collides. No social agenda will correct the situation, and no pedagogical strategy will suffice, because the power of evil is such that it can corrupt even the purest motives and the sternest resolve.[27]

The good news Paul proclaimed to the Galatians is that the release that could not be secured by human effort of any sort has come about through the action of God in Jesus Christ. Those who find their worlds invaded by this good news share the bifocal vision about which J. Louis Martyn writes so eloquently.[28] How can the assessments and identities of those around us matter if we see the triumph of God on the horizon and know its power even in the present? What difference can partial identities and malformed systems of measurement make when we know God's new creation and its liberating power?

CONCLUDING REFLECTIONS

Perhaps as Paul dictated this most passionate letter, he saw in his mind's eye the faces of women in the Galatian congregations and cast about for language that would persuade them of the impossibility of the Teachers' version of the gospel. Or perhaps he gave the women not even a passing thought. As engaging as those and other scenarios may be, neither one constitutes an answer to the question of what Galatians may contribute theologically to women in the present. If, instead of asking only about the relationship between Paul and the historical audience of this letter, or about Paul's attitudes toward women, we ask about the letter's profound theological dynamics, then Galatians emerges as a powerful voice articulating God's new creation, a creation that liberates both women and men from their worlds of achievement and identity. It is *God's* new creation, not one ushered in by human efforts. Just as Paul omits from his letter a program the Galatians might follow for expelling the Teachers or an alternate Christian form of torah, he also offers no agenda for repairing fractured gender relations in the world or even in the church.[29] Galatians is not a program. Galatians is rather a reproclamation of the gospel for those who have listened too carefully to the words of "another gospel that does not exist."[30]

PART 2

Maternal Imagery in Its Cosmic and Apocalyptic Context

Maternal Imagery in Its Cosmic
and Apocalyptic Context

Particularly for those who have been inclined to hear Paul's letters as
somehow abstract, removed from the real stuff of everyday life, the
texts explored in part 1 may have come as a pleasant surprise. Metaphors
of birthing and nursing and nurture offer an important counterpoint to
the lingering perception that Paul's language about "flesh" and "spirit"
signals a negative attitude toward the human body. The personal and
pastoral relationships suggested by these texts may also be attractive,
even if we have no way of knowing what actual relationships obtained in
these communities. And if we tend to think of Paul in exclusively hierarchical and patriarchal terms, the vulnerability that comes to the surface
in these passages is especially welcome.

These are winsome features of the studies involved in part 1, but that
winsomeness could produce a temptation to respond to Paul's use of
maternal imagery in some cozy, personal way. Even in the current cli-
mate of radical cynicism about leaders of all sorts, it is possible to hear
these texts as having to do solely with the individual Paul and his leadership style. Or they may be thought of as having to do exclusively with
social groups around the Mediterranean. But these texts have their rightful place in a larger apocalyptic context that is essential for a robust
understanding of their full scope. By using the word "apocalyptic," which
has appeared at numerous junctures in part 1, I mean not simply that
Paul's metaphors of maternity have some parallels in apocalyptic literature or that they come to Paul from the sphere of apocalyptic thought.
What I mean is that these metaphors are substantively connected to the
apocalyptic nature of Paul's theology. That relationship may be most

obvious in Rom 8, where creation's labor pains anticipate God's final redemption. Yet it also has a bearing on Gal 4:19, since it is not Paul who will birth the Galatians again but Christ who will be born among them; only Christ's intervention makes this birth possible. And when Paul engages in the subversive act of referring to himself as a nurse caring for her children or as a breast-feeding mother, he acts out the epistemology of the "new creation."

In the following chapters I explore Paul's apocalyptic theology. In chapters 6 and 7, I address Galatians, beginning with Gal 1 and 2, where Paul offers his most extensive retrospective account of the "revelation" or "apocalypse" that has invaded his own life. That is followed by an exploration of the theology of Galatians under the heading of the "singularity of the gospel." I next turn to Romans, with its reflection on the cosmic enslavement that is overturned by the apocalypse of Jesus Christ. Chapters 8 and 9 explore the understanding of Sin in Romans; chapter 10 considers the notion of community and how that community participates in apocalyptic; and chapter 11 addresses Paul's understanding of God as reflected in Romans.

I refer to these as explorations of apocalyptic theology, fully aware that the term "apocalyptic" has become problematic for many readers of the New Testament, both scholarly and lay readers. Yet I regard the word as appropriate and significant. Others have dealt at length with the history of research and have charted the historical relationships between Paul's thought and that of early Jewish apocalyptic theology.[1] My goal here is the far more modest one of sketching what I intend by the phrase "apocalyptic theology," a phrase that I will unpack in more detail in the chapters that follow.

GOD'S DECISIVE TRIUMPH: SALVATION AS DELIVERANCE

We can take as our starting point, with deliberate naïveté, the definition of apocalypticism that introduces the multidisciplinary *Encyclopedia of Apocalypticism* as "the belief that God has revealed the imminent end of the ongoing struggle between good and evil in history."[2] The wording is intentionally and appropriately broad, but on this definition it is hard to see how any reading of Paul's letters could deny that they are apocalyptic. Galatians 1:4 introduces the letter by referring to Jesus Christ as the one who rescues "us from the present evil age." First Corinthians celebrates the coming destruction of all God's enemies (15:24–28), and Rom 8 pits God's power over against that of all the forces that attempt to separate humanity from God's love (also see Rom 16:20). The Philippians hymn anticipates the bowing of all creation "in heaven and on earth and under the earth" before the name of Jesus (2:10). At numerous junctures in Paul's letters, we catch a glimpse of the ongoing struggle, the end of which is already in sight by virtue of the crucifixion and resurrection of Jesus.

In addition, Paul himself employs the language of apocalyptic. The Greek word *apokalypsis* and its cognates can refer to what appear to be specific acts of "revealing," in the sense of disclosing information (as in Gal 2:2) or in reference to a particular vision (as in 2 Cor 12:1–2), but Paul also uses the word group to refer to an event in which God invades the present ongoing struggle with salvific power as is seen especially in Rom 1:17: "God's rectification is now being revealed apocalyptically in the gospel." The present tense here is significant: God's apocalypse is not something that is still anticipated in the near or distant future, a future known only to the individual seer. The apocalypse is already taking place in the present.[3]

Yet when I describe Paul as an apocalyptic theologian, I mean more than that Paul uses a particular cluster of words or that he has passages that participate in apocalyptic eschatology. First, Paul's apocalyptic theology has to do with the conviction that in the death and resurrection of Jesus Christ, God has invaded the world as it is, thereby revealing the world's utter distortion and foolishness, reclaiming the world, and inaugurating a battle that will doubtless culminate in the triumph of God over all God's enemies (including the captors Sin and Death). This means that the gospel is first, last, and always about God's powerful and gracious initiative. Paul shares with other apocalyptic theologians (not with them alone, of course) a strongly theocentric perspective (as will be seen especially in chapter 11).

Second, it means that the invasion of the gospel *renders visible* the extent to which all human beings are in the grasp of powers larger than themselves. Chapters 8 and 9 will deal at some length with this question, which appears to have been eclipsed in recent years by concerns over ethnicity and empire. The enemies whose defeat Paul anticipates in 1 Cor 15 and Rom 8 are cosmic, but they are evidenced close at hand when humans corrupt worship (Rom 1:18–25) and distort their own calling (2:17–29). The powers are visible, not in some far-off landscape that is disconnected from human life, but in the very real experiences Paul catalog in Rom 8:35.

Third, God's reclaiming of the world means liberation for humankind. That liberation is not complete, since those who are "in Christ" still die and still experience pain and are capable of sin. Yet those who are "in Christ" have received the Spirit, whose fruits are also visible (as in Gal 5). Those who are being "rescued from the present evil age" are grafted into communities that together with one voice glorify God, communities characterized not by sameness but by unity.

ANXIOUS ABOUT APOCALYPTIC

A number of students of Paul might concede much of what I have sketched in the previous paragraphs but would still protest that the word "apocalyptic" itself has become so problematic that it ought simply to be abandoned. Douglas Campbell has recently come to this judgment and offers instead the phrase "pneumatologically participatory martyrological eschatology," PPME for short.[4] While I find Campbell's project generally congenial to my own thinking, I confess that I am unmoved by his argument about terminology, and I find the acronym more obstructing than illuminating. The notion that the word should be abandoned because it is ambiguous or has problematic connotations might well be applied to any number of words, but I suspect with little success. "Feminist," for example, is used for such a wide range of views that it is difficult to know any longer what holds them together.[5] The same might even be said of the word "Christian." If the people in my own congregation who weekly confess the faith in public worship and who study the tradition and work in the food pantry are "Christian," and those who are baptized as infants and who never again attend a worship service are "Christian," then what does the term mean?

Beyond the desire not to proliferate terminology in some futile and probably endless quest for clarity, I regard the use of the term "apocalyptic" for Pauline theology as a matter of intellectual honesty and integrity. Among the interpreters of Paul whose works most influence my own reading are Ernst Käsemann, J. Christiaan Beker, and J. Louis Martyn, all of whom explicitly adopt the terminology of apocalyptic. To withhold acknowledgment of their influence on my work by attempting to cloak my own views under other terminology strikes me as lacking in maturity and even gratitude. So, while Douglas Campbell indicates that the word itself is an adiaphoron (a rose by any other name and all that), my own conclusion is that it does in fact matter.

A different critique of the apocalyptic reading of Paul comes from R. Barry Matlock, who has put forward an extensive review of scholarly treatments of "the apocalyptic Paul," addressing major figures in twentieth-century scholarship (most prominently Schweitzer, Käsemann, and Beker).[6] In addition to the concern already noted about the ambiguity of the term itself, Matlock offers two primary criticisms. First, he argues, those who have used the term "apocalyptic" for Pauline texts have not tied their usage to a rigorous analysis of early Jewish apocalypses. This criticism does not do justice to the work of Martinus de Boer in particular.[7] It is also somewhat peculiar, since Matlock himself deals with no primary texts at all (not even Pauline texts). Second, Matlock contends that the scholars who advocate an apocalyptic reading of Paul operate with theological motives while claiming for themselves scientific objectivity. That charge could be lodged against most any trajectory in biblical scholarship, however, which means that it is not a particularly weighty criticism of the apocalyptic reading of Paul.[8]

Alongside such scholarly hairsplitting, several genuine anxieties attend proposals about an apocalyptic understanding of Paul's theology, and I want at least to name those here, although they are taken up again in the chapters that follow. One concern is that apocalyptic thinking is necessarily world-denying or escapist. Given some prominent instances of apocalyptic movements, such as the Millerites and the followers of David Koresh, these concerns are understandable. And when Paul declares that he would rather depart and be with the Lord (Phil 1:23), or that "we" are away from the Lord while we remain in the body (2 Cor 5:6), it is hard to avoid the conclusion that he regards the present world as something to be endured for the sake of the future rather than as something of intrinsic value.[9] In the larger context of his letters, however, these statements do not so much denigrate the present as they put its concerns in an infinitely larger context. Moreover, Paul is quite evidently not urging his congregations to remove themselves from the world or to practice a kind of isolationism, as we shall see in chapter 12 below. It is in the "real world" of the present that the apocalyptic gospel renders both God's power and God's wrath visible (Rom 1:17–18), and in the "real world" of the present that the Spirit generates communities liberated from the divisions of ethnicity, social status, and gender (Gal 3:28).

A second and related concern is that apocalyptic theology is dualistic. And again the letters offer ample evidence of "dualism," since Paul operates with a set of opposites that J. Louis Martyn has famously termed the "antinomies" (see my discussion of the "antitheses" of Galatians in chapter 7). These oppositions have to do with the "old age" that continues in the present time and the "new age" that God has already inaugurated in the cross and resurrection of Jesus Christ. The oppositions are especially troubling when they are aligned with groups of people, as, for instance, when 1 Cor 1:18 distinguishes between those who are perishing and those who are being saved, or when 1 Thess 5:5 separates the children of light from the children of darkness. Yet the anthropological dualism that comes to expression in such passages stands over against other passages that emphasize the universal and even cosmic scope of God's action (Rom 5:18; 11:32), suggesting that Paul's dualism is only temporary or provisional.[10] This is one of the points at which attending to Paul's strongly theocentric perspective is crucial, for it is understanding God's role that guards against the problem of identifying particular individuals or groups with these antinomies, as when human beings understand themselves to be *possessors* of the Spirit or to have achieved the status of children of the light.

Some of the anxiety that attends the term "apocalyptic theology" grows out of an understandable concern about some destructive apocalypticisms on the contemporary scene, whether those are religious or political or environmental apocalypticisms. Christian tradition offers some horrendous examples of what can happen when apocalyptic visions are coupled with unstable leadership. Yet the latter ought not prevent our taking biblical apocalypticism seriously, since otherwise those texts are virtually abandoned to their overenthusiastic misinterpreters.[11] I hope that these chapters will show that apocalyptic theology is not inherently destructive. On the contrary, Pauline apocalyptic theology concerns the unimaginable size of God's actions on behalf of the entire cosmos, including humanity itself.

CHAPTER SIX

The Apostle and the Gospel

Our exploration of maternal imagery in Paul's letters necessarily focuses attention on the congregations as receivers of nurture and Paul as the active agent. Paul is the one who is in labor, who is the nurse, who is feeding with milk. Taking those passages in isolation might permit the mistaken conclusion that Paul himself is somehow superior to or exempted from the gospel's invasive power. In this chapter I explore the way in which Paul's retrospective account in Gal 1 and 2 reflects his own understanding of having been taken over by the gospel. Contrary to a long-standing reading of those chapters, I argue that Paul's remarks here are not simply defensive; instead, they demonstrate that the gospel took over Paul's own life, rendering him an instance of "new creation" (Gal 6:15).

Paul opens his letter to the Galatian churches by identifying himself as "an apostle, not from human beings nor through a human being, but through Jesus Christ and God the Father who raised him from the dead." For many readers this introductory self-designation provides an important clue to the understanding of the letter: Paul is on the defensive. According to the conventional interpretation, something of the following scenario has occurred: the Galatians have been visited by Christians who oppose the gospel as Paul has proclaimed it. The visitors have buttressed their claims by charging that Paul did not receive his gospel or his apostolic commission from God. Instead, Paul received his gospel from the apostles in Jerusalem, and thus he is not an apostle of the first rank. Paul learns that his apostleship has been attacked, he must respond, and indeed he does so even with the first words of the letter.

There is good reason to notice Paul's negative statement about the origin of his apostleship. While his salutations elsewhere describe his vocation, those descriptions are couched in positive terms:

> Paul, called as an apostle of Christ Jesus through the will of God . . . (1 Cor 1:1)

> Paul, an apostle of Christ Jesus through the will of God . . . (2 Cor 1:1)

> Paul, prisoner of Christ Jesus . . . (Phlm 1)

> Paul, a slave of Jesus Christ, called to be an apostle, set apart for the gospel of God . . . (Rom 1:1)

Only in Galatians does Paul specify that his apostleship did not originate with or through human beings.

The notion that in Gal 1:1 Paul is on the defensive arises not only because of this peculiar feature within the text, however, but also because of the dominant exegetical tradition. Virtually all commentators on Galatians agree that the single purpose of chapters 1 and 2 is apologetic.[1] As early as Chrysostom, we find the conviction that Paul shapes his argument entirely in reaction to the claim of those who degrade his apostleship because it derives not from Christ but only from the apostles.[2]

This weighty consensus has virtually precluded examination of the purpose of Gal 1 and 2 or their function in the letter as a whole. Most commentators simply characterize this material, particularly 1:10/11–2:14, as a personal narrative or an autobiographical reflection that Paul has included to defend himself against his opponents. This reading of the letter has the effect of creating a sharp break between chapters 1 and 2 and the remainder of the letter. Chapters 1 and 2 are viewed as a personal narrative external to and irrelevant to the theological argument of chapters 3 and 4, not part of the meaty substance of the letter itself.

In his influential commentary Hans Dieter Betz raises questions about the composition and function of Galatians that provide an opportunity for reexamining this traditional view of Paul's autobiographical remarks. Betz notes that commentators offer outlines of the letter but rarely explain how they arrived at their outlines. Employing Greco-Roman rhetorical and epistolographic parallels, Betz argues that Galatians belongs to the "apologetic letter" genre. Because Paul cannot defend himself in person, he writes a "self-apology," which is situated in a fictitious court of law where Paul is the defendant and the Galatians are to be the jury. According to this analysis, the remarks contained in 1:12–2:14 constitute the *narratio* of Paul's apology, the exposition of facts that will make the defendant's denial of guilt plausible.[3]

While serious objections have been raised to Betz's analysis of the letter,[4] his work requires a reexamination of the traditional dissection of Galatians into personal narrative (chapters 1–2), theological argument (chapters 3–4), and ethical exhortation (chapters 5–6). Since Betz himself concludes that the entire letter is an apology, in which 1:12–2:14 provide the pertinent facts, he continues to support the conventional notion that what Paul writes in Gal 1 and 2 he writes entirely in order to defend his apostolate.[5]

With this judgment firmly in place, it is not surprising that Gal 1 and 2 are used extensively, and almost exclusively, for writing the history of primitive Christianity.[6] Exegetes draw upon Gal 1:11–17 when they want to understand Paul's early life, his activity as a persecutor, or his calling. Then 1:18–24 offers a supplement to the travels of Paul as portrayed in Acts. Next 2:1–10 provides a source for the discussion of the Jerusalem council, and 2:11–14 supplies numerous possibilities for the reconstruction of the divisions within the earliest communities. The entire section is consulted for details regarding the charges against Paul by his opponents in Galatia.

Whatever their value, these approaches perpetuate the tendency to view Paul's personal narrative as divorced from his theological argument. By focusing on historical reconstruction, they isolate chapters 1 and 2 from the remainder of the letter and limit the kinds of questions asked about the text.[7] If we habitually read a text only to learn about matters that exist outside it, then we lose sight of issues within the text that may be of equal importance. Indeed, we lose sight of the text altogether and read through it as if it were not there.

In two suggestive ways, Gal 1 and 2 depart from both Betz's model and the conventional model. First, why does Paul not explicitly name the charges against him? Betz notes that the rhetorical handbooks do not require an explicit reference to charges in an apology, but the one clear example he provides of the "apologetic letter" genre is Plato's *Epistle 7*, which responds to an attack in a direct and overt manner (e.g., 330B–C, 352A). Moreover, when Josephus feels compelled to write his life, he does not hesitate to enumerate the things of which he has been accused (e.g., *Life* 132–135, 189–190, 424–426). Finally, in 2 Cor 10:10–11 (cf. 11:5–6,

12–13), Paul himself refers to the attacks made against him by the "super-apostles" and to the contrasts made between himself and his opponents: "For they say, 'His letters are weighty and strong, but his bodily presence is weak, and his speech is contemptible.' Let such people understand that what we say by letter when absent, we will also do when present" (NRSV). If Paul wrote Gal 1:11–2:21 to defend his apostolate, why did he not do so directly and explicitly?

Second, in his letters Paul is normally reluctant to discuss himself or his own experiences, but here he enters into a "deliberate and provoked retrospect" that is without parallel in his letters.[8] This retrospect comprises roughly one-fifth of the text of Galatians.[9] Surely this departure from Paul's customary reticence does not arise entirely because of the accusations against him and his preaching.

These considerations suggest that Paul's autobiographical remarks in Gal 1 and 2 cannot be reduced to a single purpose and function. The autobiographical remarks of Gal 1 and 2 implicitly form the basis for Paul's later exhortation. Paul employs events out of his past, events that have to do with the exclusive nature of the gospel's claim on his own life, to urge that same exclusive claim on Christians in Galatia. He simply presents himself as an example of the working of the gospel.

That is not to say that Paul's understanding of the gospel is merely his own experience writ large. F. F. Bruce and Seyoon Kim to the contrary notwithstanding, Paul does not construct his theology out of the content or experience of his conversion.[10] Indeed, the reverse is true. It is Paul's understanding of the gospel that brings about a reconstruction or reimagining of his past.[11] Because of the "apocalypse of Jesus Christ" (1:12), Paul's own choices and actions appear in a different light. His presentation of certain aspects of his own experience is the gospel writ small, which Paul employs toward the overall goal of this letter.

In order to test these claims, I first survey Gal 1 and 2, noting features that contribute to this paradigm. Then I examine the motif of the "imitation of Paul" in Galatians and elsewhere and its relationship to our text. Finally, I explore the place of autobiographical writings in the ancient world, particularly as those writings may illumine the purpose and function of Gal 1 and 2.

GALATIANS 1 AND 2

Immediately following the salutation of the letter (1:1–5), instead of the customary thanksgiving, we find this:

> I marvel that you so quickly turn away from the one who called you in the grace of Christ to another gospel. Not that there is another gospel, but there are some who disturb you and want to pervert the gospel of Christ. But even if we or an angel from heaven should preach to you a gospel other than what we preached to you, let that one be accursed. As we have said before, I now say again: if someone preaches to you a gospel other than what you received, let that one be accursed. Am I now persuading humans or God? Or do I seek to please humans? If I were still pleasing humans, I would not be a slave of Christ. (1:6–10)

The reference to those who "disturb" believers and attempt to "pervert" the gospel is striking. The anathema of vv. 8–9 underscores Paul's anger. It is important, however, that we also see the contrast in v. 7 between the existence of those who mislead Galatian believers and the nonexistence of "another gospel."[12] There is only one gospel, and Paul makes that point over and over in these verses, where he five times uses either the noun εὐαγγέλιον (*euaggelion*, gospel) or the verb εὐαγγελίζεσθαι (*euaggelizesthai*, to preach the gospel). This sets the stage for what follows in 1:11–2:21, where Paul describes his own relationship with the gospel.

Paul follows the rhetorical questions of v. 10a and v. 10b with the assertion: "If I were still pleasing human beings, I would not be a slave of Christ." This statement is often taken to be a response to Paul's opponents, who charge that he proclaims a law-free gospel among Gentiles in order to please them. But this interpretation must ignore the adverb ἔτι (*eti*, still). The time in which Paul was pleasing to human beings was before his call, when he pleased his peers and elders by observing and promoting the law (vv. 13–14; cf. 5:11). He did not "advance beyond his peers" by loosening the law but by following it zealously.[13]

Why, then, does the contrast appear? Since Paul has just referred to those who are disturbing the Galatians, and since Paul speaks elsewhere of the influence of those troublemakers, perhaps he has in mind some of the Galatian believers themselves. They are now seeking to please outsiders in the same way Paul had done earlier, by conforming to the demand for observance of the law. As Paul describes his relationship to the gospel in 1:11–2:21, he will consistently demonstrate that there is only one gospel and that it requires the pleasing of God rather than of one's fellow human beings.

The contrast between God and human beings is carried over into vv. 11–12, as Paul announces emphatically that the gospel he preached came by means of apocalypse (NRSV: revelation). He illustrates this claim by reminding the Galatians of his earlier ἀναστροφή (*anastrophē*), his "lifestyle" in Ἰουδαϊσμός (*Ioudaismos*, Judaism).[14] He had attempted to destroy the church, had advanced in Judaism beyond his peers, and had acted zealously on behalf of tradition. In other words, Paul had lived in accordance with what he understood to be the highest claims of Judaism. While it is tempting to see a sense of guilt in his reference to persecuting the church, Paul does not linger over that action, and we should not allow the dramatic narratives in Acts to control our understanding of this passage. What Paul says of himself here and in Phil 3:2–11 gives little indication that he was haunted by guilt over his past.[15] His persecution of "the church of God" was, instead, the logical result of his zeal to please his people and to fulfill what he understood to be God's will. Between this "former lifestyle" and vv. 15–17 there is no transition sentence. Nor does Paul describe an event of revelation, a Christophany. Indeed, he confines to a temporal clause (ὅτε δέ, *hote de*, but when) all that he has to say about Christ's apocalypse and the commission to preach among the Gentiles.

The picture that emerges is of an abrupt change from zealot for the Jewish tradition to zealot for the gospel. Perhaps that abruptness appears in the text as a result of Paul's own memory, but that is merely conjecture. Here it is more important to notice how Paul juxtaposes his *former* way of life with his response to revelation without explanation or elaboration: "Immediately I did not consult with flesh and blood, nor did I go up to Jerusalem to those who were apostles before me, but I went away to Arabia and again I returned to Damascus" (1:17).

This "biography of reversal"[16] functions to demonstrate that the singular gospel demanded of Paul an extraordinary and unequivocal response. That is not to deny that Paul's comments here and elsewhere also have an apologetic purpose, but that interpretation by no means exhausts the purpose and function of this text.

Verses 18–24 continue this biography of reversal even as they describe aspects of Paul's activity. Three years after Paul's return to Damascus, he visited Cephas in Jerusalem, but saw no one else save James (vv. 18–19).[17] He then went to Syria and Cilicia. Paul was still unknown to believers in Judea, although they knew his story: "They only kept hearing, 'The one who was persecuting us now preaches the faith which then he was trying to destroy,' and they glorified God on account of me" (vv. 23–24). This report about Paul epitomizes what has already been said in vv. 11–17: the persecutor is now the proclaimer. Reinforcing the repetition is the recurrence of key terms from the earlier account: ἐκλλησία (*ekklēsia*, church) in vv. 13 and 22, ἀκούειν (*akouein*, hear) in vv. 13 and 23, διώκειν (*diōkein*, persecute) in vv. 13 and 23, εὐαγγελίζεσθαι (*euaggelizesthai*, proclaim) in vv. 11, 16, and 23 (cf. also 1:8–9), πορθεῖν (*porthein*, try to destroy) in vv. 13 and 23. The reversal Paul experiences is thus recapitulated for the reader and reinforced by the testimony of those who had good reason to be hostile witnesses, the churches in Judea.

Since Paul's account of his second trip to Jerusalem in 2:1–10 has been the focus of extensive and important historical reconstruction, here I need only draw attention to some neglected aspects of the text. Paul's assertion that he went up to Jerusalem "according to revelation" (2:2) recalls the revelation he has already experienced and features God as the central actor in this account (cf. 1:16, 24). Similarly, the Jerusalem pillars recognize the grace given to Paul (2:9) and, hence, the reader is reminded of the grace that is active in God's initial calling (1:15).

Paul emphasizes that his work was confirmed by the Jerusalem community. As the Judean churches have acknowledged God's hand in making a persecutor into a proclaimer, so now the Jerusalem pillars recognize God's action in Paul's work among the Gentiles. There is a slight movement here. At the end of chapter 1 what appears to require confirmation is the reversal in Paul himself. His personal credibility is at stake with the congregations. At the beginning of chapter 2 Paul receives from the leadership (2:2) confirmation of the shape of the gospel he proclaims. What is central here is not Paul's personal credibility but "freedom in Christ Jesus" (2:4) and proclamation among the Gentiles (2:7–9).

The movement from Paul's personal credibility to the validity of his gospel may seem to imply the existence of a clear demarcation between apostle and gospel, but such a demarcation is foreign to Paul. While Paul elsewhere suggests that the gospel can be effectively proclaimed even by those whose motives are questionable (Phil 1:15–18), that is not the case in this letter. Paul's calling as an apostle and his gospel are inextricably linked.[18] Nevertheless, there is a shift in the way he presents the material in this retrospect, for he begins with the confirmation of his own reversal by the churches and then tells of the "pillars" confirming the particular task to which that reversal led.

Until this point, the narrative has a flowing, seamless character. Paul's response to God's calling is consistent, as is the confirmation his calling and work have received. The presence of ἔπειτα (*epeita*, then) at the beginning of 1:18; 1:21; and 2:1 holds the narrative together so that we have the impression that events are moving smoothly, in accordance with revelation and grace (the presence of the "false brethren" in 2:4 notwithstanding).

At 2:11, however, matters change. The shift from ἔπειτα to ὅτε δέ (*hote de*, but when) signals a shift in events as well. No longer does Paul speak of the confirmation of his apostolate or his gospel, but of his own challenge to Cephas, one of the pillars at Jerusalem. Paul's language provides an indication of the intensity of his challenge to Cephas (at least in retrospect): "To his face I resisted him, because he was condemned" (2:11); "They acted insincerely" (2:13); "They did not walk straight toward the truth of the gospel" (2:14).

The disruption in the narration and the intensity of Paul's resistance to Cephas occur because he has reached the point at which his work no longer receives confirmation. While all could see God's reversal of Paul and could agree that he had been entrusted with the proclamation of the gospel to the uncircumcised, not all could affirm the full implications for the Gentiles of the gospel of freedom.

In the remainder of chapter 2, Paul insists again on the singularity of the gospel and prepares for the argument regarding the law and Christ in chapters 3 and 4. This transitional material in 2:15–21 looks backward as well as forward, however, and it is important that we take note of both features of the text. The assertion that justification comes only through faith in Christ Jesus and not through "works of law" (2:16) points forward to the elaborate argument of chapter 3. Verses 18–20, however, point back to the initial part of the retrospect: "For if I again build up these things which I tore down, I prove myself to be a transgressor. Through the law I died to the law, in order that I might live to God. I have been crucified with Christ. No longer is it I who live, but Christ lives in me. And what I now live in the flesh, I live in faith in the Son of God who loved me and handed himself over on my behalf."

Surely v. 18 refers to those aspects of Paul's life that were torn down by the revelation of God's Son (1:11–17). The reversal he describes in chapter 1 finds another expression in vv. 19–20: Paul died to the law and to his advancement in Judaism so that Christ might live within him (1:15–17).[19]

Exegetes frequently discuss whether the first person ἐγώ (*egō*, I) in the last part of this chapter refers to every believer or to Paul himself. The issue is complicated by the ongoing confusion regarding the referent of the "I" in Rom 7 and elsewhere.[20] Some see the first person as indicating that Paul has his own personal experience in mind;[21] others insist that this is not a personal reference but one that pertains to all Christians.[22] The difficulty in separating the general from the individual here is indicative of their interrelationship in the larger argument. Paul does not intend the first-person singular here or earlier simply to refer to "one." Nor does he speak of his own experience in order merely to defend his apostolate or to boast of his relationship to Christ. Instead, he sees in his experience a paradigm of the singularity of the gospel, and he uses his experience to call the Galatians into that singularity in their own faith-lives.

With the beginning of 3:1, the argument changes dramatically as Paul asks believers at Galatia to reflect on their own experience of the gospel. Paul does not again refer to the material in the retrospect of 1:11–2:14. Yet the conections between chapters 1 and 2 and the remainder of Galatians are closer than commentators generally recognize. What Paul has said about the reversal he has experienced is repeated at a number of points as he both reminds the Galatians of the reversals inherent in the gospel and calls on them to live out those reversals. At the beginning of chapter 3, when he appeals to their initial reception of the gospel, Paul indicates that their interest in following the law threatens to negate their earlier reversal (3:1–4). The convoluted argument regarding the law in chapter 3 culminates in the assertion that baptism means believers are no longer under the law or any other human category. They are "in Christ," and that claim is an exclusive one (3:23–29). Again, at the beginning of chapter 4, Paul writes of believers having been purchased by God from their slavery to τὰ στοιχεῖα τοῦ κόσμου (*ta stoicheia tou kosmou*, the elements of the cosmos) so that they might be heirs rather than slaves (4:1–7). As a consequence, believers must not submit again to the στοιχεῖα (*stoicheia*, 4:8–11); their submission to the law renders Paul's work futile (4:11).

The explicit exhortations of chapters 5–6 sustain the notion of reversal, beginning with 5:1 and its call to believers not to yield again to slavery. What matters is neither circumcision nor uncircumcision, but faith that works through love (5:6). Again, at the conclusion of the letter, we find this: "Neither circumcision nor uncircumcision is anything, but new creation" (6:15).

Despite the obvious differences among these texts in chapters 3–6, and the differences between them and the material in chapters 1–2, there is also a thread of continuity. The thread is not simply the end of the dominion of the law. What underlies 1:11–17; 3:23–29; 4:1–7; and so forth is the conviction that there is only one gospel and that it puts an end to all prior commitments, conventions, and value systems. Zeal for tradition, maintenance of the law, ethnic and social barriers, and observance of feast days are alike insofar as they threaten to undermine the exclusive claim of the gospel. The point is made throughout the letter, beginning with 1:6–9, but Paul develops it first with reference to himself and thereby offers his experience as a paradigm of the reversal inaugurated by the gospel.

THE IMITATION OF PAUL

If the autobiographical section in Gal 1 and 2 not only defends Paul but also presents his experience as paradigmatic of the gospel, then we may ask why that paradigm is not made explicit. Elsewhere Paul urges believers to imitate him. Why does not that exhortation appear here as well? A survey of the imitation-of-Paul texts will provide a useful answer to that question. In the letters of Paul commonly regarded as genuine, Paul refers to the imitation of himself five times:

> And you became imitators of us and of the Lord, receiving the word in much tribulation with joy from the Holy Spirit. (1 Thess 1:6)

> Therefore I exhort you, become imitators of me. (1 Cor 4:16)

> Become imitators of me even as I of the Lord. (1 Cor 11:1)

> Become fellow-imitators of me, brothers, and mark those who walk this way, as you have us as a model. (Phil 3:17)

> And whatever things you learned and received and heard and saw in me, do these things; and the God of peace will be with you. (Phil 4:9).[23]

These exhortations all appear in the context of a positive, even warm relationship between Paul and the congregation being addressed. Immediately after 1 Thess 1:6 Paul writes that believers at Thessalonica have become an example to others in Macedonia and Achaia. When he refers to his visit in Thessalonica, as discussed above in chapter 2, he employs the images of a nurse with her own child (2:7) and a nurturing father (2:11) in order to convey the nature of the relationship he established with believers. Although the relationship between Paul and the Corinthians does not appear to be entirely harmonious (e.g., 1 Cor 4:8–21; 5:2), the harsh tensions reflected in 2 Cor 10–12 have not yet arrived. Paul still speaks of believers at Corinth in familial terms and is able to express thanks for their reception of the gospel. Similarly, whatever it is that threatens the church at Philippi (Phil 3:2, 18–19), the situation does not appear to have precipitated a rupture between Paul and believers. On the contrary, the opening thanksgiving (1:3–11) indicates a strong and close relationship.[24]

It is not accidental that explicit references to the imitation of Paul occur in settings where there is a positive relationship between Paul and the recipients of the letter. Abraham J. Malherbe draws attention to a number of Pauline terms and devices in 1 Thessalonians that were standard features of Greco-Roman moral exhortation. Among these standard features was the philophronetic element, which served as the basis for exhortation. The writer would attempt to overcome the distance between himself and the audience by reminding the audience of their past relationship. That relationship, in turn, provided a way of moving into the exhortation.[25]

In Gal 1–2, Paul is unable to make an explicit call to believers to follow him or to imitate him because the relationship between Paul and Galatian Christians has been jeopardized. Paul fears that they have turned away from the gospel (1:6), that they have been bewitched (3:1). They, in turn, may even regard Paul as their enemy (4:16). The situation makes it impossible for him to begin with a reminder of their relationship and an exhortation derived from that relationship.

Although Paul does not begin the letter by appealing to the relationship between the Galatians and himself, he does make such an appeal in chapter 4, where he recalls his initial visit. Despite the fact that he was afflicted in some way, people in Galatia received him warmly and would have done much on his behalf (4:12b–15). He speaks of believers as his children and wishes, for the first time in the letter, that he could be with them.

At the beginning of this section, in 4:12, stands an enigmatic appeal: "Become as I, for also I as you." Particularly because of the elliptical character of the expression, "for also I as you," some commentators deny that this is an instance of the imitation-of-Paul motif. Paul, they insist, surely does not mean that the Galatians are to imitate him as he imitates them.[26] W. P. De Boer demonstrates that this conclusion misconstrues the relationship between the two clauses. They are not parallel or reciprocal. Instead, the first clause is a call to action and the second clause offers a past fact as a reason for fulfilling the call to action.[27] Thus, "become as I" means that the Galatians are to imitate Paul by rejecting all that threatens to remove them from an exclusive relationship to the gospel. "For also I as you" means that one reason for their imitation of Paul is that Paul has already rejected his zeal for the law and the tradition.

The presence of the imitation-of-Paul motif in Gal 4:12 raises two important issues for our study. First, if the situation prevents Paul from calling for the imitation of himself in chapter 1, why does he venture to do so in chapter 4? Here Paul builds on his earlier retrospective in chapters 1–2. "Become as I" reminds the hearers of that earlier section of the letter. In a sense, Paul assumes that the letter has been effective at least to the extent that he can appeal to the Galatians' concern for him and their earlier respect and goodwill toward him (4:13–20). An explicit appeal based on their former relationship would have been impossible at the outset, but it might be effective at this late point in the letter.

A second and more important issue concerns the character of the imitation Paul urges. In what sense is Paul to be imitated? What is it about Paul that the Galatians are to imitate? We are certainly not to imagine that Paul desires to have the Galatians imitate his life in the sense that they would repeat his course of action. Even those who may have been persuaded by the preaching of the Jewish-Christian missionaries could not be equated with the person Paul describes in Gal 1:13–14 and thus could not repeat Paul's life. These are Gentiles who could never duplicate the life Paul characterizes in Gal 1:11–2:14, especially because the fulcrum of that life is God's action (1:15), not Paul's.

What the Galatians can imitate is Paul's single-minded response to the gospel that was revealed to him. When he "immediately" returned to Damascus (1:17), he also discarded his zeal for maintaining the law and the tradition. He died not only to the law but also to the traditions and customs he had previously served. It is the reversal of those prior commitments that the Galatians are to imitate, although their commitments may be of a quite different sort (cf. 4:1–11). To become like Paul means to allow Christ to live in oneself (cf. 2:20) to the exclusion of the law or of any other tradition or category (cf. 3:27–28).[28]

AUTOBIOGRAPHICAL WRITINGS IN THE GRECO-ROMAN WORLD

We have explored Gal 1 and 2 in the context of the letter itself and in the context of the imitation-of-Paul motif. We need also to ask about their context in the Greco-Roman world. Here it becomes necessary to look at the character and function of autobiographical remarks in that world to imagine how Paul's remarks about his experience could have been heard and interpreted by his contemporaries.

Certainly Gal 1:11–2:21 is not autobiography in the modern sense. K. J. Weintraub's study of the history of autobiography supports the conventional conclusion that autobiography proper requires a self-reflective, self-conscious individuality, and that it begins with Augustine. It nevertheless is still possible to speak of writings that are autobiographical, as Weintraub concedes.[29] Arnaldo Momigliano, in *The Development of Greek Biography*, provides a useful distinction between autobiography and autobiographical. He restricts "autobiography" to works that have as their explicit purpose the narration of the author's past. The adjective "autobiographical," however, may refer to any statement an author makes regarding himself or herself.[30] This distinction appears implicitly in the work of Georg Misch, who wrote most of two volumes on the history of autobiography before he arrived at the *Confessions* of Augustine.[31] Misch's study was possible because he classified as autobiographical virtually anything written in first person or referring to the self.

In his dissertation on the function of Paul's autobiographical remarks, George Lyons employed this distinction in an attempt to demonstrate a development within autobiographical writings. Based largely on the autobiographical writings of Isocrates, Demosthenes, Cicero, and Josephus as examples of ancient autobiography, Lyons argues that during the Greco-Roman period the reasons for employing autobiography altered. While Isocrates and Demosthenes presented their autobiographical works as apologies, Cicero and Josephus set out to gain the respect of their contemporaries and to secure their own places in history.[32]

Although Lyons's review of this material is helpful, it is not clear that the works he analyzes assist us in our understanding of Paul. To begin with, the distinction between autobiography as apologetic and autobiography for the sake of gaining admiration is slight. Lyons himself acknowledges that Isocrates and Demosthenes inflate their need for self-defense in order to justify speaking of their own accomplishments.[33] While Josephus may wish to secure his place in history, he does so by dealing with the accusations that have been made against him, as noted earlier. Whatever the intent of the works Lyons studies, they are in style and form quite removed from Paul. Isocrates, Demosthenes, and Josephus each devote a complete treatise to explaining and defending their actions.[34] Although Paul provides us with a more lengthy retrospective in Galatians than anywhere else, it can scarcely be compared with Isocrates's *Antidosis*.

In order to place Paul's self-reference in its context, we need to examine the place of autobiographical remarks in Greco-Roman letters. Here we find that letter writers frequently referred to themselves, not simply because they had been accused of some offense, but because they wished to offer an example to others.[35]

Seneca's manner of referring to himself is illustrative of this practice. Seneca insists that learning occurs by means of example as much as by the handing on of precepts.[36] He draws attention to Socrates, who taught by example.[37] He also lodges a strong claim on the behavior of his student[38] and urges the student to live as if Seneca himself could observe his actions.[39] Most important, Seneca discusses his own struggles and his own problems in order to offer his correspondent an example.[40]

> "What," say you, "are you giving me advice? Indeed, have you already advised yourself, already corrected your own faults? Is this the reason why you have leisure to reform other men?" No, I am not so shameless as to undertake to cure my fellow-men when I am ill myself. I am, however, discussing with you troubles which concern us both, and sharing the remedy with you, just as if we were lying ill in the same hospital. (*Epistle 27* 1 [LCL])

> I am ill; but that is a part of my lot. My slaves have fallen sick, my income has gone off, my house is rickety, I have been assailed by losses, accidents, toil, and fear; this is a common thing. Nay, that was an understatement; it was an inevitable thing. Such affairs come by order, and not by accident. If you will believe me, it is my inmost emotions that I am just now disclosing to you: when everything seems to go hard and uphill, I have trained myself not merely to obey God, but to agree with His decisions. I follow Him because my soul wills it, and not because I must. Nothing will ever happen to me that I shall receive with ill humour or with a wry face. I shall pay up all my taxes willingly. Now all the things which cause us to groan or recoil, are part of the tax of life-things, my dear Lucilius, which you should never hope and never seek to escape. (*Epistle 96* 1–3 [LCL])

Pliny the Younger recognizes that he may appear to be boastful if he speaks about himself, but he also recognizes that self-reference is sometimes necessary.[41] Like Seneca, he refers to his own life in order to instruct others:

> My profession brought me advancement, then danger, then advancement again; I was helped by my friendship with honest men, then injured by it, and now am helped again. If you add up the years it would not seem very long, but it would be a lifetime if you count the changes of fortune. This should be a warning never to lose heart and to be sure of nothing, when we see so many fluctuations of fortune following each other in rapid succession.

> It is a habit of mine to share my thoughts with you and to
> set out for your guidance the rules and examples which shape
> my own conduct. That was the purpose of this letter. (*Epistle 4*
> 24.4–7; cf. *Epistle 7* 1 [LCL])

What do we learn from these and other autobiographical references[42] that might shed light on Paul's retrospective in Gal 1 and 2? The lengthy accounts of Isocrates, Demosthenes, and Josephus have as their subject matter the actions of the writer. Almost from beginning to end, the authors are concerned to justify their positions. Paul employs a different genre and, while he does make reference to himself, those references do not dominate the letter.

Much closer to Paul are the letters of Seneca and Pliny the Younger. Here the context is that of moral exhortation and instruction. Seneca's concern for the behavior of his pupil is comparable to Paul's involvement with the life of believers in Galatia. The letters of Seneca and Pliny the Younger demonstrate that reference to the self in Greco-Roman literature does not exclusively occur in apologetic contexts but also in didactic or paraenetic contexts. Self-reference is appropriate especially when one wishes to point beyond the self to some larger good, such as the pursuit of wisdom or virtue. It is precisely in this manner that Paul refers to his experiences in Gal 1–2: he not only defends himself and his gospel, but also offers himself as a paradigm of the work of the gospel.[43]

CONCLUSION

We have examined the function of Gal 1 and 2 in light of the context of the letter itself, the imitation-of-Paul motif, and the use of autobiographical reference in the Greco-Roman world. Each of these examinations reveals that Gal 1–2 cannot be confined to the category of apologetic. The retrospect also presents Paul as an example of the gospel's singular and exclusive power to overthrow human conventions, commitments, and values and to replace those with "the faith of Jesus Christ" (2:16). Although the severity of the tensions Paul is experiencing with the Galatians does not allow him to begin by offering himself explicitly as a paradigm of the gospel, he does do so indirectly. This paradigmatic dimension is accomplished by the repetition of the theme of the gospel's singularity, the inbreaking of apocalypse, and the insistence on the gospel's reversal of prior value systems, all presented in the form of autobiographical material.

Again, this does not mean that Paul's gospel is simply a magnification of his own experience. On the contrary, Paul sees in his experience an example of the gospel's power and employs that example for the exhortation of others. The next chapter expands this exploration further into Galatians, focusing especially on the singularity of the gospel as a way of thinking about the apocalyptic theology of Galatians.

CHAPTER SEVEN

The Singularity of the Gospel

In his letter to Galatian Christians, Paul responds to a problem that has arisen because, after his initial preaching and teaching in this region, other Christians have offered a different interpretation of the gospel. Those who have entered the Galatian churches after Paul insist that circumcision and keeping of (at least portions of) the law of Moses are necessary for full membership in the people of Israel. The advent of Jesus Christ means that Gentiles may become full partners in Israel, but it does not in any way call into question the law itself. Paul's letter responds in the sharpest manner to those who find this "other gospel" attractive, arguing that Gentile Christians *must not* take on the observance of the law. Paul's strategy in dealing with this problem is to argue both from the experience of believers and from the interpretation of Scripture that the law belongs to a past age and *must not* be observed by Gentiles who are "in Christ." Although one could scarcely speak of a consensus among Pauline scholars, this scenario is typical of the ways in which Galatians is read.[1]

For the purpose of identifying the theology reflected in this particular Pauline letter, it is important to ask whether Paul's response to the problem in the Galatian congregations constitutes the theology of the letter. That is, in order to discern the theology of Galatians, do we primarily look at Paul's response to the stated problem? For some important interpreters of Galatians, the answer to that question is apparently "yes." H. D. Betz treats the theology of Galatians by focusing on the problem, which he takes to be the threat posed to the freedom of the Galatians by outsiders who are insisting that Gentile believers in Christ must submit to the law of Moses if they are to be full members of the people of Israel.

Betz's presentation of the theology of the letter thus delineates Paul's arguments against the position of his opponents, identifying as central Paul's concept of freedom.[2]

Despite his careful articulation of the relationship between coherence and contingency in Paul's letters, J. Christiaan Beker's interpretation of Galatians appears to tip the balance toward contingency by identifying the theology of this letter with the argument Paul makes against the position taken by his opponents.[3] Because his Jewish Christian opponents have presented a version of salvation history that stresses the continuity between Abraham, the law, circumcision, and Christ, Paul is forced to insist on the disjuncture between law and Christ, between law and faith. Although Beker insists that the function of Paul's discussion about Abraham and the law in Gal 3 can be understood only within the "total context of the letter,"[4] he follows the conventional wisdom in marking 3:1 as the shift from "personal to material considerations."[5]

Both these understandings of the letter focus almost exclusively on chapters 3–4. Indeed, analyses of Galatians almost universally identify chapters 3–4 as the theological center of the letter. Since the first two chapters are regarded as a defense of Paul's apostleship, they do not enter the discussion of "theology." Similarly, the last two chapters are frequently bracketed off as paraenesis, which, by virtue of its traditional character, is not regarded as shedding light on Paul's theology. The result of this analysis of the letter is that discussions about the theology of Galatians take chapters 3–4 as their starting point and then move backward to chapters 1–2 and forward to chapters 5–6.

Such a reading of Galatians has the effect of virtually ignoring chapters 1–2 (with the possible exception of 2:16–21). These chapters enter the picture when the goal is to reconstruct something of a "life of Paul" or the history of early Christianity, but not when the issue is assessing the theological argument of the letter.[6] Similarly, chapters 5–6 are bracketed off as pragmatic advice of a traditional character that bears no material relationship to the preceding chapters.[7]

If we attend not simply to chapters 3–4 but also to the whole of the letter,[8] an alternative possibility emerges: although the letter arises out of the issue of the law, the underlying theological convictions that shape Paul's response to the problem derive not from his interpretation of the law but from his Christology. The theology reflected in Galatians is first of all about Jesus Christ and the new creation God has begun in him (1:1–4; 6:14–15), and only in the light of that christocentrism can Paul's remarks concerning the law be understood.[9] The word "christocentrism" is the right word, in that Paul presupposes from beginning to end that there is only one gospel (1:6–9), the singularity of which consists of the revelation of Jesus Christ as God's Son, whose crucifixion inaugurates the new age. This singular gospel results in a singular transformation for those called as believers, who are themselves moved into a new identity in Christ alone (2:19–21; 3:26–29) and new life in the Spirit (3:1–4; 5:16–25).[10] The new creation results in the nullification of previous identifications, whether these come from within the law (1:11–17) or from outside it (4:8–11). The position to be argued in this chapter, then, is that the governing theological antithesis in Galatians is between Christ or the new creation and the cosmos; the antitheses between Christ and the law and between the cross and circumcision are not the equivalent of this central premise but follow from it.

Three initial objections to this approach require brief comment. First, it may be thought that the argument that the theology of the letter is to be found elsewhere than in Paul's problem-solving strategy is tantamount to the view that Paul's theology is a timeless essence expressed differently in different contexts. That is not my intent. My argument is not that Paul takes from his theological storehouse the appropriate response for this setting, but that we may not arrive at the theology expressed in the letter by merely adding up responses to a particular problem. Just because the *presenting problem* concerns the law does not mean that, in Paul's perspective, the *central theological issue* at stake is the law. It is entirely possible that the Galatians themselves did not see the need to submit to the law as a theological issue. For them, it may have been an act of social identification or a pragmatic response to the demand of the outsiders. Whatever their view of the nature of the demand for circumcision, Paul sees in it the symptom of a critical theological problem.

The second objection arises as a result of introducing the term "Christology," which we customarily associate with the systematic tasks of Christian theology in later periods. I am not suggesting that Paul's argument in the letter rests on his view of the relationship between divinity and humanity in Christ or on his view of the relationship between Christ and God. Nevertheless, it is his understanding of who Jesus Christ is and what he has inaugurated and accomplished, in other words *Christology*, that stands as the focus of this letter.

Third, it may be objected that it is true but not important to say that Galatians is primarily to be understood as a christological statement. Paul makes use of traditional christologoumena (e.g., in 1:4), but—so the objection goes—those are only gestures to common tradition that have no impact on his argument and no significance for reading the letter itself. It will be my objective to show that these traditional expressions are not mere concessions to Paul's intended audience, but that they constitute an important part of the argument itself.[11]

WHY NOT OBSERVE THE LAW?

For heuristic purposes, we begin with a question that might be addressed to Paul in response to a reading of Galatians. Perhaps a group of believers from among the Galatians approach Paul, eager to find a solution that will satisfy both Paul and their more recent visitors. The question from this imaginary "compromise party"[12] runs as follows:

> Why make such a point of saying that Christians *must not* follow the law? Perhaps we Gentiles will benefit from keeping some portions of the law. It surely cannot adversely affect us, and it might help to restrain some enthusiastic or libertinistic tendencies. Would not the external sign of circumcision ensure that we Gentile Christians identify ourselves with the people of Israel and their God? You are perhaps right to contend that Gentiles are not *obliged* to follow the law, but why do you insist that we *must not* do so?

What arguments might be inferred from the letter in response to this imaginary proposal for a reasonable compromise between the two conflicting positions? Several possibilities can be considered and discarded. As is widely recognized, Paul's initial argument against the law is that it does not justify. Justification comes about only through the faithfulness of Christ (ἐκ πίστεως Χριστοῦ, *ek pisteōs Christou*; 2:16–21). To this may be added his reminder to the Galatians that they received the Spirit by hearing (ἐξ ἀκοῆς πίστεως, *ex akoēs pisteōs*) and not by means of the law (ἐξ ἔργων νόμου, *ex ergōn nomou*; 3:1–5). Such statements do not adequately respond to the compromise position, however, since the compromise does not propose that the law saves or that the Galatians came to faith through the law, but only that the law might be profitable for identifying Gentiles with Israel and for curbing the temptation to sin.

A second kind of argument Paul employs is the priority of faith over the law in the course of Israel's history. Here Abraham enters the discussion, since God grants righteousness to Abraham on the basis of faith, not on the basis of observance of the law (3:6–9). Indeed, the law comes into the world some 430 years after the promise to Abraham, a promise made to faith (3:15–18). Again, this argument does not meet the position of the compromisers, who suggest (somewhat more emphatically this time) that even if the law is historically secondary to faith and the promise made to Abraham, it still has the important functions, given by God, of setting Israel apart from the rest of the world and protecting Israel against evil.

Paul also claims that all who rely on the law are under a curse (3:10–14) and that Christ's death on the cross, itself resulting in the law's curse, removes believers from that curse. Contrary to the way in which this passage is sometimes read, Paul does not conclude that Christ therefore nullifies or curses the law. The compromisers still have room to suggest that, even if Christ's death removes believers from the law's curse, its power to discipline and direct the behavior of believers remains in force and remains necessary.

These aspects of Paul's argument about the law do not seem effective as a response to the hypothetical question, Why *not* observe the law? One remaining feature of his argument even serves to reinforce the reasonableness of the compromisers' position, and that is Paul's contention that the law was intended as a protection against sin.[13] To be sure, Paul introduces this claim in connection with the argument that the law was a temporary measure, superseded by Christ, but even in Christ the law might be understood as a curb against sin. To our sense that Paul's argument so far is something less than satisfying we may add George Kennedy's observation that Paul might easily have employed more common arguments against circumcision as unaesthetic and unnatural.[14]

I have deliberately omitted from this imaginary exchange the dominant thread in Paul's comments about the law in order to highlight the fact that the argument regarding the law in Gal 3–4 consists of statements used to bolster a previously chosen position.[15] That is, these are arguments that reinforce a position already taken, and it is that position, rather than these subordinate arguments, that leads us to understand what Paul's primary response to a compromise party would be.[16]

What the imaginary exchange deliberately omits is the antithesis Paul perceives between Christ and the law. Turning back now to Paul's comments about the law, we see that as early as the letter's first reference to the law in 2:16, it stands in direct opposition to Christ. One is either justified through the law or through Jesus Christ (2:16). The same kind of opposition dominates much of the argument in chapter 3. The Spirit came to the Galatians either through faith or through the law (3:1–5). The extremely complex section 3:10–14 turns on this opposition, since Paul sets over against each other Hab 2:4 ("The righteous one will live by faith"; v. 11b) and Lev 18:5 ("The one who does these things will live by them"; v. 12b) in order to show that the law is not from faith.

The baptismal formula employed in Gal 3:26–29 makes it clear that Paul is not simply arguing *against* some defect in the law but *for* the conviction that those who are baptized are baptized into Christ. That identification is not only primary; it is also exclusive. There can be no identification both in Christ and under the law—not even under some portion of the law understood as an aid for those in danger of succumbing to temptation in the form of libertinism.[17] Paul's response to the compromisers' proposition is clear: There can be no compromise between Christ and the law. Compromise is the thing Paul cannot do—and that not for psychological or social reasons but for profoundly theological reasons.[18] There can be no compromising of the gospel's singular and exclusive location in Jesus Christ alone. This is consistent with what Paul says about his own vocation and his "former life," as we saw in the previous chapter.

This antithesis between Christ and the law becomes explicit in 5:1–6. To receive circumcision means that one derives no benefit from Christ (5:2). Circumcision obligates one to the whole law, which means that one is set apart from the grace of Christ. Again we find the expression "in Christ" positioned antithetically over against circumcision (5:6). One may be under the law or one may be in Christ, but it is impossible to be both.[19]

THE SINGULARITY OF THE GOSPEL

We have seen that the antithesis between Christ and the law dominates Paul's argument regarding the law in Gal 3–4, and the question arises whether this same pattern holds in the remainder of the letter. Since the term νόμος (*nomos*, law) does not appear until 2:16, the letter does not begin with an explicit antithesis between Christ and the law. Instead of an attack on the law, here we find an assertion about the singular character of the gospel and its claims.

The letter opens with a salutation that immediately focuses on Jesus Christ. Although it is customary to see in 1:1 the beginnings of Paul's defense of his apostleship, even on this reading of the verse Paul points immediately to the source of his apostleship: "Jesus Christ and God [the] Father, who raised him from [the] dead." The grace reverses this order of "Jesus Christ and God" and introduces a more extended formula: "God our Father and Lord Jesus Christ, who gave himself on behalf of our sins, in order that he might deliver us from the present evil age according to the will of God and our father" (1:3–4). It is worth noting how much we learn from these few lines. Already we know that Paul's apostleship comes from Jesus Christ. Jesus is identified as one who gave himself for "our" sins. This act had as its goal "our" deliverance from the present age, which Paul identifies as evil. God, who is designated as Father, not only willed the action of Jesus Christ but raised him from the dead. The fact that Paul may be using traditional language here does not diminish the importance of this opening statement. The common "story" to which he refers is one about Jesus Christ and his actions, in accordance with God's will and as a result of God's power, as Savior ("on behalf of our sins," "to deliver us").[20] Since the letter lacks the traditional thanksgiving, in which we would expect to find indications of the subject of the letter, the suspicion arises that in Galatians the salutation itself introduces the main issue to be addressed.[21]

What Paul wishes to say about Jesus Christ becomes more focused in vv. 6–9. The Galatians have turned away from the one who called them and are turning to "another gospel." Yet Paul insists that there is no second gospel (v. 7): the gospel is singular, and the Galatians may have left its sphere for that of "another" gospel, which does not even exist. Little in vv. 6–9 allows us to identify the content or character of this singular gospel. Paul identifies it only as the word "of Christ" and as what "we" preached among the Galatians. Paul does not say that this gospel brings freedom, that it has to do with justification by faith, or that it pertains to membership in Israel. It is simply the "gospel of Christ." That formulation points back to the language identifying Christ in vv. 1–5.

If we read no further than vv. 1–9, we would surely conclude that what motivates Paul's letter to the Galatians has to do with a differing understanding of the gospel, one introduced by those who "trouble" the Galatians. Although Paul does not specify the source of the difference, the identification of the gospel he preached as the "gospel of Christ" suggests that the difference concerns the understanding of Christ.

The passage treated in chapter 6 (above), 1:10 (or 1:11) to 2:14 (or 2:21), also insists on the singular and exclusive nature of the gospel's claims. In Paul's retrospective account, he makes a sharp and uninterpreted transition from his former life (1:13–14) to his apostolic call (1:15–17). The two parts of his life, standing next to each other as they do here, support his conviction that the gospel comes from God alone and that it demands a singular and exclusive response.[22] Paul illustrates his own singular response to that gospel in 1:16b–2:21.

We have already seen the christocentrism in the central portion of the letter (chapters 3–4), but it might be objected that the ethical exhortations of the last part (5:13–6:10) derive little from the christological perspectives of chapters 1–4. Certainly it is true that the name of Christ appears seldom in this section, and commentators have often concluded from this that Paul's ethics have little material connection with his Christology. Before we agree to this partitioning, we need to look at the kinds of exhortations presented here. Richard B. Hays has argued that Paul's exhortations in this part of the letter are largely concerned with issues of freedom and slavery and address those issues within the context of communal responsibility. Although Paul does not directly invoke the name of Christ (but see 5:6, 24; 6:2), the exhortations correspond to Paul's claims about the actions of Christ, whose crucifixion resulted directly from his obedience and love.[23]

The conclusion of the letter (6:11–18) confirms the impression left by its opening that Paul is preoccupied in this letter with the Christ event, particularly with the exclusive nature of its claim upon believers. Here, where the argument of the letter culminates,[24] the antithesis between Christ and the law is first focused and then radicalized. In vv. 12–13, Paul takes up the Christ-law antithesis, but in what appears to be a highly focused way, for he contrasts a specific law, that of circumcision, with the cross of Christ. Those who urge circumcision do so only in order that they will not be persecuted because of the cross (6:12). They wish to boast in the flesh, while Paul boasts only in the cross (6:14a). At this point Paul radicalizes the contrast: in the cross of Christ, the whole cosmos has been crucified to Paul, and Paul to the cosmos (6:14b). Therefore, the primary antithesis is not between Christ and the law or between the cross and circumcision. These are but subsets of the more fundamental antithesis, which is between Christ/new creation and cosmos.[25]

ELEMENTS IN THE CHRISTOLOGY OF GALATIANS

We have seen that in Galatians Paul responds to a claim that believers must also observe the law, or at least parts of the law, by insisting that an antithesis exists between Christ and the cosmos (which includes the law). Can we be more precise about the content of the Christology of Paul's letter to the Galatians and therefore about this antithesis? What is the nature of this opposition? Is it moral, philosophical, apocalyptic?

It is clear, first of all, that Paul views Christ as an *agent of God*. The dominance of language about Christ and the scarcity of language about

God here could cause us to miss this point, but 1:1–4 and 4:3–5 make it clear that it is God who acts to send Christ and to raise him from the dead. The dominance of language about Christ should not lead us to read christomonism in Galatians, for it is God who reveals Christ, who calls Paul to proclaim Christ as God's Son (1:15–16), and who calls the Galatians (1:6; see also 3:5).

Although the letter refers to Christ's resurrection, it is *the crucifixion* that dominates Paul's Christology in Galatians. Paul sharply reminds the Galatians that Christ was presented to them publicly as "crucified" (3:1). Paul allows himself to boast only in the cross (6:14). This crucifixion results from Christ's own act of self-giving (1:4; 2:20). Because in the crucifixion the law placed Christ under a curse, that event purchased freedom from the law for those who are in Christ (3:10–14). This freedom is not merely freedom from the law (circumcision) but also from uncircumcision (5:6). In other words, the freedom Christ brings is not merely freedom from certain practices legally understood but freedom from all things—save Christ himself.

Here Betz's discussion about freedom in Galatians makes an important point: the preaching of those who followed Paul in the Galatian churches was attractive precisely because it offered a means to "protect the new Christian life from deterioration and destruction."[26] By being both "in Christ" and "under law," believers could be certain that they were full members of God's community. At some level they saw in Paul's preaching a threatening claim that they must live in—and only in—the gospel of Jesus Christ. The uncertainty of that claim and the perceived inability of this gospel to offer them concrete instructions for living out their faith made them willing to undertake the more secure avenue of the law.

Do Paul's references to the cross carry an implicit reference to resurrection as well, as is sometimes suggested? The answer to that question, at least in Galatians, must surely be no. Paul's references to the cross or crucifixion or the death of Christ are multivalent in that they carry within them references to God's action in sending Christ, to Christ's love and faithfulness in the cross, and to the curse of the law; but that multivalence does not mean that the cross for Paul includes resurrection. Although the formula of 1:1 refers to Christ's having been raised from the dead, most of the references to Jesus' death/cross in Galatians are sufficiently specific to exclude our attaching to them allusions to resurrection.[27]

More significant in Galatians is what the crucifixion expresses or reflects about Christ. One explanation Paul gives is that Christ's crucifixion stems from his self-giving love, as noted earlier. Paul also affirms that what has brought about the salvation of the Galatians is the πίστις Χριστοῦ (*pistis Christou*, lit., faith of Christ; 2:16). Although scholarly consensus has long understood this expression to refer to faith in Jesus Christ, recent studies argue persuasively for the translation "faithfulness of Christ" or "obedience of Christ."[28] This interpretation means that the references to Jesus' self-giving love in 1:4 and 2:20 ought not be sentimentalized, for the self-giving of Jesus stems from his faithfulness to God's will (1:4). Jesus does not act out of an individualized affection for believers, as a reading of 2:20 out of context might suggest,[29] but out of faithful obedience to God's intent.

In what has been said thus far there is little indication that this understanding of Christ has anything to do with Israel, but that is to neglect an important though elusive feature of Galatians. Although Christ is not confined to history, it is clear that Christ belongs to history. Born of a woman (4:4), Christ enters history. It is precisely within history, in the person of a son of woman, in the person of one crucified, that God reveals the end of history's distinctions between and among peoples. Although Christ is born under the law, his cross brings to an end both law and what we might call "unlaw." His birth under the law (4:4) means also that he is born into Israel's particular history of relationship with God. Christ is *the* offspring of Abraham (3:16), and as such he represents God's intervention in a particular history, now radicalized to include all humankind.

This observation returns us to the question raised earlier: What is the character of the antithesis between Christ and the law or, more properly, between Christ and all things? We may immediately rule out both the philosophical and the moral as descriptions of the antithesis. In Galatians, the historical locus of the Christ event means that Christ is not some eternal aeon that exists in contrast to the realm of the flesh. Neither does Paul interpret Christ and the law as ontological opposites. Similarly, Christ does not represent the moral good in contrast to evil. It is not as the good person that Christ is crucified, but as the faithful, loving Son of God.

The following may be offered by way of conclusion: Although the issue that prompts Paul to write to Galatian Christians arises from a conflict regarding the law, in addressing that problem Paul takes the position that the gospel proclaims Jesus Christ crucified to be the inauguration of a new creation. This new creation allows for no supplementation or augmentation by the law or any other power or loyalty. What the Galatians seek in the law is a certainty that they have a firm place in the church of God and that they know what God requires of them. It is precisely this certainty, and every other form of certainty, that Paul rejects with his claim about the exclusivity and singularity of Jesus Christ.

AFTERWORD

When this chapter was first published, I took up the question of whether the gospel's singularity is to be called by the name "apocalyptic" and answered that question negatively. My objections at the time were of two sorts. First, that the term itself generates some confusion, since it can refer to a movement, to a body of literature, and to a world of thought. Second, while the term does justice to the radical inbreaking of the gospel reflected in Galatians, it does not do justice to the continuity reflected in the letter (continuity with Israel's history and Israel's Scripture). As indicated in the introduction to part 2, I have changed my mind on this question of nomenclature. The term "apocalyptic" is no more ambiguous than many others in constant use in exegetical work (e.g., rhetoric, ideology, narrative), and the term has the advantage of signaling the relationship between this reading of Paul and earlier interpretations (notably those of Käsemann, Beker, and Martyn). The question of Paul's use of Scripture is far more complex than can be addressed here, especially since Richard Hays's *Echoes of Scripture in the Letters of Paul* has sparked a renewed fascination with the topic and generated a number of important studies.[30] To say that Scripture is important for Paul is not to say that Paul is interested in exegesis for its own sake or that Paul clings to Scripture as a way of maintaining continuity with tradition itself. As Francis Watson has put it, the meaning and significance of Scripture are identical: "Both are to be found in its manifold, direct and indirect testimony to God's saving action in Christ."[31]

One very particular indication that "apocalyptic" is the right term comes at the beginning of Galatians, when Paul characterizes God's saving action in Jesus Christ as God's rescue of "us from the present evil age" (1:4). Galatians itself yields only a few hints of what Paul means by that "present evil age," although those are sufficient to make it clear that this is not simply a reference to moral or philosophical shortcomings. In Romans, however, we do find extended discussion of the anti-God powers that hold humanity in slavery, and the next two chapters turn to a study of the power of Sin in Romans, first taking up Paul's initial discussion of God's wrath in Rom 1:18–32 and then exploring the problem more thematically.

CHAPTER EIGHT

"God Handed Them Over"

Commentators routinely describe the second half of Rom 1 as introducing a discussion of the human situation prior to the Christ event, a situation brought about entirely because of human behavior. Some argue that the fall of Adam stands in the background of this passage,[1] while others contend that here Paul plays on conventional Jewish critiques of Gentile idolatry and immorality.[2] In recent years the passage has become both an academic and an ecclesial battleground, on which conflicts are waged over exactly what Paul has to say about homosexual behavior, what influences shape those remarks, and how the remarks should be interpreted in the present. The passage has also figured in the attempts of some scholars to highlight inconsistencies in Paul's thought regarding sin, and in the arguments of others to show that Paul actually has no notion of "universal sinfulness." In this abundant discussion of the passage, however, little attention is addressed to the clause "God handed them over," even though the striking repetition of this clause in vv. 24, 26, and 28 is one of the hallmarks of the passage.[3]

The clause "God handed them over" is no mere rhetorical flourish, however. In this chapter, I endeavor to demonstrate that the clause signals that the human situation depicted in Rom 1 derives both from human rebellion against God and from God's own active role in a cosmic conflict. In response to human rebellion, God surrendered humanity for a time to what we may call the anti-God powers, chief among which are Sin and Death.[4] I deliberately select the verb "surrender" as a way of indicating that these anti-God powers engage in real conflict with God. This proposal places 1:18–32 firmly in the realm of cosmic apocalyptic discourse.

It also has the advantage of offering a more unified interpretation of Paul's treatment of sin in Rom 1–8 than the standard view that Paul speaks of sin as transgression in the early stages of Romans but later shifts to speak of Sin as a power.

I begin by considering the verb παραδίδωμι (*paradidōmi*), arguing that it may be understood in 1:24, 26, and 28 as "surrender" or "hand over" *to another power*. Next I take up the implications that translation would have for the interpretation of Rom 1:18–32. Finally, I consider the implications of this understanding of παραδίδωμι for a more comprehensive interpretation of sin in Rom 1–8. The chapter that follows extends this argument further into the cosmic landscape of Romans.

"GOD HANDED THEM OVER"

As indicated above, recent treatments of this passage give rather short shrift to the παρέδωκεν (*paredōken*, he handed over) clause. The relative inattention to this repetition may stem precisely from the comparison of 1:18–32 with other Hellenistic Jewish texts that castigate Gentiles for their idolatry and immorality. Along with a number of other students of Paul, I think that Paul here draws on an established Jewish tradition, one that he turns on its head at 2:1. The text most often cited is Wis 13–14, which begins with the ignorance of those who fail to see in the evidence of the world itself the work of their Creator (13:1–9), moves on to a lengthy discourse on the folly of idolatry (13:10–14:21), and then takes up the immorality that results from idolatry (14:22–31). In a Dante-esque move, the writer claims that "just penalties" will overtake the offenders (14:30–31; and see also 16:1). What Wisdom of Solomon does *not* do is attribute to God a direct role in the "handing over" of sinners.[5] Neither do any of the other texts customarily cited in connection with Rom 1:18–32 claim a direct role for God in the consequences of sinful conduct (see *Let. Aris.* 132–138; *Sib Or.* 3:8–45; *T. Naph.* 3:3; Josephus, *Against Apion* 2.236–254; Philo, *On the Special Laws* 1.13–31).[6] It appears that the similarities among these texts, which are important, cause the eye to pass quickly over the repeated παρέδωκεν (he handed over) clauses in favor of the behaviors that are said to be consequences of this handing over. The opposite move may be in order, however: the absence of the verb elsewhere, taken together with its threefold repetition here, signals its significance.

Historically, students of Romans have interpreted the παρέδωκεν (he handed over) clause along one of three major lines: (1) as permissive in the sense that God merely allows humanity to do what it wills to do;[7]

(2) as privative in that God abandons humanity to the consequences of its action;[8] or (3) as forensic in that God hands humanity over to judgment.[9] There is a great deal of overlap among these views, particularly between the first (the permissive) and the second (the privative), and the third (forensic) seems to dominate commentaries of the past few decades. None of these interpretations adequately reflects the possibility that the verb παραδίδωμι is used here, as elsewhere, to refer to the turning over of someone or something to a third party, often in a situation of conflict.[10]

The use of παραδίδωμι to refer to turning someone or something over into the custody of another or to surrender in a military context appears in a variety of sources, both biblical and nonbiblical.[11] In the LXX, παραδί-δωμι overwhelmingly refers to the handing over of an individual or (more often) a people to the power of another agent. In Deuteronomy, for example, παραδίδωμι appears over twenty times, almost always of God "handing over" a territory or a people to the possession of Israel (e.g., 2:24, 30, 31, 33; 3:2, 3; 7:2, 23, 24; 20:13, 20; 28:7). The usage in Joshua is similar, as the narration of the conquest routinely credits God with hand-ing over to Israel the city of Jericho (2:14, 24; 6:2, 16) or Ai (7:7; 8:18) or Gibeon (10:8, 12).[12] The prophetic literature, not surprisingly, frequently uses παραδίδωμι of the handing over of Israel to captivity, as when Jere-miah pronounces God's decree that Jerusalem will be handed over to Babylon (Jer 21:10; see also 22:25; 24:8; 39:28) or when Ezekiel declares that Israel's possessions will be given over to "the wicked of the earth" (7:21; see also 11:9; 16:27; 21:36 LXX [21:31 Eng.]; 23:28; 25:4). In these instances, as in Rom 1, there is an explicit connection between faithless-ness or disobedience and the "handing over."

Nothing in this broad sketch of the verb's usage is particularly star-tling. What is important to notice is that "handing over" virtually always involves handing over to another agent. Seldom does παραδίδωμι involve delivery up to an abstraction. Even in circumstances where the verb is used prophetically to warn about the consequences of disobedience or faithlessness, the "handing over" is not to some general consequence of human behavior but to another power, such as the Chaldeans, the "hands of foreigners," "the will of your enemies," or "the people of the East." The exceptions to this point only seem to underscore the general-ization. The LXX of Mic 6:16 concludes an oracle of judgment against injustice with the words:

ὅπως παραδῶ σε εἰς ἀφανισμὸν καὶ τοὺς κατοικοῦντας αὐτὴν εἰς συρισμόν· καὶ ὀνείδη λαῶν λήμψεσθε.

Translated somewhat woodenly:

> Thus I hand you over into destruction, and those who live among
> you into hissing; and you will receive scorn from the nations.

Although "destruction" and "hissing" might be construed here as abstractions, not in a grammatical sense but in the sense that they are not human powers, in context they clearly serve as references to the destruction that accompanies captivity.

A different sort of example appears in Ps 117:18 LXX (118:18 Eng.), where the psalmist declares:

> παιδεύων ἐπαίδευσέν με ὁ κύριος καὶ τῷ θανάτῳ οὐ παρέδωκέν με.
>
> The Lord harshly disciplined me, yet did not hand me over to
> death.

Being "handed over to death" might elsewhere be understood as the mere cessation of life, but the early lines of this psalm invoke the context of danger from enemies ("all nations surrounded me," v. 10), so that the "death" which the speaker has been spared is not due to disease or aging but to conflict with enemies.

In brief, in the LXX conflict with another agent or power routinely appears in the textual vicinity of παραδίδωμι.[13] Paul's letters reflect this usage as well. To be sure, he employs the verb to refer to the handing over of tradition or instruction (1 Cor 11:2, 23; 15:3), but in several instances παραδίδωμι is associated with handing over to another power. The most notable example is that of 1 Cor 5:5, Paul's instruction that the man who is living with his father's wife should be turned over to Satan for the destruction of the flesh. However difficult the passage is to interpret, it seems clear that "turning over" here is a surrender of power, since Satan consistently appears in Paul's letters as the enemy of both God and the community (e.g., Rom 16:20; 1 Cor 7:5; 2 Cor 2:11; 11:14; 12:7; 1 Thess 2:18; and cf. 1 Tim 1:20); the community is to hand the offender over to the powerful enemy, Satan. First Corinthians 15:24 likewise recalls the regular use of the LXX, as Paul looks forward to the time when the risen Jesus will "hand over" the kingdom to God, when Jesus has himself destroyed "every authority and power," that is, at the culmination of conflict with anti-God powers. Several other passages refer to the "handing over" of Jesus (1 Cor 11:23; Gal 2:20), which may itself be further indication of the pattern of handing over in settings of conflict, because Paul understands that it is the "rulers of this age" who were responsible for Jesus' death (1 Cor 2:8).[14]

Based on usage both in the LXX and in Paul's own letters, then, παραδίδωμι can refer to the surrendering of someone or something in a context of conflict. Because a number of the illustrations I have offered occur in situations of divine judgment on human life, one might think that they simply argue in favor of the third option identified earlier, that the use of παραδίδωμι merely reinforces the divine judgment on immorality and idolatry. While the sense of judgment is certainly not to be excluded, judgment alone does not adequately account for the content of the passage. To begin with, Paul does not employ κατακρίνειν (to judge) here, although he does do so in 2:1 as well as later in the letter (8:3, 34; 14:23). More important, as already noted, the very fact of the threefold repetition of the clause παρέδωκεν αὐτοὺς ὁ θεός (God handed them over) signals its importance.

Comparable instances of repetition appear infrequently in Paul's letters. First Corinthians 6:9–10 twice repeats the verb κληρονομέω (*klēronomeō*, inherit) in its warning about misconduct, and Phil 3:2 three times repeats the warning βλέπετε (*blepete*, watch out). More revealing for understanding our present text are the opening of Galatians (1:8–9), where Paul twice asserts regarding those who proclaim "another gospel," ἀνάθεμα ἔστω (*anathema estō*, let that one be accursed), and the beginning of 2 Corinthians (1:3–7), with its striking repetition of παράκλησις (*paraklēsis*, exhortation), and παρακαλέω (*parakaleō*, exhort). In both these cases the repetition identifies a major issue in the letter.

To the best of my knowledge, the closest syntactical parallel to Rom 1 comes in 1 Cor 1:27–28, where we find a threefold repetition of the verb ἐκλέγομαι (*eklegomai*, choose), with God as the subject of the verb. Rendered somewhat literally:

The foolish things of the world God chose,
the weak things of the world God chose,
the lowborn things of the world and the despised God chose.

As in Rom 1:24, 26, and 28, in Greek the verb in every case stands before the subject:[15]

τὰ μωρὰ τοῦ κόσμου ἐξελέξατο ὁ θεός
τὰ ἀσθενῆ τοῦ κόσμου ἐξελέξατο ὁ θεός
τὰ ἀγενῆ τοῦ κόσμου καὶ τὰ ἐξουθενημένα ἐξελέξατο ὁ θεός

As with the repetitions at the outset of 2 Corinthians and Galatians, this one also indicates an important concern in the letter: the absolute priority of God's election over human wisdom or achievement. A similarly

important signal is being sent in Rom 1: God's handing over of humanity is not simply a response to human action but an event in God's conflict with the anti-God powers.

GOD GAVE THEM OVER TO WHAT?

By establishing the possibility that the repeated clauses "God handed
them" over in Rom 1 suggest that God turns humanity over to the control of another agent or power, we have introduced an important new
question: to what power does God hand over humanity? Answering that
question requires a closer examination of the structure of the three
verses. All three instances of παρέδωκεν are followed by phrases consist-
ing of εἰς (*eis*, the preposition "to" or "into") plus an accusative noun: to
"impurity" (v. 24), to "dishonorable passions" (v. 26), to "a deformed
mind" (v. 28).

Verse 24	Διὸ παρέδωκεν αὐτοὺς ὁ θεὸς . . .
	εἰς ἀκαθαρσίαν
Verse 26	Διὰ τοῦτο παρέδωκεν αὐτοὺς ὁ θεὸς
	εἰς πάθη ἀτιμίας,
Verse 28	παρέδωκεν αὐτοὺς ὁ θεὸς
	εἰς ἀδόκιμον νοῦν

To be sure, the first of these statements, v. 24, inserts another phrase
between the παρέδωκεν clause and the εἰς phrase: ἐν ταῖς ἐπιθυμίαις
τῶν καρδιῶν αὐτῶν (NRSV: "in the lusts of their hearts"). This phrase
could be translated and interpreted as if it were the object to which
humanity was handed over or the circumstance of handing over, as in
the NRSV. And the LXX does sometimes employ παραδίδωμι with ἐν (*en*)
rather than with εἰς, although in those cases ἐν is often accompanied by
"the hand [or hands] of" someone (see, for example, Josh 2:24; 10:35;
Judg 2:23). Moreover, Paul does not elsewhere follow παραδίδωμι with
ἐν, and the ἐν phrase is better understood as causal;[16] that is, God
handed them over because of the desires of their hearts, desires which
have been described in the preceding lines of vv. 20–23.[17]

If the ἐν phrase is understood causally, then the three εἰς clauses may
be regarded as identifying the agent(s) to whom humanity is handed:
ἀκαθαρσία/uncleanness or impurity, πάθη ἀτιμίαις/dishonorable passions, and ἀδόκιμος νοῦς/deformed mind. At first glance, these do not
appear to be the names or descriptions of agents but of behaviors,
aspects of the human being and human behavior, thought, attitude. In

other words, they seem to be characteristics that inhere in the human. Later passages in Romans open up the possibility that Paul understands them as powers, however. The first term, ἀκαθαρσία (*akatharsia*, uncleanness) appears only one other time in Romans; 6:19 recalls that the addressees previously "presented your members as slaves to uncleanness," "when you were slaves of sin" (6:20). Here "uncleanness" offers an alternate way of speaking of the power of Sin itself. Similarly, the synoptic tradition associates "uncleanness" or "impurity" with evil spirits (e.g., Mark 1:23, 26, 27; Luke 8:29; Matt 12:43).[18]

The second term, πάθος (*pathos*, passion) appears nowhere else in Romans, but the closely related expression, τὰ παθήματα τῶν ἁμαρτιῶν in 7:5 stands as the subject of the verb ἐνεργεῖσθαι, referring to the sinful passions that work through the law to bring about death. The third phrase, ἀδόκιμος νοῦς (*adokimos nous*, deformed mind) also does not appear elsewhere in Romans, but a functionally equivalent phrase occurs in Rom 8:6–7 referring to the "mind" of the flesh that is death and is set in opposition to God. All of these expressions, then, have in view the enslavement of humanity to agents that are set over against God. Uncleanness, dishonorable passions, and deformed mind are instances of synecdoche; they refer to the anti-God powers, especially the power of Sin. Because of human refusal to recognize God, God turns humanity over—concedes humanity for a time—to another power, the power of Sin.

This proposal, which significantly recasts the forensic interpretation, coheres better with other elements in the Pauline letters than does the notion that God simply allows humanity to do what it wills or that God abandons humanity. Both of those alternatives resort to explanations of this handing over as a natural process. C. H. Dodd, for example, comments:

> All through this passage the disastrous progress of evil in society is presented as a natural process of cause and effect, and not as the direct act of God. . . . It was by men's own act that they refused to worship Him and so fell under the power of evil.[19]

Similarly, Moule characterizes this as the "working out of a natural process."[20] In those views, God seems curiously absent from the event, and the absence of God is a notion difficult to reconcile with Pauline thought, especially in Romans.[21] By contrast, Paul understands that human beings always live in the grasp of some power, whether that of God or that of an anti-God power.[22] Romans 6 affords a clear view of this understanding in the series of contrasts between "living in the realm of Sin" and having been baptized "into the realm of Christ Jesus" (6:1–3).

In Paul's understanding, people are always enslaved to something, whether to righteousness or to sin, and people are always free from something, whether from righteousness or from sin (6:12–23).

To be sure, Paul nowhere uses the phrase "anti-God powers"; this shorthand expression serves to draw together the various ways in which Paul reflects an understanding that God has other-than-human enemies.[23] As already noted, Paul often refers to Satan. In 1 Cor 2 he comments on the "rulers of this age" who were responsible for the crucifixion (2:6, 8; see also "the god of this world" in 2 Cor 4:4). Elsewhere he comments on sacrifices made to "demons, not to gods" (1 Cor 10:20) and on slavery to things that are not God (Gal 4:8; and see also 1 Cor 8:5). The argument of 1 Cor 15 makes little sense apart from some concrete notion that God has enemies that must finally be defeated, chief among which is death itself (1 Cor 15:26, 54–57). The concluding lines of Rom 8 offer a veritable litany of these powers, and the strong affirmation that none of these powers can bring about separation from the love of God implies that they actually undertake to do just that; they intend to separate humanity from its proper Lord, and they array themselves against God.[24] Unlike the author of *1 Enoch*, Paul does not speculate about the origin of the anti-God powers, nor does he concern himself with a systematic account of their relationship to God, but their reality and their cosmic significance are clear for him.[25] And the existence of these anti-God powers underlies Paul's repeated claim in Rom 1 that God "handed over" humanity.

GOD'S SURRENDER IN THE LARGER DRAMA OF ROMANS

Turning now to the implications of this argument regarding 1:24, 26, and 28 for reading the remainder of Romans, I touch on two points, both of which return in the next chapter. One has to do with Paul's understanding of Sin as reflected in this letter, and the other with the cosmic apocalyptic perspective of the letter.

First, Paul's understanding of Sin: At least since the work of Martin Dibelius, it has been conventional to distinguish in Paul's letters between sin as a transgression, an individual action that occurs in a context of free choice, and Sin as an external force that holds humanity in its grasp.[26] The first of these understandings is associated most closely with Rom 1–3, and the second with Rom 5–7. For some interpreters, Paul's understanding of sin is "ambiguous," as when J. Christiaan Beker characterizes Paul as moving from a notion of "responsible culpability" for sin in Rom 1 and 2 to a notion of the human as Sin's "victim" in Rom 5:12–19.[27] Others regard Paul's treatment of sin, especially in 1:18–3:20, as simply inconsistent or incoherent, notably Heikki Räisänen and E. P. Sanders.[28]

In recent years some students of Paul have tried to resolve the problem by contending that Paul's personification of Sin as a power is merely metaphorical, that what he "really" means is simply that people have choices to make and they routinely make mistakes. In his study of the structure of Rom 6, Bruce N. Kaye argues that Paul varies his language for sin according to the varying argumentative contexts within the letter, but that the "basic concept" of sin remains constant throughout; sin is "sinful act" or the "guilt consequent upon such acts."[29] Approaching the problem from a study of personification in Paul and contemporary literature, Günter Röhser has similarly concluded that Paul regularly refers to human action and not to a suprahuman power.[30] The more recent works of Stanley Stowers and Troels Engberg-Pedersen have sounded the same note, reducing sin to misdeed or misdirection throughout the letter.[31]

By offering a unified understanding of Sin as a power, the proposal I am making flies in the face of the traditional view as well as the more recent reaction to it. The prevailing interpretation of 1:18–32 draws attention to the fact that Paul does not personify sin at this point in the letter; in fact, neither ἁμαρτία (*hamartia*) nor its cognates occur here. My reading of the passage, by placing more stress upon the presence of the παρέδωκεν clauses ("God handed them over") and the conflict they represent, brings it closer to the remainder of the letter. When God is three times said in Rom 1 to have "handed over" humanity to the powers of uncleanness, dishonorable passions, and a deformed mind, that action places humankind in the power of Sin. To be sure, there is human action in 1:18–32 (as there is with the action of Adam in chapter 5 and the "all" of 5:12), but this combination of human action and divine action is not as odd as is usually thought. To turn to Luke–Acts for an analogy, Luke is quite capable of saying both that the death of Jesus is part of God's plan (e.g., Acts 2:23; 3:14–15) and that the Jerusalem Jews put Jesus to death on the cross (e.g., Luke 24:46–47; Acts 2:23; 3:14–15).

It may be that confirmation of this reading of "God handed them over" comes at Rom 11:32, when Paul writes that "God imprisoned all in disobedience that he might be merciful to all."[32] The attribution to God of the action of confining or imprisoning "all" offers a shorthand reference back to the scenario of 1:18–32. In turn, it provides an explanation of the goal of God's "handing over"; that is, God concedes humanity to the anti-God powers for a time, less for punishment than for mercy.[33]

Both the handing over and the release from that handing over come to expression at several important points in the letter. In 3:24, as he returns to the declaration of God's righteousness announced in 1:16–17, Paul writes of God's grace "through the redemption in Christ Jesus." The language of redemption signals that God has now bought back from slavery the humanity once "handed over" to the anti-God powers.[34] Similarly, the claim in 8:3 that in sending Jesus God has "condemned sin in the flesh" indicates, not merely God's condemnation in the sense of moral disapproval or disapprobation, but God's actual defeat of Sin as a power. In 8:32, the notion of "handing over" returns explicitly with the statement that "God did not spare his own son but handed him over [παρέδωκεν] on behalf of all of us" (see also 4:25 and Isa 53:12 LXX).[35] For Paul, the cross is the point at which the "handing over" to the anti-God powers reaches its undoing, since it is here that "God handed over his own Son" (Rom 8:31–32), which is not victory for the powers but their unmasking and the sure sign of their defeat.[36]

With that last comment regarding the handing over of Jesus Christ to the anti-God powers precisely for their defeat and for human redemption, we come to the second conclusion, namely, the cosmic apocalyptic character of Romans. The significance of this proposal extends beyond that of merely establishing that Paul may have been more consistent than is often thought or that he had a more thoroughgoing view of sin than has recently been propounded. The larger issue at stake here is the reclamation of the apocalyptic character of Romans. That character is already signaled in Rom 1, not only in the repetition of παρέδωκεν (handed over) but already in the repetition of ἀποκαλύπτεται in vv. 17–18 (*apokalyptetai*, is being apocalyptically revealed), and perhaps already in v. 4 with the phrase ἐν δυνάμει (*en dynamei*, with power / powerfully). If that is the case, then we need to be alert to the possibility that apocalyptic figures all along the way. Although argued passionately by Ernst Käsemann and J. Christiaan Beker, and developed in the works of Charles B. Cousar and Martinus de Boer,[37] that feature of Romans has fallen into neglect in recent years. Major voices have emphasized the continuity between Romans and the story of Israel in ways that have nearly eclipsed the apocalyptic character of the letter. Yet, if the previous generation has rightly insisted that Romans is about more than the standing of an individual before God, it is now time to insist that Romans is also about *more than* God's covenant faithfulness with Israel. Romans situates the people of Israel, as well as the people outside Israel, within a conflict that is nothing less than cosmic in its horizon and its implications. God has signaled in the death and resurrection of Jesus Christ that the time of handing over, of confining all to sin, is past. God has condemned not only Sin (8:3) but also all the anti-God powers (8:31–39) in this definitive action to reclaim the world for God's own self.

CHAPTER NINE

The Cosmic Power of Sin in Paul's Letter to the Romans

No form of Christian teaching has any future before it except such as can keep steadily in view the reality of the evil in the world, and go to meet the evil with a battle-song of triumph.

Gustaf Aulén[1]

"Here at Christ Church, we don't have sin." Stunning as it may be, this statement was made to a pastor of my acquaintance early in his current pastorate. What precisely the statement was intended to convey remains obscure, but it conjures up the range of ways in which contemporary Christians convey their discomfort with talk about sin (at least as sin pertains to themselves). A friend told me that she could not sing "Amazing Grace" since she had never been a "wretch" who required saving. Congregations seeking a more "positive" worship experience relegate prayers of confession to the dustbin with the explanation that people prefer not to think about sin.

The people who inhabit these anecdotes would surely find themselves ill at ease with Paul's letter to Christians at Rome. More than anywhere else in the New Testament, the language of sin flourishes here.[2] The noun *hamartia* (ἁμαρτία, sin) and words related to it (sinner, to sin, sinful) appear 81 times in the undisputed letters of Paul, and 60 of those instances are in Romans. In Rom 5–8 alone, the noun *hamartia* occurs 42 times. Often it acquires particular intensity because it serves as the subject of a verb: sin "came into the world" (5:12), sin "increased" (5:20), sin "exercised dominion" (5:21; cf. 6:12, 14), sin "produced" (7:8), sin "revived" (7:9), sin "dwells" (7:17, 20). Clearly sin has a leading role in the letter to the Romans.

Given this striking linguistic evidence, it may be surprising to notice that some important scholarly works of recent years show a certain reluctance in the discussion of Paul's understanding of sin. A major concern of Stanley Stowers in *A Rereading of Romans* is to undermine the notion that Romans contains an understanding of universal sinfulness. Stowers contends that the point of 1:18–3:26 is first to demonstrate the decline and degeneration of Gentiles and then to demonstrate that Jesus Christ is God's solution to the problem of Gentile sin. Romans does affirm that the Gentile world stands under God's judgment, but no vigorous argument about sin is to be found here: "*In the trivial sense*, Paul believes that all humans sin, but that is far from saying that all are unrighteous, all fail to understand, all fail to seek God, all have turned away, and not a single person fears God (3:10ff.)."[3] Troels Engberg-Pedersen sounds a similar note in his recent work *Paul and the Stoics*. He argues that when Paul asserts in 3:9 that "all are under sin," he does not mean "necessarily 'to sin' or 'to be a sinner in such a way that one constantly or at least regularly sins.'" Instead, being "under sin" may mean only "that one *risks* sinning, *risks* doing actual sins."[4]

To be sure, one purpose of these comments is to counter—and rightly so—claims made by earlier scholars who all too readily interpreted Paul's letter as a reasonable and reliable indictment of Jews and Judaism.[5] Nevertheless, the entirely appropriate desire not to bear false witness against the neighbor cannot excuse interpreters from taking seriously what is surely an important feature of Paul's letter. And a treatment of Romans that does not give a robust account of Paul's understanding of sin just will not work.

READING ROMANS: WIDE-SCREEN VERSUS PAN AND SCAN

Although any comparison between the careful scholarly treatments just mentioned and the highly selective anecdotes of the opening paragraph distorts both sides, there is one common thread that does connect them. *In each case, the comments about sin consider sin strictly as a feature of human activity or human experience.* The parishioner who claimed that there was no sin at Christ Church commented on the relative health of the congregation. Those who regard it as offensive to sing "Amazing Grace" or to offer a corporate prayer of confession do so because they think of sin as something a human being or group of human beings has done or not done. Stanley Stowers complains that the notion of universal sinfulness in Romans results in a portrait of the human condition that cannot distinguish between Moses and Hitler.[6] What drives Stowers's complaint is the assumption that sin is a behavior, one that is hideously present in the activity of Adolf Hitler and infinitely less so in the activity of Moses.

This all seems quite self-evident. The difficulty arises when we notice that Paul does not confine his comments about sin to human behavior, to sin as misdeeds, omitted deeds, even to perverted thoughts and plans. Instead, as we have already noted in the preceding chapter, sin is Sin—not a lowercase transgression, not even a human disposition or flaw in human nature, but an uppercase Power that enslaves humankind and stands over against God. Here, Sin is among those anti-God powers whose final defeat the resurrection of Jesus Christ inaugurates and guarantees.[7] That larger picture of the cosmic battle is necessary to understand Paul's language in Romans, but that larger picture is missing in much recent discussion of Romans.[8]

An illustration from the world of film may be helpful. A major complaint of film aficionados is the way in which movies shown on television or VHS tape are subjected to pan-and-scan editing. Pan-and-scan editing crops the edges from film in order to compensate for the discrepancy between the wide screens in movie theatres and the boxy television screens in most homes. While satisfying to those who dislike the black bands of letterboxed editions and who want their television screens full of picture, pan-and-scan editions can actually distort the filmmaker's work. For example, the number of actors who are visible may be substantially reduced, which in turn exaggerates the importance of the actors who remain in view.[9]

Perhaps it is unavoidable that readers of biblical texts perform something equivalent to pan-and-scan editing as we interpret. Invariably, we "shrink" the text, never quite able to attend to the whole of it. Yet our reading of Paul's letter to Rome may offer a most impressive example of this editing process, precisely because the letter itself involves so many twists and turns (to say nothing of the history of its interpretation). In a number of recent studies, what seems to have been left on the cutting-room floor (underinterpreted or entirely neglected) in the interpretation of Romans concerns the larger apocalyptic dynamic of Paul's theology, particularly the cosmic character of his remarks about Sin. That apocalyptic framework is not only essential for understanding the letter as a whole and the place of Sin in particular but also crucial to understanding the urgency of Romans in the contemporary context.

Here with utter seriousness I will take Paul's frequent use of Sin (*hamartia*) as the subject of a verb and describe Sin itself as a major character in the letter—a character who enslaves, who brings death, who ensnares even God's Torah, and whose demise is guaranteed by God's action in the death and resurrection of Jesus Christ. What may at first glance seem an exaggeration will, in my judgment, illumine the apocalyptic struggle that forms the wide-screen version of Romans.

THE RÉSUMÉ OF SIN

Paul's remarks in Romans allow for the construction of a veritable résumé of Sin's achievements. Taking Sin's actions chronologically, the first claim made is that in the transgression of Adam, *Sin entered the world* (5:12–21). Assuming that his Roman audience knows the biblical story, Paul does not retell it but simply touches on it as the beginning of the activity of Sin.

Having established a base of operations,[10] *Sin became an enslaving power.* This feature of Sin's résumé Paul exposes at two different points in the letter and at some length, surely in itself an indication of its importance. Paul explicitly identifies Sin as humanity's slaveholder in chapter 6, yet Sin's enslaving power first comes into clear view in 3:9 as the culmination of the human rebellion and the divine "handing over" in 1:18–2:29.

Although the noun *hamartia* does not enter the picture until 3:9, Paul's depiction of Sin's activity properly opens with 1:18.[11] Paul announces the subject in 1:18 with the solemn declaration that now God's wrath is revealed against "all ungodliness and wickedness of those who by their wickedness suppress the truth." The nature of this suppressed truth is nothing other than God's own work as creator, something humanity denied by its behavior (vv. 19–23). Through the refusal to honor or give thanks to God, and through idolatry—corrupt practices of worship!—humanity suppressed the truth.[12] As is well-known, the repetition of the phrase "God gave them up" structures the remainder of chapter 1. Because human beings did not acknowledge God as God, God "gave them up" to impurity (v. 24), to degrading passions (v. 26), to a debased mind (v. 28). This handing over results in the relentless array of misconduct Paul itemizes in stark detail.[13]

As we saw in the last chapter, scholars often posit a tension between what Paul affirms in this passage about human refusal to acknowledge God and later sections of the letter that speak of Sin as a power. The beginning point of this grand depiction of Sin is humanity's willful choice to deny God, even to create its own gods. Paul's depiction of humankind opens with an action taken by humanity itself rather than by another power. With the claim that God delivered up humanity to impurity, passion, and debased mind, however, there is an indication of a larger conflict.[14] An as-yet-unnamed someone or something challenges God for control of humanity. That is not to overlook the initial action: humanity's refusal of God's lordship meant that God turned humanity over for a time to the lordship of another.

In 1:18–32 the vigorous recital of the behaviors associated in Jewish literature with Gentiles virtually invites the audience to energetic assent.[15] We can readily imagine Phoebe reading the letter to a gathering of believers at Rome, at least some of whom would nod their heads in smug agreement with the condemnation of "those" other people who do such dreadful things.[16] At 2:1 Paul springs the trap on just such a reader, observing that the willingness to condemn others also constitutes a form of denying God. Romans 2:1–16 sharply rebukes the one who judges others, perhaps by way of anticipating chapter 14, with its more extended affirmation of the perils of judging others. All are responsible before God, who is the only true judge (14:10–12). In 2:17–29, Paul explicitly addresses Jews with the possibility that they instruct others while not themselves learning, that they rightly perceive circumcision as a value without understanding the requirement attached. Paul W. Meyer is right to insist that this address not be understood as implying some flaw peculiar to Judaism but as revealing the difficulty inherent in sincere religious conviction.[17] In other words, the end of chapter 2 addresses those who genuinely undertake to pursue God's will.

This section of the letter culminates in 3:9 with the conclusion that "all, both Jews and Greeks, are under the power of Sin." The NRSV supplies the noun "power" where none exists in the Greek text, yet "power" is surely to be inferred.[18] Those behaviors paraded in 1:18–2:29 are not simply symptoms of an intellect set against God. Quite the opposite: 2:17–24 concerns precisely those who intend to honor God. Instead, Paul's review of human behavior points to the reality of a power named Sin that holds human beings in its grasp. So firm is the control that even the great advantages conveyed upon Israel by God cannot immunize Israel against Sin's power (3:1–8).

In chapter 6, Sin's enslaving grasp comes into full and unmistakable view. The chapter opens as a rebuttal of the possible conclusion that God's grace permits antinomianism: "Shall we persist in Sin so that grace may increase?" (6:1). Paul responds with an extended contrast that plays on the language of life and death. Those baptized into Christ's own death are simply dead to Sin—its power is shattered. All ambiguity falls aside in the second half of the chapter, where the image of Sin as slave-owner is explicit. Sin was formerly the owner of these slaves (6:16–20). In that condition, they were enslaved to "impurity" and to "iniquity" (6:19). The only possible outcome of this slavery to Sin was death (6:20–22).

Not only did Sin enter and enslave, but also *Sin's résumé includes the unleashing of its cosmic partner, Death.* When Paul introduces the extravagant contrast between Adam and Christ in 5:12–21, he connects the entry of Sin with that of Death: "Death came through sin, and so death spread to all because all have sinned" (5:12). Death itself "exercised dominion" (5:14, 17). Death is the very "wage" of Sin (6:23). Not surprisingly, the language of Death is, like that of Sin noted earlier, more extensive in Romans than in Paul's other letters.[19] Elsewhere Paul may anticipate his own physical mortality as the opportunity to be with Christ (Phil 1:21–23; 2 Cor 5:1–9), but here Death is a force unleashed by Sin (see also 1 Cor 15:56).[20]

Perhaps the most disturbing element in the résumé of Sin is the claim made in chapter 7 that *Sin is capable of exerting power even over the law.* In his landmark study of Romans 7, "The Worm at the Core of the Apple," Paul W. Meyer redirected attention from preoccupation with the supposedly divided "I" (*egō*) to the workings of Sin; Sin continues to be the topic in 7:7–25, now focused as the question, "Is the law of God itself the equivalent of Sin?"[21] Paul vehemently denies the equation, yet he simultaneously insists that Sin has used the law for its own purposes. A series of expressions conveys this point:

> Sin "seizing an opportunity [base of operations] in the commandment, produced in me all kinds of covetousness" (v. 8 NRSV).

> Sin "seizing an opportunity [base of operations] in the commandment, deceived me and through it killed me" (v. 11 NRSV).

> Sin brought death by "working death in me through what is good" (v. 13 NRSV).

Because Sin is capable of using *even the holy law of God*, it can produce the crisis described in vv. 14–20. In Meyer's view, then, the "law of sin" (7:23, 25; 8:2) is the law as it has been possessed by Sin.[22] Sin has proved capable of producing a cleavage in God's own "holy, just, and good" law: "The transcendentally (*kath' hyperbolēn*) demonic nature of sin is its power to pervert the highest and best in *all* human piety, typified by the best in Paul's world, his own commitment to God's holy commandment, in such a way as to produce death in place of the promised life."[23]

Brought together, these "achievements" of Sin's résumé create the portrait of a cosmic terrorist. Sin not only entered the cosmos with Adam; it also enslaved, it unleashed Death itself, it even managed to take the law of God captive to its power. This résumé of Sin's accomplishments requires something more than a generous God who forgives and forgets, and something entirely other than a Jesus who allows people to improve themselves by following the example of his good behavior. Sin cannot be avoided or passed over; it can only be either served or defeated.

The most important element in Paul's treatment of Sin in Romans, however, is the gospel itself. Before the first word about God's wrath has been uttered, Paul has already introduced the gospel as God's own saving power (1:16–17). When he returns to that point in 3:21–26 to unpack it, he explicitly identifies God's offering up of Jesus Christ in death as the apocalypse of God's gracious defeat of Sin. As God once handed humanity over to Sin, God has now handed over the Son Jesus Christ for Sin's defeat (1:24, 26, 28; 8:32). God's power revealed in the gospel, then, is far greater than God's mere ability to forgive the sins of those who assent to a set of propositions about Jesus Christ. It is God's own power to redeem all of creation (see 8:19–23 and chapter 4 above) from the grasp of powers arrayed against God.[24]

Because of God's powerful and gracious victory, Paul can contrast the achievement of Adam with that of Christ (5:12–21). By presenting the implacable consequences of Adam's transgression, Paul sets up the comparison that follows in order to show that the consequences of Christ's obedience are even more astonishing than are the consequences of Adam's transgression. To begin with, the consequences are diametrically opposed to one another, the entry of Death on the one hand and justification on the other. In addition, the two actions start from different positions, since Christ's act does not simply begin where Adam's ended, but Christ's act begins with the entire human consequence of Adam's act. Most important, the grace that follows from Christ's act "abounded all the more" (5:20); it multiplied even more than had the fearsome implications of Sin. No longer is Sin the enslaving power; it is now grace that exercises dominion.

The question that presses immediately is what it means to say that God has rescued humanity from Sin, that there is genuine death to Sin, when the evidence of human conduct runs overwhelmingly in the opposite direction. Romans itself demonstrates that Paul understands that being a "slave of righteousness" and "free from Sin" does not carry with it immunity to transgression. Whether the admonitions of 12:1–15:13 address some particular problem in the Roman house churches or whether they are such as Paul would offer anywhere, they clearly display a frank realism about human behavior. (At the very least, Paul's dealings with the Corinthians should have undermined any exaggerated notions he had about Christian perfection.) To be freed from the power of Sin is not the same thing as being without flaw or incapable of transgression (sin in the lowercase). On the other hand, being free from the power of Sin means that the gospel actually does change human lives. In Romans, as elsewhere in Paul's letters, the gospel brings about transformation of the mind so that the human eye may see what God is doing and perceive God's will (12:1–2; see also 2 Cor 5:16–17). Paul addresses the Romans as people who are gifted by God with hope (Rom 5:1–5) and joy (15:13) and peace (5:1; 14:17; 15:13). These are not simply private spiritual possessions but instead manifest themselves for the upbuilding of the common life, as comes to expression often in 12:1–15:13.

THE RÉSUMÉ OF SIN AND THE COSMIC STORY

To take seriously the résumé of Sin will require an enlargement of our view of Romans. Recent decades of Pauline scholarship have rightly called into question those interpretations that treat Romans as having to do largely with the relationship between God and the individual. The scholarly pendulum has swung in the opposite direction, emphasizing the concern in Romans for God's dealings with Israel and the Gentiles. Yet even that important correction does not suffice, since the widescreen version of Romans is not only about the relationship among ethnic groups, between God and humanity, or God and the individual. It concerns the much larger apocalyptic battle in which God wages war against anti-God powers, including the powers of Sin and Death.[25]

In addition to the depiction of Sin and Death as cosmic powers, the sheerest view Romans affords us of this apocalyptic conflict comes in Rom 8. At the culmination of Paul's celebration of the future glory of a creation liberated from futility and decay, he returns to the present to ask who might threaten "us," that large family of God's children (8:33): "Who will bring any charge against God's elect?" The scene here is one of conflict, and Paul delights in parading before his hearers the names of those Powers that might seek to harm God's chosen: hardship, distress, persecution, famine, nakedness, peril, and the sword. No mere survivors, "we" are "more than conquerors" in the face of the litany of powers that follows, the first of which is Sin's cosmic partner, Death. The gospel of God's handing over of Jesus Christ to crucifixion, of the resurrection, and of the triumphant place at God's right hand has already secured victory over all these things (8:34). When Paul speaks of the "love of God in Christ Jesus," it is no sentimental valentine but a fierce love that rescues creation itself (8:39).

The closing lines of Romans epitomize this conflict. In 16:20 Paul completes a warning about deceitful people with the words, "The God of peace will shortly crush Satan under your feet" (NRSV).[26] As one of the names given in biblical and postbiblical literature to the one opposed to God, Satan is more than adequate as a shorthand reference to the anti-God powers, prominent among whom is Sin itself.[27] Any lingering notion that the anti-God powers, including Sin, are to be defeated by human strength fails on these words. The Romans are admonished to be wise and to avoid evil (16:19), but it is God who crushes Satan beneath their feet.

Corroboration for this apocalyptic battle between God and the anti-God powers appears across the Pauline corpus. First Thessalonians, widely regarded as Paul's earliest letter, does not explicitly speak of the defeat of God's enemies, but the battle imagery of 4:13–18 and 5:1–11 is consistent with an expectation that the Parousia is something more than the point in time at which Jesus returns to collect his faithful followers. It is a triumphant victory in contested territory. More explicit is Gal 1:4, with its description of Jesus Christ as "the one who gave himself on behalf of our sins that he might rescue us from *the present evil age* according to the will of God the Father." The most explicit treatment comes in 1 Cor 15, with its anticipation of "the end, when he [Jesus] hands over the kingdom to God the Father, after he has destroyed every ruler and every authority and power. For he must reign until he has put all his enemies under his feet. The last enemy to be destroyed is death" (15:24–26 NRSV). Here there is no ambiguity: God has enemies with real power, chief among them Death itself. In 1 Cor 15, where Paul insistently couples denial of the resurrection with denial of God's own power, Death takes the leading role among God's enemies. Yet Sin also makes an appearance here, once again linked with Death, in 15:56.

BUT SOMEONE WILL SAY . . .

The most immediate objection to this understanding of Sin in Romans is that it takes literally something that is simply a metaphorical device. Commentary after commentary identifies as an anthropomorphism Paul's practice of making *hamartia* the subject of a verb (e.g., 5:12, 13, 20). On this line of reasoning, Paul is merely making his writing vivid by means of a standard literary device. At least two possible arguments in favor of this objection should be mentioned. In the first place, Paul occasionally refers to sin as merely something a person does that is wrong, as in the use of the verb "sin" in 2:12 and 3:23. Yet this argument is not persuasive because it is exactly in these passages that Paul undertakes to demonstrate the workings of Sin's power. That he finds himself drawing on the language in a variety of ways (verb, noun, adjective) is not surprising. A second possible argument in favor of the notion that Paul is merely using a literary device notes that Paul also employs other terms, such as "grace" and "righteousness," in ways that are analogous to his use of Sin. In Rom 5:20, for example, Paul speaks of grace abounding, and in 6:15 he contrasts being "under law" with being "under grace." In context, however, grace may well be a power analogous (and opposed) to the power of Sin, precisely because here grace is a shorthand reference to God's saving power revealed in the gospel of Jesus Christ.

To speak of Sin as a power is not to claim to peer into Paul's mind and see there the existence of a literal character by the name of Sin. Yet both Paul's language about Sin itself and the cosmic apocalyptic thrust of his letter seem to require us to take seriously the notion of Sin as a power that sets itself over against God. To dismiss it as only a literary device runs the risk of trivializing.

A second possible objection is that, whatever Paul may have believed, contemporary Christians cannot find themselves in this cosmic apocalyptic battleground. The shadow of Rudolf Bultmann's insistence that the New Testament be demythologized lingers, most strenuously represented in recent discussion of Paul by Troels Engberg-Pedersen. Engberg-Pedersen claims, with admirable directness, that "we" simply cannot take seriously the mythological element in Paul: "by far most of Paul's basic world-view, in other words, the basic apocalyptic and cosmological outlook that was his, does not constitute a real option for us now—in the way in which it was understood by Paul."[28] It may well be that Paul's understanding of the gospel as God's invasion of a world enslaved to Sin and Death is not within our imaginative powers, although the vast appetite for the stories of J. K. Rowling and J. R. R. Tolkien prompts me to suspect otherwise. At the very least, it would seem to be the obligation of Christians to entertain the possibility that Paul might be right and "we" might be wrong.

Even those who do wish to take the language seriously may be troubled by the imagery, however. Particularly Christians who daily see the consequences of a willingness—even eagerness—to engage in military action in God's name rightly resist any facile baptism of human conflict with language drawn from biblical texts. Yet the text will not let us off the hook. It stands as an invitation, not to identify our battles with God's own or to cloak our aggression in Paul's terminology, but as an invitation to see that the conflict imagery Paul employs has to do with God's actions on behalf of creation, not human actions distorted to replace God's own.

WHAT IS AT STAKE?

As prominent as the vocabulary of Sin is in Romans, it is only one piece of a rich and dense argument. Research and publication on Romans is a booming enterprise. Lively interest in Paul's interpretation of the Old Testament, the ethnic conflicts that appear to stand behind the letter, ongoing interest in Paul's understanding of Judaism, argumentative style, the roles of the women named in Rom 16, the extensive discussion of the purpose of the letter—most of these are more congenial topics than that of Paul's treatment of Sin. It is easy to imagine someone asking whether we might not just leave this issue aside for something more attractive, especially since conversation about Sin renders most of us tiresome or judgmental, or perhaps both.

Fraught with danger as the topic may be, it is an essential feature of the wide-screen Romans, the one in which God invades creation in the death of Jesus Christ, releases human beings from the grasp of Sin, and transforms those believers into God's own children, who await their ultimate final redemption as slaves of righteousness. Apart from the larger theological context, these other issues are distorted by a pan-and-scan editing process that isolates their importance. Without an understanding of the enslaving grasp of Sin, ethnic tensions between Jew and Gentile are mere social relations, while for Paul they are a matter of the unity of humankind in doxological response to God's action for all humankind. Without an understanding of Sin's power to corrupt even the law, the question of law observance for Gentiles becomes simply a matter of lowering the price of admission so as to attract as many converts as possible. Paul's interpretation of the Old Testament is merely a series of intriguing intellectual guessing games, unless it is understood that he puts Scripture and everything else available to him at work for the urgent task of conveying God's actions. Yet the wide-screen edition of the gospel as viewed in Romans has to do with God's revealing invasion in Jesus Christ of a cosmos in the grip of Sin and of Death, subject to peril and sword and all the rest of the Powers of this age. Without viewing that wide-screen edition, the rest of these issues may stimulate the intellectual appetite, but they offer little that is of nutritional value.

This apocalyptic context is no less essential for understanding our own situation. A visit to the front pages of the daily newspaper should be sufficient to nudge us back to this uncomfortable topic. In 1995, well before the events of September 2001 and their aftermath, Andrew Delbanco published *The Death of Satan*, in which he traced what he termed the "unnaming" of evil, the gradual decline of talk about evil in American cultural life.[29] Evil is either altogether denied or reified in "the blamable other—who can always be counted on to spare us the exigencies of examining ourselves."[30]

Paul's language is that of Sin rather than evil, of course. Paul's Romans urgently demands not simply that we recognize the Sin in the world out there, or even that we recognize the evil in ourselves—in our very best selves. Paul's Romans shows us that the battle against evil is not fought by reducing it to a laundry list of transgressions and trying really hard to avoid them. Nor is it fought by identifying evil in other people and restraining or eradicating them. Evil is God's own enemy. The gospel Paul proclaims is that God has not left us alone and powerless. In Jesus Christ, God has already broken Death and Sin and will finally crush Satan on our behalf. Confidence in that word is the beginning of peace and joy and the obedience of faith.

CHAPTER TEN

The Apocalyptic Community

The last two chapters have emphasized both the cosmic power of Sin and Death and Paul's conviction that their defeat has already begun. God may soon crush Satan under the feet of believers (Rom 16:20), but in the meanwhile the question is this: What about those believers? My question does not concern the identity of the historical recipients, those who first hear Paul's letters read aloud, but instead concerns the nature and function of the community implied by the letters. What do Paul's letters suggest about that community? Does Paul's apocalyptic interpretation of the gospel in any distinctive way yield what could be called an apocalyptic interpretation of the community?

Instead of surveying all the letters for Paul's comments about the believing community or looking especially at the passages that explicitly take up problems of community life (as in 1 Cor 12–14), here I return to Romans to see what can be teased out from this letter. My reason for doing so is not that I regard Romans as more systematic or less situational than Paul's other letters, but I think it will be instructive to ask about the implications for community life precisely in a letter that seems to have less to offer.

Problems immediately present themselves. Paul uses the term ἐκκλη-σία five times in this letter, but all of those instances occur in chapter 16, and only once does the word refer to a gathering in Rome (16:5).[1] There is little in this letter that addresses the nature or mission of the church in any focused sense: here we find no Eph 4 or even 1 Cor 12. Yet the opening of the letter gives thanks for the faith or faithfulness (πίστις, *pistis*) of those in Rome and expresses the desire to be with them, to be mutually encouraged (1:8, 12). When Paul turns to his travel plans in chapter 15, he expresses the hope that he will receive support from gatherings of believers in Rome, and the extended greetings in chapter 16 presuppose the existence of groups of believers. More important, the body of the letter itself speaks directly to and about a gathered community. *The question, then, is what can be inferred from the letter about Paul's understanding of this community that has been brought into being by the apocalypse of God's rectification in Jesus Christ.*

Three further questions will shape this exploration of the theological identity of this community:

1. What does the letter suggest about how its addressees are to understand themselves?
2. What behavior is to characterize this community?
3. What are the boundaries of this community?

We anticipate that these questions will lead us to the conclusion that Romans understands the community as one created entirely by God's rectifying initiative, just as Israel itself came into being and continues to exist because of God's initiative. The community consists of those who know themselves to be God's own slaves, weapons in God's battle with powers that are aligned against God. Because it is one body in Christ, this community seeks the upbuilding of others within the boundaries of the community, while at the same time it reaches out for the other, the outsider. The community is obligated to those on the outside—both Jew and Gentile— because the gospel itself extends to include all people, even all of creation.

THE APOCALYPTIC COMMUNITY: MEMORY

We begin with the question of how the Romans are to understand themselves. In her important book on the construction of identity in early Christianity, Judith Lieu attends to the role of textual memory in shaping the identity of an individual or a community, that is, to the "relationship between *who we are* and *the past we tell.*"[2] Does the textbook of American history, while recounting events of the founding of the United States, remember or forget the roles played by religious leaders? How exactly does it represent the native inhabitants or women or African slaves? Among Lieu's prominent examples is the book of *Jubilees*, with its rewriting of Genesis to meet the interpretive needs of the Hasmonean period.

Paul writes in a different genre than does the author of *Jubilees*, to be sure, yet we can see the way in which what is said about the past endeavors to shape and identify the communities Paul addresses. First Thessalonians offers perhaps the best example of Paul's use of the past, since what is said about what has already taken place has a great deal to do with the initial preaching in Thessalonica and the warm relationships established there, as Paul attempts to consolidate that community in anticipation of the Parousia. The identity of the community (ἐκκλησία, *ekklēsia*) Paul addresses in 1 Thessalonians is determined by its relationships (brought into being by God) and by its future. Among the Galatians, the memory of the gospel has been corrupted, as Paul sees it, so that he undertakes what J. Louis Martyn has termed a repreaching of the gospel.[3]

In Romans, by contrast, Paul cannot appeal to experiences he and the Roman Christians share, for the obvious reason that he has not yet been to Rome. Chapter 16 may offer something of a substitute for such memories, in the form of its brief comments on individual relationships and on the work done by various individuals on behalf of the gospel. Instead of appealing to shared experience, as Paul writes this letter he attempts to shape a common memory of what has happened in the gospel, in the hope that that common interpretation will shape the future—that is, the future understanding of the Romans and their relationship with Paul, and hopefully their support for his trip to Jerusalem and then to Rome and from there to Spain.

The letter contains at least one hint that Paul understands himself to be shaping or correcting memory. At 15:15, as he is moving into a discussion of his travel plans, Paul comments that he has dared to write by way of *reminding* the audience. The bulk of the letter scarcely reads as a reminder, however, and in 1:15 Paul claims that he wants to preach the gospel in Rome as he has done elsewhere. Since this verb is otherwise restricted in Paul's letters (and outside them) to the *initial* declaration of that good news, we may assume that this language of "reminder" is a rhetorical device, a euphemism indicating that what has preceded in the letter is not actually a reminder, in the sense that the Romans already knew it.[4] Instead, Paul is "reminding" them of what he fears they have not known or understood: he is shaping a new memory.

Perhaps all of the body of Romans, especially all of chapters 1–11, falls under this heading of a reminding declaration of the gospel. *But how does that reminder intersect with, and offer to shape, an understanding of the community's identity?*

To take up that question, I turn first to Rom 5 and 6, since here for the first time the first-person pronoun "we" *unambiguously* refers to believers. Earlier in the letter it is often quite unclear to whom the first-person plural refers, as anyone who has lingered over the pronouns in Rom 3 can attest. (Where is "we" the plural of authorship? Where does "we" refer to a specific group, and who constitutes that group?) Even when chapter 4 introduces "our father" Abraham, the identity of the "our" is somewhat murky. But as chapter 4 ends and chapter 5 opens, "we" are those who stand in grace, who boast in the hope of God's glory, who have received God's love through the Holy Spirit. And in chapter 6, the reference to baptism makes identification of the "we" unambiguous. Here the community of those who have been called into faith is in view. What does Paul say to and about this community? What memory is he reinforcing, creating, correcting?

One of the striking features of this passage is that, almost as soon as it is clear that Paul is speaking directly to and about the community of believers in 5:1–5, he turns again in v. 6 to the death of Christ and its saving power: We were then weak, we were ungodly, we were sinners, we will be saved from wrath. This passage (chapters 5 and 6) brings together what Paul has already said about the saving power of the gospel (1:16; 3:21–26) and the ineluctable grasp of Sin (especially in 3:9). And it does so not simply to intensify the earlier argument *but also to locate the Roman addressees themselves squarely within this account.*

As Rom 5 develops, the cosmic apocalyptic character of the account comes to the foreground.[5] The Adam-Christ typology (or antitypology) serves to bring to full expression what has been put only obliquely up until now: the conflict between the powers of Sin and Death and the power of God and Jesus Christ. Sin and Death entered the world, Death extended itself throughout humanity (5:12), Death ruled as a king (5:14, 17, 21), Sin increased (5:20), Sin was an enslaver of humanity (6:6, 17, 20). All of this reign is overturned by Jesus Christ, through whom grace superabounded, so that it is now grace itself (i.e., the gospel itself) that rules (5:21). The controlling question in chapter 5, as Eugene Boring put it succinctly, is this: "Who is in charge? Who is in control of the world and humanity?"[6]

This account, this memory of the past, tells the Romans *how* to remember who they are. It locates them within the conflict. Their death with Christ in baptism and new life in anticipation of the resurrection takes place because of Christ's triumph over Sin and Death. The death and new life of the baptized are part and parcel of the apocalyptic drama, since those who were once slaves of Sin were also its weapons, its artillery for the conflict. Paul urges them now to understand themselves as weapons of rectification (6:13; see also 13:12).[7]

This reference to the baptized as weapons already hints that the conflict between God and the Powers of Sin and Death is ongoing, but that conflict comes into clear view in chapter 8, when Paul lists those enemies that will not prevail. In 8:12–39 Paul again offers something of an account of the past. The addressees have already received a spirit of adoption that allows them to cry out to God as father (8:15). All of creation itself exists in a state of subjection (8:20). Believers have already received the firstfruit of the Spirit (8:23); they have already been saved in hope (8:24). Verses 28–30 articulate this history dramatically with a series of affirmations about what God has already done for believers.

This account of the past also reaches forward into the future, however, to a time when glory is to be revealed (8:18), when all of God's children are to be revealed (8:19).[8] Creation itself will be freed even as the children of God are glorified (8:21). Adoption will be complete, as will the redemption of the body (8:23).

These references to the future move in an unanticipated direction, however. At several junctures, just where those who have read 1 Thess 4 and 1 Cor 15 might expect Paul to launch into a vivid depiction of the return of Christ and God's final triumph, we find instead that Paul plunges his audience even more deeply into the present.[9] Where he might have taken them out of the world to reorient their angle of vision,[10] he instead touches on the future but then returns to the present situation of conflict, in which threats come from circumstances of persecution and deprivation as well as from the Powers themselves.[11]

Here also the identification of believers as slaves and weapons gives way to a different identification. Where Paul had already addressed them as slaves and weapons of rectification, now he insists that what God's Spirit has given them is *not* a spirit of slavery but one of adoption (8:15); they are God's own offspring. This is not simply an inconsistency in Paul's vocabulary. Instead, it is an act of interpretation: this is what it means to be slaves of righteousness and weapons. It means to become children of God.[12]

In the section of the letter that immediately follows, Rom 9–11, there is yet another shaping and reshaping of memory. Ross Wagner has rightly described the narration of Israel's history at the beginning of chapter 9 as "a highly selective and abbreviated retelling of Israel's history."[13] Here what is important to know about that history is that Israel's history is the history of God's choices. God always made choices, beginning with the calling of Isaac and Jacob, and also with the hardening of Pharaoh's heart. Other recountings of Israel's history also select, as in the case of *Jubilees* or in Stephen's recital in Acts 7, with its relentless account of God's promise and Israel's rejection. Romans 9 is also relentless, but the focus here is on God's choices and their results for the constituting of Israel. Romans 11 similarly emphasizes God's choice, since the One who chose to graft Gentiles into the tree can also choose to remove them. Just as Israel always consisted of those whom God chose, so also the Gentiles are part of the tree because of God's choice. Since believers—both Jews and Gentiles—are part of the tree solely because of God's choice, no room exists for human presumption or hubris or false conclusions about God's decisions.

Among the things Paul is undertaking in this letter, then, consciously or otherwise, is an announcement of the gospel, a reminder (as Paul writes in chapter 15) that places Roman Christians within the larger community of those whom God has chosen, those who know themselves to have been freed from the tyrannical powers of Sin and Death, who wait together for their full redemption along with that of all creation.

THE APOCALYPTIC COMMUNITY: BEHAVIOR

That last sentence provides the segue to my second and third questions, since the reference to those who *wait together* for their full redemption anticipates the explication of what it is that those *wait-ers* do in the meanwhile. If chapter 8 plunges the audience more deeply into the present, what practices characterize the present? What does the community look like? (Once again, it is important to recall that the question concerns what the letter suggests or calls for, with no assumptions being drawn about actual practice.)

Elements of an answer to that question lie ready to hand in chapters 12–16. First, the community is engaged in concrete actions of support for one another, actions that reflect their common indebtedness to the gospel. The collection Paul is taking to Jerusalem he understands as the appropriate sharing by Gentiles that corresponds to what has been shared with them by Jews. Although he never says so explicitly, it appears that one of the ways in which Paul hopes he will be supported at Rome is with assistance for his upcoming mission to Spain (see 15:24, 28). Paul's recommendation of Phoebe draws attention to her patronage; it also asks that she be supplied with whatever she might need, clearly again reflecting the assumption that the community is obligated to financial support and to hospitality. These actions are anticipated in 12:8, characterizing the giver as generous, and in 12:13, urging readers to share in the needs of the saints.

Another feature of the community that comes to expression here is its labor on behalf of the gospel. Along with many other exegetes, I take the several references in chapter 16 to toil (vv. 6, 12) and to fellow workers (vv. 3, 9) as referring to people who have been engaged in work of an apostolic sort (to say nothing of the apostles Andronicus and Junia).[14] That does not mean heroic labor of an individualistic persuasion, of course. Paul identifies these individuals as part of a pattern of work to which believers are called on behalf of the gospel. Here we could also cite 12:6–8 with its list of spiritual gifts used in the community, including the gifts of prophecy, service, instruction, and exhortation.

This section of the letter also assumes that the community is engaged in prayer and thanksgiving. Unlike 1 Corinthians, there is no direct discussion of the conduct of worship, yet 15:30 finds Paul requesting that the Romans struggle with him in the battleground of prayer on behalf of his mission in Jerusalem. The assumption is that the prayer of those gathered in the homes of Prisca and Aquila, Aristobulus, Narcissus, and others actually matters for what happens when Paul arrives in Jerusalem with the collection. This feature of the closing section of the letter is perhaps already anticipated, not only in the comments about prayer in chapter 8, but also in 15:1–13, which notably emphasizes prayer and praise and Gentiles glorifying God alongside Jews.

All of these features—the concrete acts of support, labor, and prayer —may be related to the admonitions of 14:1–15:13. Even though chapter 16 without complaint or criticism acknowledges the existence of various house churches in Rome, in 14:1–15:13 they are analogized with a single household in which all of them, whatever their differences, serve a single Lord. The discussion in chapter 5 of who is in charge provides the basis for this analogy. If the baptized are slaves of righteousness, then they all serve in the house of the same Lord (and see 12:11).

THE APOCALYPTIC COMMUNITY: BOUNDARIES

When we move to the final question, the question of boundaries, we know at the outset that one of the boundaries marking out this community is the shared memory of God's action to defeat the enslaving powers of Sin and Death through Jesus Christ. A related boundary is the memory of God's persistent calling and saving of Israel, a calling and saving that now has been shown to include both Israel and the Gentiles, just as previously both Israel and the Gentiles were caught in the grasp of Sin. But how does this community understand its internal coherence? How and why and to what extent is the community to be separated from those on the outside?

This is a question that comes into play more explicitly in other Pauline letters, especially 1 Thessalonians and 1 Corinthians. In 1 Thessalonians Paul makes a sharp distinction between the behavior he expects from believers and that of "the Gentiles who do not know God" (4:5 NRSV); he also distinguishes the eschatological hope of Christians from those "who have no hope" (4:13 NRSV). The question of relationships with outsiders is, of course, more pronounced in 1 Corinthians, where Paul castigates believers for going to court before outsiders, advises about marriage with unbelievers, and addresses questions having to do with outsiders who may be present in the community's gatherings—to say nothing of the major challenge posed by food offered to idols. In both these letters, it is quite clear that relationships with outsiders pose a problem. Romans does not address such problems explicitly. Nevertheless, there is concern here about reinforcing the community's sense of mutual belonging, and that concern introduces the question of boundaries and the stance toward outsiders. Our clearest access to this set of issues comes, of course, in Rom 12 and 13.

Chapter 12 opens with a radical appeal that recalls the language of chapter 6. In chapter 6, Paul urges the letter's recipients to present themselves to God, to present their members as weapons of rectification, weapons of the gospel, and in 12:1 he urges them to present their bodies to God as a living sacrifice. The "newness of life" of 6:4 is here echoed in the call to a renewed mind (12:2).[15]

Beginning from this appeal, much of chapter 12 draws on traditional ethical admonitions to address issues of community life. Pivotal to this passage is the assertion that "while many, we are one body in Christ, and members one of another" (12:5). It is from this understanding of the oneness of believers in Christ that Paul can appeal for right thinking, for the proper and energetic use of the spiritual gifts, for hospitality and mutual concern. It is not at all clear that this passage responds to specific problems at Rome, although at several points the admonitions seem to anticipate the treatment of conflicts in chapters 14 and 15 (slaving in the Lord, 12:11; persisting in prayer, 12:12; sharing in the needs of the saints, 12:13; not being arrogant, 12:16).

Chapters 12 and 13 culminate in an appeal for wakefulness based on the fact that believers know what time it is: "Our salvation is nearer than when we began to believe" (13:11). Here the behavior of those within the community is implicitly contrasted with that of outsiders. Believers live in the daylight: they are not to be characterized by the "works of darkness," including dissipation, sexual misconduct, and quarreling. Even though Paul does not engage in the explicit contrast between insider and outsider that we find in 1 Thessalonians, the demarcation suggests itself.

Demarcation between inside and outside is also suggested by language that distinguishes between the present, in which believers live in the realm of the gospel, and the past, during which they lived as slaves of Sin and Death. The opening of chapter 8 explicitly distinguishes between those who live in the realm of the flesh and those who live in the realm of the Spirit. By implication, demarcation of insider and outsider is already made when 6:4–5 refers to those who have died in baptism and who now live in anticipation of the resurrection. Nothing could be sharper than this line between those who are living and those who remain in the power of Death. In this sense, the boundary around the community is sharply defined.[16]

But as Judith Lieu wisely notices, boundaries are often deceptive. What looks to be fixed and definite is, in fact, "permeable" and "contested."[17] Before we conclude that Paul is in the business of creating exclusive societies that exist only for themselves, we should note features of the letter that move in another direction. First, despite the fact that the letter in several ways distinguishes insider from outsider, nothing in the letter stigmatizes those on the outside. Nothing here corresponds to the disparaging remarks of 2 Peter about the false teachers or to 1 John's castigation of the "children of the devil," to say nothing of Qumran's instruction to "hate all the Children of Darkness, each commensurate with his guilt and the vengeance due him from God" (*Serek Hayaḥad* [1QS] 1.10–11).

Indeed, we can take that point a step further. Not only does Paul refrain from such negative characterization of those on the outside; he also displays concern for them. In a recent article on Paul and the "common good," Victor Paul Furnish acknowledges that Paul draws sharp "moral" as well as "spiritual distinctions between the Christian community and society in general."[18] Yet Furnish also observes that Paul "does not summon his converts to withdraw from society," and at least in some instances "Paul specifically encourages believers to include all people within their circle of concern,"[19] as in Rom 12:14–21 and also in Rom 13.

The concern Paul extends to all people should not come as a surprise to an audience that has attended carefully to Rom 5. The contrast Paul sets forth between the death accomplished by Adam and the life accomplished by Jesus Christ only works if both actions include all of humanity. Where there had been condemnation for all, now there is rectification and life for all (5:18).[20] Romans 8 extends that "all" to include creation itself. As 11:32 expresses it, God "confined all in disobedience so that God might have mercy on all." To return to the history of Israel as recounted in chapters 9–11, if it is God who calls, then clearly the boundaries also belong to God, so that the believing community has an obligation not to treat these boundaries as human property.

Whatever it means for these communities to be "one body in Christ," then, it does not mean isolation from the world. I find that a fairly remarkable point, since it would presumably have been easier to consolidate congregations theologically and socially by drawing more sharply the line around the community. (Paul seems to be able to build up without also tearing down, something lost on a number of contemporary voices.)

The most difficult boundary question, of course, is that of Israel. A number of recent treatments of Romans would address this question, or perhaps avoid it, by advocating a two-covenant hypothesis; the gospel is for the Gentiles and has no relationship to the covenant between God and Israel. Other recent treatments address or avoid the question by understanding the church as largely an extension of Israel's story. Neither of these approaches seems to me to account for the complexity of Romans, where Paul affirms the calling of Israel, while at the same time undermining some of the features that constitute Israel.[21] The image of Gentiles being grafted into the tree raises a host of questions about the church and Israel, but Paul leaves most of them aside. He does not later develop this image of the tree, drawing instead on the language of "one body." The church (congregation) as imagined in Paul's Romans involves Jews and Gentiles (the Jew first, and also the Greek, as Paul puts it) in a shared vocation that demands their mutual respect.

CONCLUSION

It is perhaps obvious that, of the three questions I have put to Romans concerning the *ekklēsia* (questions regarding memory, behavior, and boundary), those regarding memory are the most dominant. It is the memory of enslavement to the cosmic powers of Sin and Death and the memory of liberation from that enslavement by God's rectifying action in Jesus Christ that shapes Paul's comments about the church's boundaries and about the church's practices. However urgent we might understand to be Paul's treatment of the questions of boundary and behavior in chapters 12–16, that treatment is preceded both literarily and logically by his carefully worked out analysis of God's defeat of Sin and Death and its implications for all of humanity. In other words, Paul's ecclesiology is subsidiary to his soteriology—not the other way around.[22] Both soteriology and ecclesiology participate in an apocalyptic gospel: a radical intervention by God to rescue humanity from its enslavement.

The final chapter expands on this understanding of God. For the present I offer a tentative suggestion that is neither ecclesiological nor soteriological but historical. I share the view that the purpose of Romans is actually the "purposes" of Romans, that Paul has several purposes in mind. Yet I think this attention to the "memory" being shaped or reshaped by the letter suggests that one of Paul's concerns about the congregations at Rome has to do with their grasp of the gospel (as Paul perceives it). Especially if many Roman Christians are Gentiles who come via the synagogue (i.e., the *sebomenoi*), Paul may know or fear that they understand the gospel largely as a way of gaining admission into Israel without undergoing circumcision. The gospel affords them a means to social alignment with Israel and its tradition, a way previously available to them only through circumcision. And he may know or fear that some, at the other extreme, have come to disdain Israel because most Jews in Rome have rejected the gospel. While Paul affirms the permanence of God's calling to Israel, he also wants the Romans to understand that the gospel concerns humankind as a whole; indeed, it concerns the entirety of creation. The church, then, rightly knows that God has acted in Jesus Christ for the whole of creation, even as the church lives out its own vocation as the body of Christ.

CHAPTER ELEVEN

The God Who Will Not Be Taken for Granted

Among the striking observations in Donald Juel's treatment of Mark 16 is that "Jesus is out, on the loose, on the same side of the door as the women and the readers."[1] This unsettling way of putting things builds on Juel's earlier observation that the tearing of the heavens at Jesus' baptism declares that the protective barrier between humanity and God is gone and that God, "unwilling to be confined to sacred spaces, is on the loose in our own realm."[2] The inescapability of God not only unsettles Mark's narrative; in Juel's view, it also unsettles interpreters, scholarly and otherwise, who desire to wrest control over the text from "the divine actor who will not be shut in—or out."[3]

That God is "on the loose" serves not only as a challenging reading of Mark's Gospel; it also is a provocative way of epitomizing Paul's letter to the Romans, one that may stand as an apt conclusion to these chapters. Admittedly, this leap from Mark to Romans is disconcerting—and for good reasons. Any movement from interpreting a narrative to interpreting a letter brings with it certain challenges. And the movement from Mark's particular Gospel, with its narrative gaps and awkward syntax, to the careful argumentation of Romans only heightens the difficulties.[4] Yet in its own distinctive way, Romans no less than Mark's Gospel reflects the understanding that God is "on the loose," that God cannot be contained either in the argumentation of Paul or by the craftiness of Paul's interpreters.

GOD AS TAKEN FOR GRANTED

Paul's letter to believers at Rome, a city he had not yet visited and a group of believers most of whom he had not met (although see the greetings in chapter 16), has generated a nearly endless procession of questions and proposals. Research in recent years has addressed a number of important questions about the purpose and occasion of Romans, its rhetorical genre, and its audience.[5] Yet it remains the case, as Nils Dahl observed about New Testament theology in general, that students of this letter pay too little attention to God.[6]

One recent major study of Pauline theology that does begin with God is J. D. G. Dunn's *The Theology of Paul the Apostle,* a work that identifies Romans as offering interpreters their best access to Paul's theology.[7] Dunn opens his exploration of Pauline theology with a chapter on God, yet he early on depicts God as belonging among Paul's "taken-for-granteds," by which he means that "'speech about God' was part of the shared speech of the first Christian congregations." Because these common beliefs were also thoroughly Jewish, "Paul did not have to explain or defend his belief in God," since it was a "fundamental" part of his own tradition. Dunn goes on to say that Paul's "conversion had not changed his belief in and about God," so that "his most fundamental taken-for-granted remained intact."[8] Elsewhere Dunn insists that those things that are "taken for granted" are not things to which Paul is indifferent;[9] nevertheless, the expression "taken for granted" appears to imply that God belongs among the presuppositions of Paul's thought, that the precise issue of God's identity has no real impact on Paul's theology. Indeed, Dunn speaks of several "levels" in Paul's theology, so that Paul's inherited view of God and Israel occupy one level while the events of Jesus' death and resurrection occupy another level.[10] The chapter on Jesus Christ stands at considerable remove from the initial discussion of God, and here it becomes clear that what changes in Paul's theology following his conversion changes because of his encounter with and understanding of Jesus Christ, while his understanding of God remains stable. It is Christ who endows Paul's work as "theologian, missionary, and pastor" with its coherence. When Dunn sums up Paul's theology, he identifies its "focal and pivotal point" as Christ. Christ is a mediator figure for Dunn, not simply in the sense of being God's agent, but also in the sense that Christ becomes the occasion by which human beings experience God.[11]

The distance Dunn appears to place between God and Christ raises numerous questions. Francis Watson has unpacked the sheer impossibility of speaking of God in Paul's thought apart from reference to Christ and the Spirit and vice versa.[12] Even the opening words of Romans reflect the difficulty involved. To affirm that Paul is *both* "a slave of Jesus Christ" *and* "set apart for the gospel of God" surely means that those two designations belong to one another, which makes it difficult to distinguish the "taken-for-granted" understanding of God from the new event of Jesus Christ. How can God and Christ occupy two levels when God's gospel and Jesus Christ here stand connected to one another?

What concerns me at present is the unfortunate expression "taken for granted," with its apparent implication that the gospel involves no real challenge to Paul's previous understanding of God. Dunn correctly claims that Paul always knew that God was one, Creator, sovereign, judge, and faithful to Israel.[13] Yet surely these descriptors are strained when Paul speaks of the Gentiles of Thessalonica as God's beloved (1 Thess 1:4), or when he concludes that "neither circumcision nor uncircumcision is anything" (Gal 6:15 NRSV), or when he identifies God as the one "who raised Jesus our Lord from the dead" (Rom 4:24 NRSV). How can a "taken-for-granted" God possibly justify the *ungodly* (Rom 4:5)? Dunn's "taken-for-granted" God provides us with scant means of understanding the repeated "now" of Paul's letter to the Romans (e.g., 3:21; 5:9, 11; 6:22; 8:1; 13:11). The impossibility of restricting the identity of God to predefined categories emerges into plain sight in Romans. Indeed, it is not too much to say that the God of Romans is very much "on the loose." The God of the promises of Scripture (1:2) is faithful, but faithfulness does not imply predictability. God is also free, not to be confined to human expectations about God's judgments and responses.

Perhaps the first hint of God's freedom comes already in the salutation of the letter. Here Paul describes the gospel as "promised beforehand through his prophets in the holy scripture" (1:2 NRSV), language that reflects God's commitment to Israel, the people from whom the prophets come and for whom God sends them. In other words, this line invokes the ancestral expectations of God's faithfulness. Yet, when Paul describes his apostleship, he anticipates "the obedience of faith among all the Gentiles" (1:5 NRSV). Already the scope of God's actions extends in new directions: God is faithful to the promise but not restricted in fulfilling it.[14]

Indeed, the letter contains a string of arguments that might be summarized as "God will not be restricted. God is on the loose." By way of anticipation, the first major section of the letter insists that God is not restricted even by the implacable forces of Sin and Death (1:18–8:39). If that is the case, then clearly God's freedom will not be restricted by some narrow, fixed definition of election (chapters 9–11). And, finally, God cannot be limited to a sliver of human life that is designated "ethics" (12:1–15:13).

GOD'S FREEDOM IN RESPONSE TO SIN AND DEATH

As E. P. Sanders famously observed, in Paul's thinking the solution precedes the problem, but in the structure of Paul's argument in Romans, the problem precedes the solution.[15] Although, as we have seen in chapter 6, the apocalypse Paul refers to in Gal 1 and Phil 3 has invaded his life and destroyed that life and its understandings (Paul's preexisting "solutions"), in Romans an initial declaration of the gospel in 1:17 yields to an extensive statement of the problem of the human condition as the gospel reveals that problem. And Paul expounds the situation in unrelenting terms. From 1:18 through 3:20, he depicts the extent of Sin among both those under the law and those outside it. As one, humanity falls short of God's glory (3:20), whether by the refusal to acknowledge God or by an acknowledgment twisted into self-congratulation. With the declaration of God's intervention of grace in 3:21–31, readers may imagine that this exploration of the human condition has come to an end, but in chapter 5 it returns, as the recollection of Adam serves to show how the powers of Sin and Death have captured all of humanity. Again, the end of chapter 5 declares the "free gift of grace" (5:15), and chapter 6 finds humanity transferred to the dominion of righteousness, but once more 7:7–25 introduces the problem of Sin's grasp of the Law, so that even the impulse of humanity to do the good is maimed by Sin.

Leander Keck has perceptively observed that these three passages move in the manner of a spiral, with Paul "each time going deeper into the human condition, and each time finding the gospel the appropriate antidote."[16] This spiral, then, involves not only Sin, in that Sin captures humanity in its grasp, but also God's own intervention. Here Paul's understanding that God is "on the loose" comes into play, for God's intervention also "spirals," in the sense that God's action encompasses more as the spiral continues.

The first stage in the spiral comes to its climax in 3:19–20, followed by a statement of the good news in 3:21–26, a text that is often regarded as a restatement of 1:16–17. Exegetical problems abound here, but the general logic of the passage is sufficiently clear: all human beings fall short of God's glory, and all are rectified freely through the grace of redemption in Christ Jesus, grace that results from God's own action in putting Christ forward. The act Paul describes is unilateral in the sense that it is God alone who accomplishes this event.

Yet there is also a qualification having to do with faith, since 3:22 stipulates that "the rectification of God" is "through the faithfulness of Jesus

Christ for all who believe."[17] I am inclined to think that the phrase "all who believe" does not limit the range of God's righteousness; instead, "all who believe" acknowledges that only those to whom faith has come have received the gift of seeing God's action for what it is. The phrase works in a fashion similar to 1 Cor 1:18, which frankly acknowledges two irreconcilable views of the cross; to some it appears foolish, and to others it is God's power.[18] Yet most recent commentators understand this statement as somehow limiting the scope for God's action, so that God's saving righteousness applies only to believers.[19] For example, Brendan Byrne describes faith as the "vehicle" of the operation of redemption, since through faith "God is able to draw sinful human beings into the scope of the divine righteousness."[20] Regarding Paul's comments on faith in Rom 3–4, Dunn goes so far as to say that God "would not justify, could not [sic!] sustain in relationship, those who did not rely wholly on him."[21] Granting that conventional (and certainly majority) view for the present, we would conclude that the first cycle reflects the conviction that the gospel reveals that now God deals with sin differently. The implacability of human rejection meets with God's own offering up of his Son, an offering that has its effect on all those who believe.

This is not, however, Paul's final statement in Romans about the scope of God's redemptive action. In the second stage of the spiral, Paul introduces not only the extent of human rebellion against God but also humanity's capture by the powers of Sin and Death. Sin "entered" the world through the transgression of Adam, bringing with it Death and its unavoidable, unyielding grasp. But Paul finds that the universal consequence of Adam's action has an equally universal consequence in Christ's gracious death: "Therefore, just as the trespass of one brought condemnation for all people, so the right act of one led to the rectification of life for all people" (5:18).

Numerous attempts to limit this statement fail, since the comparison Paul makes will only work if the scope of God's gospel includes "all."[22] To contrast Adam's death-giving act, an act that invades the entire human sphere, with Christ's life-giving act, and then insist that Christ's action pertains only to some, or only to those who respond, would make no sense at all. Charles B. Cousar puts it directly: "Nothing is said about Christ's having made life 'potentially' available to all and that faith is necessary to turn the potentiality into reality. (Certainly death is not pictured as a potential destiny.)"[23] Even if the first stage of the spiral imagines that God's redemptive action concerns only those who believe, the second does not.[24]

In its third stage, the spiral cannot become more inclusive, but it does become more invasive. As we saw already in chapters 8 and 9 (above), Sin's power is such that it can make use *even* of God's good and holy instrument, the law, and can corrupt even the laudable desire to do what is right.

Again in this final stage of the spiral, Paul writes about the response of God. In this instance, however, the response is not the putting forward of Christ as God's righteousness for those who believe. Neither is it the death of Jesus that defeats death for all. Now the response of God is to condemn Sin itself (8:3) and to liberate not only humanity (7:25) but also all of the cosmos. The final section of Rom 8 brings the spiral of God's action to its completion: God "did not withhold his own Son" recalls the language of 3:21–31 as well as 5:6–21, with its claim that Jesus' death reveals that God's grace suffices even for human rebellion. The God who defeated Sin in Jesus' death will finally defeat all those other powers arrayed against the power of God (see also 1 Cor 15:24–28).

The downward spiral of the human condition is more than matched by what we might regard as an "upward" spiral of God's intervention. God cannot be restricted by Sin and Death, for God will finally defeat both those enemies and all others. God is "on the loose."

GOD'S FREEDOM AND THE ELECTION OF ISRAEL

Despite intense scholarly disagreements about the contours and even the coherence of Rom 9–11, there is widespread agreement that this portion of the letter fundamentally concerns the faithfulness of God.[25] Important features of Rom 1–8 make the question of God's faithfulness an urgent one. If there is "no distinction" between Jew and Greek, as Rom 1–3 forcefully contends, then what has become of Israel's election? If Israel's election is to be understood as null and void, what does that imply about God? As Wayne Meeks notes, if God has abandoned the calling to Israel, then Gentiles have no reason to trust that God will not also abandon them.[26]

In response to this potentially disastrous conclusion, Paul crafts an argument about God's faithfulness. He insists that the "word of God" has not failed (9:6), that God has by no means rejected Israel (11:1–2). With Isaiah, he recalls that God has continually held out God's hands to Israel (10:21).[27] God is not fickle, but that does not mean that God is predictable.[28] This section of the letter does not permit the reduction of faithfulness to predictability; it is by no means clear that Paul's understanding of God's faithfulness would sit well with Matthew, for whom the events in Jesus' life fulfill quite specific passages of Scripture (e.g., 1:22–23; 2:17–18). In fact, Paul's argument on behalf of God's faithfulness actually rests upon some astonishing claims about God's freedom.

The most obvious assertion of God's freedom comes in 9:6–30, with its recital of Israel's history as the history of God's calling. The opening description of Israelites as people to whom belong "the adoption, the glory, the covenants, the giving of the law, the worship, and the promises" (9:4 NRSV) might suggest that these are Israel's *possessions*, but what follows permits no such conclusion. God *chose* to show mercy on Isaac; God *chose* to harden Pharaoh's heart. Pivotal to Paul's argument are the words of vv. 11–12, which the NRSV regrettably confines to a parenthesis: "so that God's purpose of election might continue, not by works but by his call." The phrase "purpose of election" joins two nouns, "purpose" and "election," that do not otherwise appear together in the New Testament. Either of them might have served to make the point of God's initiative, but together they constitute an exclamation mark that underscores God's role. The additional expression "not by works but by his call" places the entire statement in boldface: only God's choosing accounts for Israel's status with God.

If God chooses some and not others, that reflects only God's freedom and offers no basis for complaint (9:19–23). Indeed, God elects also "from the Gentiles" (9:24), a point Paul paradoxically reinforces by quoting Hosea's lines about the restoration of Israel. That God's freedom is at work here becomes even clearer when this passage is placed alongside other Jewish texts, as Neil Richardson has demonstrated. For example, the author of *Jubilees* introduces a note about the relative merits of Jacob and Esau before Abraham's pronouncement of blessing on Jacob (*Jub.* 19:13–14; 22:10–24); and Philo emphasizes that God knows in advance what their characters will only later reveal (*Allegorical Interpretation* 3.88–89). Although these and other authors comment on God's election, Paul is distinctive in his silence about any hint of merit.[29]

Another example of the freedom that characterizes God's faithfulness comes in Rom 9:32b–33, as Paul draws from Isaiah's language about the "stumbling stone." The complex questions about the text of Isaiah and its transmission and interpretation—not to mention the disputed identity of the stumbling stone in Romans itself—makes appeal to this passage intensely risky.[30] The point I am making, however, does not depend on resolving those questions. Having noted the paradox of Gentiles winning a race they were not running while the running Israel fails at the same race, Paul asserts that "they [i.e., Israel] have stumbled over the stumbling stone" (9:32b NRSV). He then introduces a modified form of the LXX of Isa 28:16, which depicts God laying a stone that will be fixed, secure, foundational. But in the center of the quotation, he inserts a portion of Isa 8:14, and in so doing he replaces the foundation stone with a stone of stumbling. In other words, as Paul Meyer puts it, here Paul attributes to God an action of "placing in the midst of his people a base of security that is at the same time an obstacle over which they stumble."[31] By making what was to be a sound foundation into something that trips Israel up but can nevertheless be trusted (see the end of v. 33), God here becomes a trickster on behalf of Israel's redemption.

God's freedom again comes to expression in the argument about God's dealings with Israel and the Gentiles in chapter 11. As Paul understands events of the present and future, Israel's unbelief has led to salvation for the Gentiles, which will in turn prompt Israel's jealousy (11:11–12). A number of scholars connect Rom 11 with the "eschatological pilgrimage" tradition, according to which the last days will see the restoration of Israel, in response to which the Gentiles will stream into Jerusalem.[32] If that pilgrimage tradition is somehow in play here, then Paul attributes to God a complex inversion of the tradition. Here it is not Israel's triumph (its restoration) but Israel's failure (its rejection of the gospel) that invites the Gentiles to recognize God. In addition, in Rom 9–11 it is the Gentiles who lead Israel to its redemption rather than the other way around. Most important, many texts associated with the eschatological pilgrimage tradition are concerned with the vindication of Israel—its liberation from oppression by external powers, the return of the exiles (see, e.g., Isa 60:1–22; Jer 31:1–24; Ezek 20:33–34; Zech 8:1–23; 14:10–11; Bar 4:36–37; 5:1–9; *Jub.* 1:15–18). By contrast, Paul is less concerned with the vindication of Israel than with the vindication of God.

These indications of God's freedom do not exhaust either the possibilities or the problems of Rom 9–11. They may, however, suffice to undermine any notion that God's faithfulness can be predicted in advance, in the sense of being a "taken-for-granted." Even as God fulfills the ancient promises to Israel, God also cannot be restricted to a petty understanding of that fulfillment. To refer to Paul's own language about knowing in 2 Cor 5 may be helpful here. In that important passage, Paul distinguishes knowing in a human way (κατὰ σάρκα, *kata sarka*) from knowing "now," in the light of God's apocalypse in Jesus Christ (5:18). Not only Christ but also all people are understood differently, as is the cross itself (1 Cor 1:18). By the same token Rom 9–11 implies that God's faithfulness is not faithfulness that can be perceived in a merely human sort of way. For a writer who knows that the cross is God's power and wisdom, but not all have been granted the gift to see it, it would seem clear that God's faithfulness may also be perceived differently by those who have received the gift of sight. What looks like rejection or even fickleness is merely God's own brand of faithfulness. The blessing at the end of chapter 11 appears to underscore this very point, with its declaration of the unsearchability of God's judgments and inscrutability of God's ways.

GOD'S FREEDOM AND THE PROBLEM OF ETHICS

With the conclusion of Rom 11, Paul moves to the final section of the body of the letter, a section often designated as "ethical" or "paraenetic."[33] The assumption is that Paul has now turned from his exposition of God's activity to an exposition of the demands made on believers by that activity. There are numerous problems with such a schematization, not least of which is the way God's own activity continues to dominate in 12:1–15:13. As in chapters 1–11, in this section also God is "on the loose," here in the sense that God's demands cannot be confined to a single slice or portion of human life.

The two verses that open this section of the letter are generally understood as providing an overview of what is to follow. Stanley Stowers has described these verses as insisting that the Romans "are to renew their minds,"[34] but how exactly are the Romans to accomplish such an impressive feat? Paul opens with an appeal to "the mercies of God," a phrase that—at the very least—locates what follows in connection with God's merciful activity to humankind, activity first introduced as early as chapter 1 but recently recapitulated with reference to Israel and the Gentiles in chapters 9–11.

"By the mercies of God" is far more than an appeal to God's activity, as if God has now carried out the divine part of the bargain and it is up to human beings to take up their assigned portion so that the total task will be complete. "By" (διά, *dia*) often refers to the means or instrumentality through which something takes place, not simply to attendant circumstances. It is by and only by God's mercies that human beings are able to undertake the life Paul evokes in 12:1–2. Not even the admonitions Paul offers can be fulfilled apart from God's continued intervention.

God's role does not disappear even in the admonition "be transformed by the renewing of your minds" (12:2 NRSV). The passive voice, "be transformed," is essential: human beings do not transform their own minds. Indeed, in 1:21–22 Paul has explicitly associated futile and sense-less thinking with the problem of Sin, from which humanity must be delivered. The passive voice here is almost certainly a divine passive, referring to God's renewal of the mind.

A glance at the next few chapters shows that this is not, for Paul, merely introductory chatter about God that serves to decorate the transition into a section that otherwise imagines the human being as an independent ethical agent.[35] It is God who assigns gifts (12:3), Christ's body that governs how members relate to one another (12:5), God's prerogative (and no one else's) to judge the dietary practices of fellow believers. The culminating pleas of 15:1–2 and 15:7 both end in prayers that understand God as the one who grants the gift of fulfillment for these admonitions:

> May the God of steadfastness and encouragement grant you to live in harmony with one another, in accordance with Christ Jesus, so that together you may with one voice glorify the God and Father of our Lord Jesus Christ. (15:5–6 NRSV)

> May the God of hope fill you with all joy and peace in believing, so that you may abound in hope by the power of the Holy Spirit. (15:13 NRSV)

There may be a sense of comfort in that reminder about God's role, but the remainder of 12:1–2 is apt to generate discomfort rather than comfort. As is widely recognized, Paul here employs language that usually has its home in cultic situations.[36] "Sacrifice" clearly belongs in the context of religious observance, but the Greek word translated "worship" (λατρεία, *latreia*) also is not a general term for obeisance to the divine but carries specific connotations of the cult.

In this context of cultic language, Paul urges Roman Christians to "present your bodies." The adjectives "living" and "holy" prompt readers to infer a critique against other sacrificial cults; that is, Paul implicitly identifies the Christian's sacrifice as superior to that of pagan rituals or even the sacrificial practices in Jerusalem. That critique certainly finds its place in Hebrews, but Paul's concern is to assert a positive claim about the comprehensive nature of the gospel's work. The "body" (σῶμα, *sōma*) includes the physical being but refers to the entire person. In addition, the phrase here is "your bodies," rather than the singular "your body," suggesting that the appeal is to the entire body of believers rather than just to solitary individuals. In a classic discussion of this passage, Ernst Käsemann articulated both features well, commenting that the body, in Paul, is the human

> capacity for communication and the reality of his incorporation within a world that limits him. God lays claim to our corporeality because he is no longer leaving the world to itself, and our bodily obedience expresses the fact that, in and with us, he has recalled to his service the world of which we are a part.[37]

The call, then, is for believers together to present themselves to God as their appropriate form of worship. The text offers nowhere to hide. Here it is clear that Paul has no place in his thinking for a distinction between Christian behavior and the "rest" of life. The cultic language employed here cannot be confined to cultic act. To present "your bodies" is to present all that there is. Again, Käsemann is helpful by insisting that there is no longer room for cultic thinking, since the very use of cultic language in Rom 12:1–2 paradoxically demonstrates how extensive is the upheaval in human life. There is no longer anything "profane," and there is no longer anything "holy" except "the community of the holy people and their self-abandonment in the service of the Lord."[38] Here we find Paul's version of the rending of the temple veil in Mark's Gospel. No place offers safety from the God who reclaims the world for himself. God's demand is of all.

GOD IS "ON THE LOOSE"

In his reflection on the completion of the work of the Society of Biblical Literature's Pauline Theology Group, Paul W. Meyer observed that many participants in the discussion had moved away from discussions of Paul's *theology* (as a fixed content, even as a coherent set of ideas) and toward discussions of Paul's *theologizing* (as an ongoing activity). Meyer noted, however, that contributors to the discussion often reflected the assumption that Paul began from a fixed point (his theological convictions) and modified that fixed point as developments required (theologizing). His own proposal was that the actual process was the reverse, that Paul's theology or convictions are not his starting point but his end product; in other words, Paul revised and recast his convictions in the light of events.[39] Crucially, for Meyer, this discovery of Paul's theology does not reflect only changing pastoral situations, much less some quirk in Paul's mental processes. Instead, this fluidity in Paul's theology has to do with the gospel itself. It is nothing less than the crucifixion and resurrection of Jesus that "*forces* the revision and recasting of all the traditional language, concepts, convictions and categories."[40]

The preceding brief and very preliminary reflection on God's activity in Romans confirms Meyer's suggestion. Paul's opening announcement about the gospel's power for salvation (1:16 NRSV) creates enormous ambiguities, as a glance at any critical commentary will confirm. Only as the letter unfolds does it become clear that God's power for salvation is all that is capable of defeating the enormous reign of Sin and Death. God's power for salvation encloses the previously excluded Gentiles and extends even to the present deafness of Israel, and God's power for salvation enables and demands the total service of those who are "called to belong to Jesus Christ" (1:6). The identity of this God is emphatically not a "taken-for-granted." No less than the God of Mark's ending is the God of Romans "on the loose."

Abbreviations

AB	Anchor Bible
ABR	*Australian Biblical Review*
ACW	Ancient Christian Writers
ALGHJ	Arbeiten zur Literatur und Geschichte des hellenistischen Judentums
ANTC	Abingdon New Testament Commentaries
BDAG	Bauer, W., F. W. Danker, W. F. Arnst, and F. W. Gingrich. *Greek-English Lexicon of the New Testament and Other Early Christian Literature.* 3d ed. Chicago, 1999.
BETL	Bibliotheca ephemeridum theologicarum lovaniensium
BHT	Beiträge zur historischen Theologie
BZNW	Beihefte zur Zeitschrift für die neutestamentliche Wissenschaft
CBC	Cambridge Bible Commentary
CBQ	*Catholic Biblical Quarterly*
CJT	*Canadian Journal of Theology*
CNT	Commentaire du Nouveau Testament
ConBNT	Coniectanea neotestamentica
CRBR	*Critical Review of Books in Religion*
DBAT	*Dielheimer Blätter zum Alten Testament und seiner Rezeption in der Alten Kirche*
EKKNT	Evangelisch-katholischer Kommentar zum Neuen Testament
ETR	*Etudes théologiques et religieuses*
ExAud	*Ex auditu*
ExpTim	*Expository Times*

FRLANT	Forschungen zur Religion und Literatur des Alten und Neuen Testaments
HDR	Harvard Dissertations in Religion
HNT	Handbuch zum Neuen Testament
HNTC	Harper's New Testament Commentaries
HR	*History of Religions*
HTKNT	Herders theologischer Kommentar zum Neuen Testament
HTR	*Harvard Theological Review*
IBS	*Irish Biblical Studies*
ICC	International Critical Commentary
Int	*Interpretation*
JBL	*Journal of Biblical Literature*
JSNT	*Journal for the Study of the New Testament*
JSNTSup	Journal for the Study of the New Testament: Supplement Series
KEK	Kritisch-exegetischer Kommentar über das Neue Testament (Meyer-Kommentar)
KJV	King James Version
LCL	Loeb Classical Library
LS	*Louvain Studies*
LSJ	Liddell, H. G., R. Scott, H. S. Jones. *A Greek-English Lexicon*. 9th ed. with revised supplement. Oxford, 1996
LXX	Septuagint
MM	Moulton, J. H., and G. Milligan. *The Vocabulary of the Greek Testament*. London, 1930. Reprint, Peabody, MA, 1997
NAB	New American Bible
NASB	New American Standard Bible
NCB	New Century Bible
NIB	*New Interpreter's Bible*
NICNT	New International Commentary on the New Testament
NIGTC	New International Greek Testament Commentary
NIV	New International Version
NJB	New Jerusalem Bible
NLT	New Living Translation
NovT	*Novum Testamentum*
NovTSup	Novum Testamentum Supplements
NPNF[1]	*Nicene and Post-Nicene Fathers*, Series 1
NRSV	New Revised Standard Version
NTAbh	Neutestamentliche Abhandlungen
NTL	New Testament Library

NTS	*New Testament Studies*
OBT	Overtures to Biblical Theology
PG	Patrologia graeca. Edited by J.-P. Migne. 162 vols. Paris, 1857–1886
PW	Pauly, A. F. *Paulys Realencyclopädie der classischen Altertumswissenschaft.* New edition G. Wissowa. 49 vols. Munich, 1980
RB	*Revue biblique*
RSR	*Recherches de science religieuse*
RSV	Revised Standard Version
SBLDS	Society of Biblical Literature Dissertation Series
SBLSBS	Society of Biblical Literature Sources for Biblical Study
SBLTT	Society of Biblical Literature Texts and Translations
SBM	Stuttgarter biblische Monographien
SJT	*Scottish Journal of Theology*
SNTSMS	Society for New Testament Studies Monograph Series
SP	Sacra pagina
StudBib	Studia Biblica
TDNT	*Theological Dictionary of the New Testament.* Edited by G. Kittel and G. Friedrich. Translated by G. W. Bromiley. 10 vols. Grand Rapids, 1964–1976
THKNT	Theologischer Handkommentar zum Neuen Testament
TLZ	*Theologische Literaturzeitung*
TTZ	*Trierer theologische Zeitschrift*
TynBul	*Tyndale Bulletin*
USQR	*Union Seminary Quarterly Review*
WA	Weimar Ausgabe, the critical edition of Luther's works
WBC	Word Biblical Commentary
WUNT	Wissenschaftliche Untersuchungen zum Neuen Testament
ZBK	Zürcher Bibelkommentare

Notes

PART 1. MATERNAL IMAGERY IN THE LETTERS OF PAUL

1. Peter Lampe, *From Paul to Valentinus: Christians at Rome in the First Two Centuries* (Minneapolis: Fortress, 2003), 19–27.

2. Wayne A. Meeks, *The First Urban Christians: The Social World of the Apostle Paul* (New Haven, CT: Yale University Press, 1983), 28–29; Carolyn Osiek and David L. Balch, *Families in the New Testament World: Households and House Churches* (Louisville: Westminster John Knox, 1997), 5–35; Walter Scheidel, "Germs for Rome," in *Rome the Cosmopolis* (ed. Catharine Edwards and Greg Woolf; Cambridge: Cambridge University Press, 2003), 158–76.

3. The descriptions of Carolyn Osiek and Margaret Y. MacDonald are evocative:

> House-church meetings must have been noisy and bustling places. The sounds of a woman in labor somewhere in the background, the crying of infants, the presence of mothers or wet nurses feeding their children, little toddlers under foot, children's toys on the floor—all could have been part of the atmosphere.

(*A Woman's Place: House Churches in Earliest Christianity* [Minneapolis: Fortress, 2006], 67). See also Suzanne Dixon, *The Roman Family* (Baltimore: Johns Hopkins University Press, 1992), 98–132; Keith R. Bradley, *Rediscovering the Romans Family: Studies in Roman Social History* (Oxford: Oxford University Press, 1991).

4. Translations of biblical texts are my own unless otherwise noted.

5. I deal only in passing with 1 Thess 5:3; Gal 1:15; and 1 Cor 15:8. The first is a conventional association between eschatological expectation and the pangs of childbirth (see chapter 2), the second is prophetic imagery (e.g., Isa 49:1), and 1 Cor 15:8 deals less with Paul's understanding of the gospel and apostleship than with the circumstances surrounding his call.

6. See below, chapter 1, on the reasons for this translation, which differs from that of the NRSV because of a notorious text-critical problem. The text-critical problem and the resulting translation are not urgent for the point under discussion since, even if it is resolved in favor of "gentle," we still have another double metaphorical transference here.

7. In his discussion of the marriage analogy in Rom 7:1–6, C. H. Dodd comments that Paul "lacks the gift for sustained illustration of ideas," probably because of a "defect of imagination" (*The Epistle of Paul to the Romans* [Moffatt; New York: Ray Long and Richard R. Smith, 1932], 103). Generalizing about Paul's use of metaphor is perilous, but my impression is quite different from that of Dodd; Paul employs metaphors well, and his mixed metaphors (the ones Dodd would regard as defective) often appear in settings where he is striving to convey a particular point *and* to avoid another. For example, the analogy in Rom 7:1–6 logically requires Paul to say that the law has died, but he refuses to do that, affirming instead that believers died to the law.

8. Earl J. Richard identifies Paul's use of maternal imagery with his founding visit and his use of paternal imagery with the process of growth and discipline. In so doing, however, he considers only the maternal imagery in 1 Thess 2:7 and does not take into account the other passages under discussion here. Richard also fails to note that all of 1 Thess 2:1–12 concerns Paul's founding visit, including the paternal metaphor of 2:11. See *First and Second Thessalonians* (SP; Collegeville, MN: Liturgical Press, 1995), 86, 106.

9. J. Louis Martyn rightly characterizes *gennan*, the verb for begetting that appears in Phlm 10 and 1 Cor 4:15, as Paul's "missioning verb" (*Galatians* [AB 33A; New York: Doubleday, 1997], 451). Norman R. Petersen similarly comments on Philemon that fatherhood is "a metaphor describing one who brings an individual into the church, whether through preaching or through baptizing, or through both" (*Rediscovering Paul: Philemon and the Sociology of Paul's Narrative World* [Philadelphia: Fortress, 1985], 85, n. 69).

10. John L. White attempts to trace both Paul's Christology and his ecclesiology to his conception of God as Father; God's generativity brings about both the Son Jesus Christ and the Christian community ("God's Paternity as Root Metaphor in Paul's Conception of Community," *Foundations and Facets Forum* 8 [1992]: 271–95). Much in White's article is suggestive, but in my judgment he has not taken adequate account of the presence of maternal imagery (although see 280, n. 19).

11. See also Mic 4:10; *1 En.* 62:4; *2 Bar.* 56:6; *4 Ezra* 4:42; and the discussion in chapter 2 below.

12. The translation is that of M. Wise, M. Abegg, C. Cook, and N. Gordon, in *Poetic and Liturgical Texts* (ed. Donald W. Parry and Emanuel Tov; vol. 5 of *The Dead Sea Scrolls Reader*; Leiden: Brill, 2005). See the discussion of this text in chapter 1 below.

13. See especially Maud W. Gleason, *Making Men: Sophists and Self-Presentation in Ancient Rome* (Princeton, NJ: Princeton University Press, 1995); John J. Winkler,

The Constraints of Desire: The Anthropology of Sex and Gender in Ancient Greece (New York: Routledge, 1990); David M. Halperin, John J. Winkler, and Froma I. Zeitlin, eds., *Before Sexuality: The Construction of Erotic Experience in the Ancient Greek World* (Princeton, NJ: Princeton University Press, 1990); and Thomas Laquer, *Making Sex: Body and Gender from the Greeks to Freud* (Cambridge, MA: Harvard University Press, 1990). For an important attempt to read a Pauline letter in conversation with issues of gender construction, see Dale B. Martin, *The Corinthian Body* (New Haven, CT: Yale University Press, 1995).

14. Winkler, *The Constraints of Desire,* 21.

15. Max Black, "Metaphor," in *Models and Metaphors* (Ithaca, NY: Cornell University Press, 1962), 25–47; originally published in *Proceedings from the Aristotelian Society* 55 (1954).

16. Samuel R. Levin, "Standard Approaches to Metaphor and a Proposal for Literary Metaphor," in *Metaphor and Thought* (ed. Andrew Ortony; Cambridge: Cambridge University Press, 1979), 124–35.

17. Eva Feder Kittay, *Metaphor: Its Cognitive and Linguistic Structure* (Oxford: Oxford University Press, 1987), 316–24.

18. Wayne C. Booth, "Metaphor as Rhetoric: The Problem of Evaluation," in *On Metaphor* (ed. Sheldon Sacks; Chicago: University of Chicago Press, 1979), 63.

19. Ted Cohen, "Metaphor and the Cultivation of Intimacy," in *On Metaphor,* 1–10.

20. Mark Turner, *Death Is the Mother of Beauty: Mind, Metaphor, Criticism* (Chicago: University of Chicago Press, 1987).

21. Ibid., 24.

22. Ibid., 25.

23. Ibid., 55.

24. I refer especially to the work carried out in the Society of Biblical Literature's Pauline Theology Group.

25. Steven J. Kraftchick, "Death in Us, Life in You: The Apostolic Medium," in *Pauline Theology,* vol. 2 (ed. David M. Hay; Minneapolis: Fortress, 1991), 156–81; and my response, "Apostle and Church in 2 Corinthians," in ibid., 187–93.

26. This approach may be contrasted with that of Victor Paul Furnish, for whom Paul's theology is located more narrowly in his "*critical reflection on the beliefs, rites, and social structures in which an experience of ultimate reality has found expression*" ("Paul the Theologian," in *The Conversation Continues: Studies in Paul and John in Honor of J. Louis Martyn* [ed. Robert T. Fortna and Beverly R. Gaventa; Nashville: Abingdon, 1990], 25). The italics are in the original.

27. Meeks, *The First Urban Christians,* esp. 84–94.

28. Even without taking maternal imagery into account, there are problems with this strategy. As Dale B. Martin has observed, Paul sometimes "uses patriarchal rhetoric to make an antipatriarchal point" (*Slavery as Salvation: The Metaphor of Slavery in Pauline Christianity* [New Haven, CT: Yale University Press, 1990], 142).

29. An English translation of *The Acts of Paul* by Wilhelm Schneemelcher and Rodolphe Kasser is conveniently available in *New Testament Apocrypha* (2nd ed.; ed. Wilhelm Schneemelcher; 2 vols.; Louisville: Westminster/John Knox Press, 1991–92) 2:237–70; quotation on 262–63.

30. Origen, *Commentary on the Epistle to the Romans Books 6–10* (trans. Thomas P. Scheck; Fathers of the Church; Washington: Catholic University of America Press, 2002), book 8, chapter 10 (p. 174).

31. Methodius, *The Symposium* (trans. Herbert Musurillo; ACW; London: Longmans, Green, 1958) 9 (p. 67).

32. Gregory of Nyssa, *Commentary on the Song of Songs* (trans. Casimir McCambley; Brookline, MA: Hellenic College Press, 1987), 157. A similar connection appears in Theodoret, who writes that the "apostles' hearers met the flowing apostolic streams as if they were breasts to be valued more highly than any wine and any gladness" (*The Song of Songs Interpreted by Early Christian and Medieval Commentators* [trans. and ed. Richard A. Norris Jr.; The Church's Bible 1; Grand Rapids: Eerdmans, 2003], 34). And the Venerable Bede identifies the breasts of the Song of Songs with the "church's teachers when they are ministering the milk of elementary instruction to Christ's little ones." While he does not specify the names of the teachers, in the same paragraph he goes on to quote 1 Cor 2:2 and Rom 9:5 (ibid., 262).

33. See the account in *The Acts of Paul*, in *New Testament Apocrypha*, 2:237–70.

34. Guerric of Igny, "Sermon 45: The Second Sermon for Saints Peter and Paul," *Liturgical Sermons* (2 vols.; Spencer, MA: Cistercian Publications, 1970–71), 2:154. This sermon is an extended interpretation of Song 4:5, in which Guerric identifies Peter and Paul as the breasts of the church.

35. *The Prayers and Meditations of Saint Anselm* (trans. Benedicta Ward; London: Penguin Books, 1973), 152.

CHAPTER 1. APOSTLES AS INFANTS AND NURSES

1. The phrase is Helmut Koester's ("1 Thessalonians—Experiment in Christian Writing," in *Continuity and Discontinuity in Church History: Essays Presented to George Hunston Williams an the Occasion of His 65th Birthday* [ed. F. Forrester Church and Timothy George; Leiden: Brill, 1979], 33–44).

2. "Gentle" is also the translation of the NEB, the NASB, and the NAB. The NIB reads, "Instead, we lived unassumingly among you. Like a mother feeding and looking after her children."

3. C. J. Ellicott, *A Critical and Grammatical Commentary on St. Paul's Epistle to the Thessalonians* (London: John W. Parker & Son, 1858), 21; Helmut Koester, "The Text of 1 Thessalonians," in *The Living Text: Essays in Honor of Ernest W. Saunders* (ed. Dennis E. Groh and Robert Jewett; Lanham, MD: University Press of America, 1985), 225.

4. Koester, "Text of 1 Thessalonians," 225; Béda Rigaux, *Saint Paul: Les épitres aux Thessaloniciens* (Paris: J. Gabalda, 1956), 418.

5. Context appears to be the deciding issue for many scholars: E. von Dobschütz, *Die Thessalonicher-Briefe* (KEK; 7th ed.; Göttingen: Vandenhoeck & Ruprecht, 1974 [orig. 1909], 93); Martin Dibelius, *An die Thessalonicher I–II; An die Philipper* (HNT; 2nd ed.; Tübingen: J. C. B. Mohr, 1923), 9; C. G. Findlay, *The Epistles of Paul the Apostle to the Thessalonians* (Cambridge, MA: Cambridge University Press, 1925), 32–33; William Neil, *The Epistle of Paul to the Thessalonians* (London: Hodder & Stoughton, 1950), 40; Bruce M. Metzger, *A Textual Commentary on the Greek New Testament* (London: United Bible Societies, 1970), 629–30; Ernest Best, *A Commentary on the First and Second Epistles to the Thessalonians* (London: Adam & Charles Black, 1972), 40; Ronald Ward, *Commentary on 1 and 2 Thessalonians* (Waco, TX: Word, 1973), 61–62; I. H. Marshall, *1 and 2 Thessalonians* (NCB; Grand Rapids: Eerdmans, 1983), 70; Koester, "Text of 1 Thessalonians," 225; Earl J. Richard, *First and Second Thessalonians* (SP; Collegeville, MN: Liturgical Press, 1995), 82; Joël Delobel, "One Letter Too Many in Paul's First Letter? A Study of (ν)ήπιοι in 1 Thess 2:7," *LS* 20 (1995): 126–33. Metzger apparently speaks for many when he invokes Daniel Mace's dictum that "no manuscript is so old as common sense" (*The Text of the New Testament: Its Transmission, Corruption, and Restoration* [New York: Oxford University Press, 1964], 230–33). What counts as "common sense," of course, fluctuates from one period of time to another and from one culture to another.

By contrast with the above, F. Zimmer argues that νήπιοι fits the context better than does ήπιοι ("1 Thess. 2:3–8 erklart," in *Theologische Studien: Festschrift B. Weiss* [ed. C. R. Gregory et al.; Göttingen: Vandenhoeck & Ruprecht, 1897], 264–65); see also J. J. Janse van Rensburg, "An Argument for Reading νήπιοι in 1 Thessalonians 2:7," in *A South African Perspective on the New Testament: Essays by South African New Testament Studies presented to Bruce Manning Metzger* (Leiden: Brill, 1986), 252–59.

6. "The Text of 1 Thessalonians," 224–25; see also Traugott Holtz, "Der Apostel des Christus: Die paulinische 'Apologie' 1 Thess 2,1–12," in *Als Boten des gekreuzigten Herrn: Festgabe für Bischof Dr. Werner Krusche zum 65. Geburtstag* (ed. Heino Falcke, Martin Onnasch, and Harald Schultze; Berlin: Evangelische Verlagsanstalt, 1982), 170; Trevor Burke, "Pauline Paternity in 1 Thessalonians," *TynBul* 51 (2000): 75.

7. In response to an earlier version of this chapter, Timothy B. Sailors notes that Rom 2:20 places "infants" in parallel with "the foolish," concluding that the connotation of "infants" in that passage is "very much" negative ("Wedding Textual and Rhetorical Criticism: The Text of 1 Thessalonians 2.7," *JSNT* 80 [2001]: 91). It may be that my comment should be nuanced somewhat, but the series in Rom 2 contains four groups in order: the blind, those in darkness, the foolish, and infants. What they appear to have in common is need of assistance rather than a negative assessment per se.

8. Sailors contends that the term is used with a neutral sense in the 75 percent of instances in literature of "the first centuries BCE and CE" ("Wedding Textual and Rhetorical Criticism," 11–12).

9. C. G. Findlay, who concludes that νήπιοι results from an early and widespread dittography, nevertheless points out that, if the reading were ἤπιοι, Paul's intent would be to describe the apostles as "simple, guileless, unassuming" (*Epistles to the Thessalonians*, 42).

10. See, for example, the comment by C. H. Dodd on Rom 7:1–6: "He lacks the gift for sustained illustration of ideas through concrete images (though he is capable of a brief illuminating metaphor). It is probably a defect of imagination" (*The Epistle of Paul to the Romans* [London: Hodder & Stoughton, 1932], 121). A more sustained discussion of the topic appears in Herbert M. Gale, *The Use of Analogy in the Letters of Paul* (Philadelphia: Westminster, 1964).

11. The verb γίνομαι is also used with an adjective, as in 1 Thess 2:1, 8, 10. The point is that Paul might well use a noun here, not that he must do so. On the frequency of γίνομαι in this passage, see Paul Schubert, *Form and Function of the Pauline Thanksgivings* (Berlin: Töpelmann, 1930), 19–20.

12. So also J. E. Frame, *A Critical and Exegetical Commentary on the Epistles of St. Paul to the Thessalonians* (ICC; Edinburgh: T&T Clark, 1912), 100.

13. Others who favor νήπιοι include Leon Morris, *The First and Second Epistles to the Thessalonians* (NICNT; Grand Rapids: Eerdmans, 1959), 76–78; Jean Gribomont, "Facti sumus parvuli: La charge apostolique (1 Th 2, 1–12)," in *Paul de Tarse: Apôtre du notre temps* (ed. L. De Lorenzi; Rome: Abbaye de S. Paul, 1979), 311–38; Stephen Fowl, "A Metaphor in Distress. A Reading of NHΠIOI in 1 Thessalonians 2.7," *NTS* 36 (1990): 469–73; Jeffrey A. D. Weima, "'But We Became Infants Among You': The Case of NHΠIOI in 1 Thess 2.7," *NTS* 46 (2000): 547–64; Gordon D. Fee, *To What End Exegesis? Essays Textual, Exegetical, and Theological* (Grand Rapids: Eerdmans, 2001), 70–74; Sailors, "Wedding Textual and Rhetorical Criticism," 81–88; Gene L. Green, *The Letter to the Thessalonians* (Pillar NT Commentary; Grand Rapids: Eerdmans, 2002), 127. In addition, Daniel Marguerat concludes that, either way the text-critical problem is resolved, the text works to distinguish the apostle from those who practice rhetoric irresponsibly ("L'apôtre, mère et père de la communauté," *ETR* 75 [2000]: 373–89, esp. 386).

Charles Crawford ("The 'Tiny' Problem of 1 Thessalonians 2, 7: The Case of the Curious Vocative," *CBQ* 54 [1973]: 69–72) also argues for the reading νήπιοι, but for reasons not yet discussed. Crawford revises the suggestion of an eighteenth-century scholar, Daniel Whitby, that νήπιοι is a vocative ("But in your midst, babes, we were like a nurse"). The same argument has been advanced recently by Christine Gerber, *Paulus und seine 'Kinder': Studien zur Beziehungsmetaphorik der paulinischen Briefe* (BZNW 136; Berlin: Walter de Gruyter, 2005), 278, 290–91. While that translation would resolve the difficulties of the mixed metaphor, it is grammatically indefensible.

14. For this approach, see Sailors, "Wedding Textual and Rhetorical Criticism," 93–95.

15. Abraham Malherbe, "'Gentle as a Nurse': The Cynic Background to 1 Thess ii," *NovT* 12 (1970): 203–17. Malherbe does not discuss the text-critical problem of 2:7 in this article. In a letter, however, he indicates that the Pauline usage elsewhere, the context, and the topos decide the debate in favor of ἤπιοι (letter to Beverly Gaventa, February 13, 1989); see also *The Epistle to the Thessalonians* (AB 32B; New York: Doubleday, 2000), 145–46.

16. Discussion continues about the purpose of 1 Thessalonians; see the essays in *The Thessalonians Debate: Methodological Discord or Methodological Synthesis?* (ed. Karl P. Donfried and Johannes Beutler; Grand Rapids: Eerdmans, 2000).

17. This noun *titthē* is not employed in the New Testament, LXX, or Josephus.

18. Mary Rosaria Gorman, *The Nurse in Greek Life* (PhD diss., The Catholic University of America, 1917; Boston: Foreign Languages Print Co., 1917), 7–8.

19. Ammonius 470 (113–118; p. 122 in the edition of K. Nickau). Cf. Eustathius, Il., 6.399, p. 650. I learned of the discussion in Ammonius through von Dobschütz, *Die Thessalonicher-Briefe*, 94. One study of Greek words for nursing and nurture does not even discuss the term τίτθη (Claude Moussy, *Recherches sur* τρέφω *[trephō] et les verbes grecs significant "nourrir"* (Paris: Librairie C. Klincksieck, 1969).

20. For a critique of Malherbe's comparison of 1 Thess 2:1–12 with Cynic texts, see Wolfgang Stegemann, "Anlass und Hintergrund der Abfassung von 1 Th 2,1–12," in *Theologische Brosamen für Lothar Steiger* (ed. G. Freund and E. Stegemann; DBAT 5; Heidelberg: Theologische Seminar, 1985), 399–401. Stegemann argues that the Pauline text is not comparable with the texts Malherbe cites, since (1) Paul is not presenting himself or his gospel for the first time but is reminding believers of their earlier experience; and (2) while Dio is attacking the authenticity of other philosophers, Paul is discussing his own teaching. In addition, as Stephen Fowl observes, "no matter which variant we read, Paul never says that he was as gentle as a nurse. The most one could claim is that Paul claimed he was gentle and then he went on to talk about how his love for the Thessalonians was similar to a nurse's love for her child" ("A Metaphor in Distress," 470).

Karl Paul Donfried has suggested that the background of the nursing image in 2:7 is to be traced to the cult of Dionysus, which was important in Thessalonica, since the myth involved nymphs who nursed the infant Dionysus ("The Cults of Thessalonica," in *Paul, Thessalonica, and Early Christianity* [Grand Rapids: Eerdmans, 2002], 24–25, 28). The ubiquity of nurses in the Roman world makes it difficult to limit the associations in this way, however.

21. See Gorman, *The Nurse in Greek Life*, 9–33, and the abundant references cited there; also G. Herzog-Hauser, "Nutria," PW 17, col. 1495.

22. See the discussions in Thomas Wiedemann, *Adults and Children in the Roman Empire* (New Haven, CT: Yale University Press, 1989), 144; Keith R. Bradley, "The Social Role of the Nurse in the Roman World," in *Discovering the*

Roman Family: Studies in Roman Social History (Oxford: Oxford University Press, 1991), 13–36.

23. Indeed, in some texts the word τροφός is used of a woman who is, in fact, the mother of the character (e.g., Theocritus, *Idylls* 27.65; Sophocles, *Ajax* 849). Keith Bradley demonstrates that nurses, especially wet nurses, were employed for children across the social spectrum and across a broad geographical range ("The Social Role of the Nurse," esp. 17–20). See chapter 3 below for further discussion of nurses, particularly wet nurses.

24. The similarities between these two passages were noted as early as Zimmer, "1 Thess. 2:3–8," 268.

25. The translation is that of M. Wise, M. Abegg, C. Cook, and N. Gordon, in *Poetic and Liturgical Texts* (ed. Donald W. Parry and Emanuel Tov; vol. 5 of *The Dead Sea Scrolls Reader;* Leiden: Brill, 2005). The similarities between this passage, previously identified as 1QH 7.19–23, 25, and 1 Thess 2:7 are noted by O. Betz, "Die Geburt der Gemeinde durch den Lehrer," *NTS* 3 (1957): 322; W. Grundmann, "Die NHΠIOI in der urchristlichen Paränese," *NTS* 5 (1959): 200; Traugott Holtz, *Der erste Brief an die Thessalonicher* (EKKNT; Zurich: Benziger, 1986), 83 n. 342.

26. Norman Friedman, *Form and Meaning in Fiction* (Athens: University of Georgia Press, 1975), 289; cited in Alan Culpepper, *Anatomy of the Fourth Gospel* (Philadelphia: Fortress, 1983), 181.

27. I. A. Richards, *The Philosophy of Rhetoric* (London: Oxford Univeristy Press, 1936), 93.

28. Ibid., 93–95, 124–25.

29. Philip Wheelwright, *Metaphor and Reality* (Bloomington: Indiana University Press, 1961), 70–91.

30. Wayne Booth, *A Rhetoric of Irony* (Chicago: University of Chicago Press, 1974), 22–23.

31. Wolfgang Clemen, *Shakespeares Bilder: Ihre Entwicklung und ihre Funktionen im dramatischen Werk* (PhD diss., University of Bonn, 1936; Bonn: Hanstein, 1936), 144; Eng. trans., *The Development of Shakepeare's Imagery* (Cambridge, MA: Harvard University Press, 1951). Quoted in Rene Wellek and Austin Warren, *Theory of Literature* (3rd ed.; New York: Harcourt, Brace & World, 1956), 302 n. 37.

32. I have deliberately set aside discussion of paternal imagery because it is abundantly treated in the commentaries. Another means of holding the shifting imagery together is found in Stephen Fowl, who suggests that, by introducing "infants," Paul has created a problem, since that term suggests both gentleness and dependency, and Paul has just insisted that the apostles are not demanding and dependent. To curb the generativity of his first metaphor, then, Paul introduces the metaphor of the nurse to reclaim the caring role of the apostles ("A Metaphor in Distress," 472). I do not think Paul is restricting his first metaphor so much as holding together several distinct understandings.

33. Zimmer likewise concludes that what is in view is the affection of a nurse for the children she has reared ("1 Thess. 2:3–8," 268).

34. Stegemann suggests that "as if" (ὡς ἐάν, *hōs ean*) may signal that Paul knows it is unlikely that a nurse would be caring for her own children ("1 Th 2, 1–12," 409). Gerber adds an important observation: nurses worked on the basis of a contract, which means that caring for one's own children would involve working without reimbursement (reinforcing Paul's earlier insistence that he did not act from greed) (*Paulus und seine 'Kinder,'* 291–92).

35. Of course, the use of such outrageous imagery for describing the apostles is consistent with the proclamation of a crucified Christ. See Paul Meyer's suggestive essay on the need to reclaim the historical event of the crucifixion as the central element in New Testament theology ("Faith and History Revisited," *Princeton Seminary Bulletin NS* 10 (1989): 75–83; now republished in *The Word in This World: Essays in New Testament Exegesis and Theology* (ed. John T. Carroll; Louisville: Westminster John Knox, 2004), 19–26.

36. Wayne Meeks, *The First Urban Christians* (New Haven, CT: Yale University Press, 1983), 86–88.

37. "In a very real sense the New Testament was born when that first letter of Paul was written" (Raymond Collins, *The Birth of the New Testament: The Origin and Development of the First Christian Generation* [New York: Crossroad, 1993], 213).

CHAPTER 2. THE MATERNITY OF PAUL

1. See Carolyn Osiek and Margaret Y. MacDonald with Janet H. Tulloch, *A Woman's Place: House Churches in Earliest Christianity* (Minneapolis: Fortress, 2006), 53–63.

2. Verse 12 does not explicitly call for the imitation of Paul (compare 1 Cor 4:16; 11:1; Phil 3:17), but the implication is clear. See W. P. De Boer, *The Imitation of Paul* (Kampen: J. H. Kok, 1962), 188–96; B. R. Gaventa, "Galatians 1 and 2: Autobiography as Paradigm," *NovT* 28 (1986): 319–22 (see chapter 6 below); R. B. Hays, "Christology and Ethics in Galatians," *CBQ* 49 (1987): 281–82.

3. For the use of the term "Teachers," see J. Louis Martyn, "A Law-Observant Mission to Gentiles: The Background of Galatians," *Michigan Quarterly Review* 22 (1983): 221–36; now available in *Theological Issues in the Letters of Paul* (Nashville: Abingdon, 1997), 7–24.

4. So J. B. Lightfoot, *St. Paul's Epistle to the Galatians* (6th ed.; London: Macmillan, 1880), 178; E. D. Burton, *The Epistle to the Galatians* (ICC; Edinburgh: T&T Clark, 1921), 248. However, a number of commentators identify v. 19 as an anacoluthon, placing a period at the end of v. 18 and a dash following v. 19. So Pierre Bonnard, *L'épître de saint Paul aux Galates* (CNT 9; Neuchâtel: Delachaux et Niestlé, 1953), 94; Heinrich Schlier, *Der Brief an die Galater* (5th

ed.; KEK; Göttingen: Vandenhoeck & Ruprecht, 1971), 213; Franz Mussner, *Der Galaterbrief* (HTKNT 9; Freiburg: Herder, 1974), 312.

5. This situation has now changed somewhat (see the Afterword at the end of this chapter), although it is still worth noticing the relative lack of attention to this and other passages in which Paul uses maternal imagery.

6. Typical of this line of thinking is the commentary of Ronald K. H. Fung: "This section [4:12–20] manifestly differs from the others in the present division (III, 2:15–5:12) in that whereas the others are directly doctrinal, this section is Paul's personal appeal to his Galatian converts and has little doctrinal content" (*The Epistle to the Galatians* [NICNT; Grand Rapids: Eerdmans, 1988], 195).

7. Chrysostom, *Homilies on Galatians, Ephesians, Philippians, Colossians, Thessalonians, Timothy, Titus, & Philemon* (NPNF[1]; Grand Rapids: Eerdmans, 1956), Homily 4. Note also Pierre Bonnard's comment that in vv. 19–20 Paul overcomes with love the bitterness revealed in vv. 16–19 (*Aux Galates*, 94).

8. Since H. D. Betz finds discourses on friendship in the ancient world that compare friendship with parental relationships, he takes 4:19 to be yet another part of the friendship topos (*Galatians* [Hermeneia; Philadelphia: Fortress, 1979], 233–34).

9. See chapter 4 below.

10. Reading *teknia* (with ℵ[2], A, C, D[2], Ψ) rather than *tekna* (with ℵ*, B, D*, F, G); the NRSV translates, "My little children." The manuscript evidence seems weighted in favor of *tekna*, but the difference in meaning is negligible.

11. See also Phlm 10.

12. The connections are probably to be found in the relationship between these metaphors and Paul's understanding of apostolic authority.

13. For example, Betz (*Galatians*, 233 n. 150) refers to Plato, *Lysis* [*Friendship*] 207E, which compares the love of parents for their child with the respect people have for a wise man. In several passages from Aristotle's *Nicomachean Ethics* are references to the nature of parental love, sometimes distinguishing maternal love from paternal love (8.1.3 [1155a, 15–20]; 8.8.3 [1159a, 28–34]; 8.12.2–3 [1161b, 17–34]; 9.4.1 [1166a, 6f]; 9.7.7 [1168a, 25–27]). Plutarch (*On Having Many Friends* 93F–94A) and Cicero (*On Friendship* 8) also compare friendship with parental love.

14. Betz, *Galatians*, 233.

15. Ibid., 233–34. Albrecht Oepke (*Der Brief des Paulus an die Galater* [3rd ed.; THKNT 9; Berlin: Evangelische Verlagsanstalt, 1973], 108) also points to the mystery religions, in which the mystagogue is called the "father" of the novices, but thinks that Paul's usage probably has its precedents in Old Testament traditions (see Num 11:12; 2 Kgs 2:12). While Oepke regards the notion of rebirth as generally absent in Paul, he thinks that it is distantly hinted at here.

16. Betz, *Galatians*, 233–34. Here Betz follows the translation of K. W. Tröger, "Die sechste und siebte Schrift aus Nag Hammadi-Codex VI," *TLZ* 98 (1973): 498–99. This translation is accepted also by Jean-Pierre Mahe, *Hermes en Haute-*

Egypte (Quebec: Les Presses de L'Université Laval, 1978), 67, 93; but see *The Nag Hammadi Library in English* (New York: Harper & Row, 1977), 293.

17. The translation is that of M. Wise, M. Abegg, C. Cook, and N. Gordon, in *Poetic and Liturgical Texts* (ed. Donald W. Parry and Emanuel Tov; vol. 5 in *The Dead Sea Scrolls Reader*, Leiden: Brill, 2005). This text, previously identified as 1QH 3.7–10, has been the focus of much debate. Early discussions of this hymn identified the child with the Messiah, but that interpretation has largely been rejected in favor of the notion that the text portrays the birth of the community of the righteous. Thus Matthew Black writes in *The Scrolls and Christian Origins* (New York: Charles Scribner's Sons, 1961), 150: "The eschatological setting of the hymn suggests that its subject is the 'birth-pangs of the Messiah' in the sense of the emergence through trial and suffering of the redeemed Israel." So also Helmer Ringgren, *The Faith of Qumran* (Philadelphia: Fortress, 1963), 193; Marinus de Jonge, "The Role of Intermediaries in God's Final Intervention in the Future according to the Qumran Scrolls," in *Studies on the Jewish Background of the New Testament* (ed. O. Michel et al.; Assen: Van Gorcurn, 1969), 58–59; John J. Collins, *The Apocalyptic Imagination: An Introduction to the Jewish Matrix of Christianity* (New York: Crossroads, 1984), 136; Dale Allison, *The End of the Ages Has Come: An Early Interpretation of the Passion and Resurrection of Jesus* (Philadelphia: Fortress, 1985), 8–9.

Mussner denies that there is any parallel between Gal 4:19 and 1QH[a] 3.7–10, because in Paul there are two pregnancies, but that is an overly precise reading of the metaphor (*Galaterbrief*, 312 n. 102). Betz also denies any relationship between the two texts, apparently appealing to the earlier notion that 1QH[a] 3.7–10 refers to the birth of an individual rather than a community (*Galatians*, 234).

18. See also Acts 2:24, which refers to God's raising of Jesus from the dead as "loosing the *pangs* [*ōdin*] of death." On the woman in Rev 12, see Adela Yarbro Collins, *The Combat Myth in the Book of Revelation* (HDR 9; Missoula: Scholars Press, 1976), 57–100; John M. Court, *Myth and History in the Book of Revelation* (Atlanta: John Knox, 1979), 106–21.

19. The suggestion is sometimes made that the image of birth in 4:19 anticipates the quotation from Isa 54:1 in 4:27. See, for example, Dieter Luhrmann, *Der Brief an die Galater* (ZBK; Zürich: Theologische Verlag, 1978), 74. J. Louis Martyn has connected the birth imagery in the two passages in his argument that Hagar and Sarah in Gal 4:21–31 represent, not Judaism and Christianity, but two forms of Christian mission—that is, two births ("The Covenants of Hagar and Sarah," in *Faith and History: Essays in Honor of Paul W. Meyer* [ed. John T. Carroll, Charles H. Cosgrove, and E. Elizabeth Johnson; Atlanta: Scholars, 1990], 160–92; now available in *Theological Issues in the Letters of Paul*, 191–208.

20. Allison, *The End of the Ages Has Come*, 6 n. 6.

21. See Albrecht Oepke's comment that Paul "erlebt sozusagen im kleinen die Wehen des Messias" (*An die Galater*, 109).

22. Burton, *Galatians,* 248–49. Because of the birth imagery in the first part of this verse, it is reasonable to ask whether *morphousthai* refers to the formation of an infant in the mother's womb. In fact, *morphousthai* can connote gestation, but that usage of the word appears to have been quite limited. Pedro Gutierrez argues that *morphousthai* frequently refers to gestation, but the evidence is scanty (*La paternité spirituelle selon saint Paul* [Paris: J. Gabalda, 1968], 217).

23. Ernst Käsemann rightly contends that Gal 4:19 is not a text about spiritual perfection but about "apocalyptic expectation" (*Perspectives on Paul* [Philadelphia: Fortress, 1971], 31).

24. Lietzmann, *An die Galater* (4th ed.; HNT 10; Tübingen: J. C. B. Mohr [Paul Siebeck], 1971), 28.

25. The line between theological language and moral language is much less distinct than I may seem to suggest here, especially in Paul. See Hays, "Christology and Ethics in Galatians."

26. R. Hermann, "Über den Sinn des μορφοῦσθαι Χριστὸν ἐν ὑμῖν in Gal 4, 19," *TLZ* 80 (1955): 713–26; Mussner, *Galaterbrief,* 313.

27. On Paul's use of the word group, see John Koenig, "The Motif of Transformation in the Pauline Epistles" (ThD diss., Union Theological Seminary, New York, 1970).

28. On this as a central issue in Galatians, see chapters 6 and 7 below.

29. J. Louis Martyn, "Apocalyptic Antinomies in Paul's Letter to the Galatians," *NTS* 31 (1985): 410–24; now available in *Theological Issues in the Letters of Paul,* 111–24. Independent of Martyn's work, Charles Cousar comes to remarkably similar conclusions in an essay read at the 1989 meeting of the Society of Biblical Literature, "Galatians 6:11–18: Interpretive Clues to the Letter."

30. So also Koenig, "The Motif of Transformation," 112–19.

31. Similarly Morna Hooker connects "formation of Christ" with conformity to Christ; see "Πίστις Χριστοῦ," *NTS* 35 (1989): 342.

32. See also Phil 3:10–11. See also J. D. G. Dunn's comment that the process ends only when the body is transformed to be like Christ's body (Rom 8:11; Phil 3:21) ("1 Cor 15:45—Last Adam," *Christ and Spirit in the New Testament: Studies in Honour of C. F. D. Moule* (ed. Barnabas Lindars and Stephen Smalley; Cambridge, MA: Cambridge University Press, 1973), 137.

33. So also Schlier, *An die Galater,* 214 n. 2. F. F. Bruce modifies this interpretation slightly, arguing that the community is born through Christ's growth in individuals (*The Epistle to the Galatians: A Commentary on the Greek Text* [NIGTC; Grand Rapids: Eerdmans, 1982], 212). What this apocalyptic community looks like is the subject of chapter 10 below.

34. J. Louis Martyn, *Galatians* (AB 33A; New York: Doubleday, 1997), 418–30.

35. Brigitte Kahl accounts for the extensive presence of maternal imagery in Gal 4 differently, construing it as a subversion of the masculine imagery of Gal 3

("No Longer Male: Masculinity Struggles behind Galatians 3.28?" *JSNT* 79 [2000]: 37–49).

36. Martyn, *Galations*, 429.

37. Ibid., 429–30.

38. Another of the important features of Martyn's treatment of this passage is his translation of v. 19b: "until Christ is formed in your congregations" (*Galatians*, 425). See also Richard B. Hays, *Galatians* (*NIB* 11; Nashville: Abingdon, 2000), 296.

39. Susan Eastman, *Recovering Paul's Mother Tongue: Language and Theology in Galatians* (Grand Rapids: Eerdmans, 2007).

40. Ibid., p. 8. Ursula K. Le Guin's discussion appears in "Bryn Mawr Commencement Address," in *Dancing at the Edge of the World: Thoughts on Words, Women, Places* (New York: Grove Press, 1989), 147–60.

41. Eastman, *Mother Tongue*, 6.

42. Ibid., 100–105.

43. Ibid., 110.

44. Ibid., 177.

45. Ibid., 118.

46. There may also be a bit of unintended irony here. Early on, Eastman voices a concern about the speculative nature of Martyn's method of reconstruction (21 n. 49), but her own reconstruction is also speculative. To a very large extent, that is unavoidable in historical work.

47. Ibid., esp. 181.

CHAPTER 3. MOTHER'S MILK AND MINISTRY

1. To a limited degree, my proposals are anticipated in the work of J. Francis ("'As Babes in Christ'—Some Proposals Regarding 1 Corinthians 3.1–3," *JSNT* 7 [1980]: 41–60), who notes the claims to authority implicit in Paul's use of what Francis refers to as the "nurse image." I contend that Paul is not merely reinforcing his own claims to authority but also laying the groundwork for a radically different understanding of authority.

2. See, for example, the following discussions: H. A. W. Meyer, *Critical and Exegetical Handbook to the Epistles to the Corinthians* (2 vols.; Edinburgh: T&T Clark, 1877), 2:83–84; Archibald Robertson and Alfred Plummer, *A Critical and Exegetical Commentary on the First Epistle of St. Paul to the Corinthians* (2nd ed.; ICC; Edinburgh: T&T Clark, 1914), 52–53; Hans Lietzmann, *An die Korinther I–II* (HNT; Tübingen: J. C. B. Mohr [Paul Siebeck], 1923), 15; Johannes Behm, "βρῶμα," *TDNT* 1:642–45; Heinrich Schlier, "γάλα," *TDNT* 1:645–47; Ulrich Wilckens, *Weisheit und Torheit: Eine exegetisch-religionsgeschichtliche Untersuchung zu 1. Kor. 1 und 2* (BHT 26; Tübingen: J. C. B. Mohr, 1959), 52–53. There

are ancient precedents for this interest in correlating "milk" and "solid food" with levels of instruction; see Judith L. Kovacs, "Echoes of Valentinian Exegesis in Clement of Alexandria and Origen: The Interpretation of 1 Cor 3, 1–3," in *Origeniana Octava: Origen and the Alexandrian Tradition* (ed. L. Perrone; BETL 164; Leuven: Leuven University Press, 2003), 317–29; idem, *1 Corinthians Interpreted by Early Christian Commentators* (The Church's Bible; Grand Rapids: Eerdmans, 2005), 47–53.

3. Morna Hooker, "Hard Sayings: 1 Corinthians 3:1," *Theology* 69 (1966): 19–22; quotation on 21. Hooker suggests that it is the Corinthians who have introduced the "milk and meat" imagery into the conversation, accusing Paul of giving them only baby food. Paul employs their language but turns it against them. J. Francis characterizes the problem as "not a failure of progression but a failure of basic comprehension" ("As Babes in Christ," 57).

4. C. K. Barrett, for example, contends that the teaching among the mature "rests on" proclamation of the cross, "but it is a development of this, of such a kind that in it the essential message of the simple preaching of the cross might be missed, or perverted, by the inexperienced." He concludes that the two teachings differ in form but not in content, just "as meat and milk are both food" (*A Commentary on the First Epistle to the Corinthians* [HNTC; New York: Harper & Row, 1967], 81). See also John Calvin, *First Epistle of Paul the Apostle to the Corinthians* (trans. John W. Fraser; Edinburgh: Oliver & Boyd, 1960), 66; C. F. Georg Heinrici, *Der erste Brief an die Korinther* (KEK; Göttingen: Vandenhoeck & Ruprecht, 1896), 116; Rudolf Schnackenburg, "Christian Adulthood according to the Apostle Paul," *CBQ* 25 (1963): 356–57; Karl Maly, *Mündige Gemeinde: Untersuchungen zur pastoralen Führung des Apostels Paulus im 1. Korintherbrief* (SBM; Stuttgart: Katholisches Bibelwerk, 1967), 58; Wilhelm Thüsing, "'Milch' und 'feste Speise' (1 Kor 3,1f. und Hebr 5,11–6,3): Elementarkatechese und theologische Vertiefung in neutestamentlicher Sicht," *TTZ* 76 (1967): 235–38; Rolf Baumann, *Mitte und Norm des Christlichen: Eine Auslegung von 1 Korinther 1,1–3,4* (NTAbh; Münster: Aschendorff, 1968), 267; Gordon Fee, *The First Epistle to the Corinthians* (NICNT; Grand Rapids: Eerdmans, 1987), 124–26; Wolfgang Schrage, *Der erste Brief an die Korinther* (2 vols.; EKKNT; Zurich: Benziger, 1991–95), 1:280–82.

5. In addition to the literature cited above, see the discussions of the New Testament usage of this imagery in Walter Grundmann, "Die ΝΗΠΙΟΙ in der urchristlichen Paränese," *NTS* 5 (1959): 188–205; Thüsing, "'Milch' und 'feste Speise,'" 233–46, 261–80; and Ronald Williamson, *Philo and the Epistle to the Hebrews* (ALGHJ; Leiden: Brill, 1970), 277–308.

6. Victor Paul Furnish, in whose honor this chapter was first written, carefully distinguishes the two in his annotations of 1 Corinthians in *The HarperCollins Study Bible* (ed. Wayne A. Meeks; San Francisco: HarperCollins, 1993), 2144–45.

7. On this distinction, see the discussion above in the introduction to part 1, noting also the demur of Susan Eastman, *Recovering Paul's Mother Tongue: Language and Theology in Galatians* (Grand Rapids: Eerdmans, 2007).

8. Apparently, the dangers of these substitutes were recognized, and male nurses were used only in emergencies (see Ralph Jackson, *Doctors and Diseases in the Roman Empire* [London: British Museum Publications, 1988], 102).

9. O. Larry Yarbrough, "Parents and Children in the Letters of Paul," in *The Social World of the First Christians: Essays in Honor of Wayne A. Meeks* (ed. L. Michael White and O. Larry Yarbrough; Minneapolis: Augsburg Fortress, 1995), 126–41; discussion of the *nutritor* is on 132–33.

10. Keith R. Bradley, "Child Care at Rome: The Role of Men," *Historical Reflections/Réflexions historiques* 12 (1985): 485–523; repr. in *Discovering the Roman Family: Studies in Roman Social History* (New York: Oxford University Press, 1991), 37–75.

11. Ibid., 40–41.

12. Ibid., 49–51.

13. Ibid., 61.

14. In an earlier article Bradley does comment that a *nutritor lactaneus* "may have fed infants from a bottle, though the evidence that bottle-feeding was practised at all is very slender" ("Wet-Nursing at Rome: A Study in Social Relations," in *The Family in Ancient Rome: New Perspectives* [ed. Beryl Rawson; Ithaca, NY: Cornell University Press, 1986], 214).

15. I omit 14:33b–36 because, along with many commentators, I regard this as a non-Pauline interpolation. On that question, see Fee, *First Corinthians*, 699–708, and the literature cited there. See also Raymond Collins, *First Corinthians* (SP; Collegeville, MN: Liturgical Press, 1999), 515–16.

16. For a suggestive treatment of the household language in 1 Corinthians, see Stephen C. Barton, "Community Formation in Corinth," *NTS* 32 (1986): 225–46.

17. "Sister" (ἀδελφή) itself occurs in 7:15 and 9:5. For instances in which the plural ἀδελφοί clearly refers to "brothers and sisters," see BDAG, 18.

18. On this feature of Paul's letters, see Klaus Schäfer, *Gemeinde als "Bruderschaft": Ein Beitrag zum Kirchenverständnis des Paulus* (Frankfurt: Peter Lang, 1989).

19. Yarbrough's article, "Parents and Children in Paul," helpfully surveys this aspect of Paul's family language in 1 Corinthians and elsewhere and speculates on its moral implications. In my judgment, however, he considerably understates the significance of the maternal language in Paul.

20. On the factionalized nature of the Corinthian congregation, see the excellent work of Margaret Mitchell, *Paul and the Rhetoric of Reconciliation: An Exegetical Investigation of the Language and Composition of 1 Corinthians* (Louisville: Westminster/John Knox, 1993).

21. Thomas Laquer, *Making Sex: Body and Gender from the Greeks to Freud* (Cambridge, MA: Harvard University Press, 1990), quotation on 62. According to Laquer, this one-sex model dominated understandings of sexual differences until the end of the seventeenth century.

22. For a fascinating reading of 1 Corinthians in light of this discussion of the body, see now Dale Martin, *The Corinthian Body* (New Haven, CT: Yale University Press, 1995).

23. See the discussion of Quintilian in Maud W. Gleason, *Making Men: Sophists and Self-Presentation in Ancient Rome* (Princeton, NJ: Princeton University Press, 1995), 113–21.

24. Maud W. Gleason, "The Semiotics of Gender: Physiognomy and Self-Fashioning in the Second Century C.E.," in *Before Sexuality: The Construction of Erotic Experience in the Ancient Greek World* (ed. David M. Halperin, John J. Winkler, and Froma I. Zeitlin; Princeton, NJ: Princeton University Press, 1990), 412. See also Gleason, *Making Men*.

25. John J. Winkler, *The Constraints of Desire: The Anthropology of Sex and Gender in Ancient Greece* (New York: Routledge, 1990), 50.

26. Ibid., 21.

27. This is not to claim that Paul was consistently indifferent to gender distinctions. His argument in 1 Cor 11:2–16 that it contravenes nature for women to have heads uncovered and for men to shave their heads is prime evidence that he was very much influenced by such social constructs.

28. Fee nicely underscores this point (*First Corinthians*, 129–30).

29. Elizabeth Castelli, *Imitating Paul: A Discourse of Power* (Louisville: Westminster/John Knox, 1991), 105.

30. Martin, *The Corinthian Body*, 64.

31. In a sense this interpretation contributes to the case of those who see 1 Cor. 3:1–4 as a transition from chapter 2 to chapter 3 (over against those who identify 3:1–4 as the conclusion to the argument in chapter 2 and others who identify it as the introduction to chapter 3). Most of those who read 3:1–4 as transitional, however, see it as marking a shift from the discussion of wisdom to a renewed discussion of factions at Corinth. Both of those issues are present but so is the nature of apostolic ministry; on this point, see Brendan Byrne, "Ministry and Maturity in 1 Corinthians 3," *ABR* 35 (1987): 83–87. For 3:1–4 as transitional, see Hans Conzelmann, *1 Corinthians* (Hermeneia; Philadelphia: Fortress, 1975), 71; Fee, *First Corinthians*, 121–22; David W. Kuck, *Judgment and Community Conflict: Paul's Use of Apocalyptic Judgment Language in 1 Corinthians 3:5–4:5* (NovTSup 66; Leiden: Brill, 1992), 155.

32. In a private communication, C. Clifton Black writes: "Paul's maternal language registers as a stunning, altogether appropriate image for the stewardship of God's mysteries (4:1), which, like Christ, must appear by worldly standards of judgment scandalous and utterly foolish."

CHAPTER 4. THE BIRTHING OF CREATION

1. Sarah is never mentioned by name, but she is to be inferred from the reference to "a free woman" in Gal 4:22. Although the allegory has conventionally

NOTES TO PP. 51–52

been understood as a contrast between Christians as the children of Sarah and Jews as the children of Hagar, J. Louis Martyn has proposed that the contrast intended is between two Gentile missions, the circumcision-free mission Paul is conducting (the free children of Sarah) and the law-observant mission of the Teachers (the enslaved children of Hagar; *Galatians* [AB 33A; New York: Doubleday, 1997], 431–66). See also the extended discussion in Susan Eastman, *Recovering Paul's Mother Tongue: Language and Theology in Galatians* (Grand Rapids: Eerdmans, 2007).

2. An additional text that might be included in this list is 1 Cor 15:8: "last of all, as to one untimely born, he appeared also to me" (NRSV). The word ἔκτρωμα refers to a birth that does not come to full gestation, whether a premature birth, a miscarriage, or an abortion (BDAG, 311; Num 12:12; Job 3:16; Eccl 6:3; Philo, *Allegorical Interpretation* 1.76). It seems clear that Paul applies the word to his own vocation as an apostle, but exactly what he intends is disputed; see Raymond F. Collins, *First Corinthians* (SP; Collegeville: Liturgical Press, 1999), 537.

3. The redundancy of "apocalyptically revealed" is unfortunate, but the translation aims at capturing something of the word ἀποκαλύπτειν, which Paul employs not simply for the uncovering of something merely hidden from view but also for the activity of God in the gospel, as in Rom 1:17–18. Ernst Käsemann's expression is apt: "God has begun to reclaim for himself the world which belongs to him" ("Worship and Everyday Life: A Note on Romans 12," in *New Testament Questions of Today* [Philadelphia: Fortress, 1969], 191). And see the discussion of the verb in Martyn, *Galatians*, 99.

4. Pelagius comments on the fact that there are differing interpretations of "creation" in this passage (*Pelagius's Commentary on St. Paul's Epistle to the Romans* [trans. Theodore De Bruyn; Oxford Early Christian Studies; Oxford: Oxford University Press, 1993], 110). The primary alternatives put forward are the following: all of creation except human beings (i.e., nonhuman creation), nonhuman creation together with unbelievers, and all of humanity apart from believers. For the history of interpretation as well as additional bibliography, see John Reumann, *Creation and New Creation: The Past, Present, and Future of God's Creative Activity* (Minneapolis: Augsburg, 1973), 98–99; C. E. B. Cranfield, *Introduction and Commentary on Romans I–VIII* (vol. 1 of *The Epistle to the Romans*; ICC; Edinburgh: T&T Clark, 1975), 413–14; J. D. G. Dunn, *Romans 1–8* (WBC 38A; Dallas, TX: Word Books, 1988), 464–65; Olle Christoffersson, *The Earnest Expectation of the Creature: The Flood-Tradition as Matrix of Romans 8:18–27* (ConBNT 23; Stockholm: Almqvist & Wiksell, 1990), 13–46.

5. Among recent scholars who argue for nonhuman creation are Cranfield, *Romans*, 1:411–12; Ulrich Wilckens, *Der Brief an die Römer: Römer 6–11* (EKKNT 6.1; Zurich: Neukirchen-Vluyn, 1978), 152–53; Dunn, *Romans*, 469–70; Christoffersson, *Earnest Expectation*, 139; Joseph A. Fitzmyer, *Romans* (AB 33; New York: Doubleday, 1993), 506; John Bolt, "Creation and Redemption in Romans 8:18–27," *CJT* 30 (1995): 34–51; Brendan Byrne, *Romans* (SP; Collegeville: Liturgical Press,

1996), 255–56; Douglas Moo, *The Epistle to the Romans* (NICNT; Grand Rapids: Eerdmans, 1996), 514; Edward Adams, *Constructing the World: A Study in Paul's Cosmological Language* (Studies of the New Testament and Its World; Edinburgh: T&T Clark, 2000), 175–78. Dissenters, those who affirm that "creation" here includes humanity, include A. Viard, "Expectatio creaturae (Rom. VIII, 19–22)," *RB* 59 (1952): 340; Ernst Käsemann, *Commentary on Romans* (Grand Rapids: Eerdmans, 1980), 232–33; Susan Eastman, "Whose Apocalypse? The Identity of the Sons of God in Romans 8:19," *JBL* 121 (2002): 273–76.

6. Dunn, *Romans*, 470. See also Jan Lambrecht, "The Groaning Creation: A Study of Rom 8:18–30," *LS* 15 (1990): 7; Moo, *Romans*, 515; Byrne, *Romans*, 257.

7. Ernest Best, *The Letter of Paul to the Romans* (CBC; Cambridge: Cambridge University Press, 1967), 98–99; Sylvia C. Keesmaat, *Paul and His Story: (Re)Interpreting the Exodus Tradition* (JSNTSup 181; Sheffield: Sheffield Academic Press, 1999), 101.

8. N. T. Wright, *Romans* (*NIB* 10; Nashville: Abingdon, 2002), 596–97.

9. Adams, *Constructing the World*, 180, 182.

10. Philip F. Esler, *Conflict and Identity in Romans: The Social Setting of Paul's Letter* (Minneapolis: Fortress, 2003), 263.

11. On the word and its usage in both Jewish and non-Jewish texts, see Adams, *Constructing the World*, 77–81.

12. One earlier argument was that creation included nonbelievers, but that position has little support in recent discussion. For supporters, see G. W. Lampe, "The New Testament Doctrine of κτίσις," *SJT* 17 (1964): 400; John C. Gager, "Functional Diversity in Paul's Use of End-Time Language," *JBL* 89 (1970): 329.

13. Adams, *Constructing the World*, 178.

14. BDAG, 313; LSJ, 527. On the range of connotations of ἑκών, especially in early literature, see GailAnn Rickert, *ΕΚΩΝ and ΑΚΩΝ in Early Greek Thought* (American Classical Studies 20; Atlanta: Scholars Press, 1989).

15. Commentators generally agree that the "one who subjected" is God. See also chapter 8 below.

16. John Bolt, who argues that κτίσις has to do with nonhuman creation, sees an inclusive understanding of κτίσις as subordinating creation to redemption and as interpreting creation anthropocentrically ("Creation and Redemption in Rom 8:18–27"). While that view is represented in some scholarly literature (e.g., Lampe, Reumann), I hope it is clear that the position I am advocating actually reinforces the cosmic scope of Rom 8 rather than limiting it to the future of believers.

17. Jouette Bassler notes the repetition of πᾶς in 1:16–2:11 (*Divine Impartiality: Paul and a Theological Axiom* [SBLDS 59; Chico, CA: Scholars Press, 1982], 128.

18. In this section, I translate "sons" to indicate when Paul himself uses the Greek word υἱοί in distinction from the word τέκνοι, which I translate "children." In neither case do I think that Paul understands these groups to contain only males.

19. The word υἱός does appear earlier in the letter, but only in reference to Jesus Christ as God's Son (1:3, 4, 9; 5:10; 8:3).

20. Eastman, "Whose Apocalypse?" 266.

21. Ibid. Both of these points rely on the earlier observations of Keesmaat, *Paul and His Story*, 266.

22. Martyn, *Galatians*, 99, 407.

23. In addition, it is not always clear in Romans to whom Paul refers when he uses the first-person plural (note 3:9, 19; 4:1). That flexibility should warn against assuming a too-easy identification between "we" and "sons of God" and "Christians" or "believers." See below, chapter 10.

24. Wright, *Romans*, 597.

25. Luzia Sutter Rehmann, "To Turn the Groaning into Labor," in *A Feminist Companion to Paul* (ed. Amy-Jill Levine with Marianne Blickenstaff; Cleveland: Pilgrim, 2005), 74–84, quotation on 76. See also her monograph, *Geh, frage die Gebärenin* (Gütersloh: Chr. Kaiser / Gütersloher Verlagshaus, 1995).

26. Rehmann, "To Turn the Groaning into Labor," esp. 75–76.

27. As is rightly noted by Eastman, "Whose Apocalypse?" 269: "In the prophets, 'labor pains' precede Israel's promised redemption."

28. To be sure, contemporary readers may well think of awaiting a baby who is to be adopted, but in the Roman world adoption largely concerned the adoption of adult sons for the sake of preserving inheritance. James M. Scott has argued vigorously that Paul's understanding of adoption is to be traced to the OT, especially to 2 Sam 7:14 (*Adoption as Sons of God: An Exegetical Investigation into the Background of ΥΙΟΘΕΣΙΑ [hyiothesia] in the Pauline Corpus* [WUNT 2.48; Tübingen: J. C. B. Mohr (Paul Siebeck), 1992]). Others note the absence of the term υἱοθεσία in the LXX and the absence of evidence for the practice of adoption in Judaism and conclude that Paul's references to adoption here and in Gal 4 reflect his knowledge of contemporary practice (see James C. Walters, "Paul, Adoption, and Inheritance," in *Paul in the Greco-Roman World: A Handbook* [ed. J. Paul Sampley; Harrisburg, PA: Trinity Press International, 2003], 42–76). For present purposes, the origin of this notion is less important than the fact that, on either reading, there is a shift from the laboring of all creation to the action of God in adopting and redeeming.

29. On the enslaving character of Sin in Romans, see chapters 8 and 9 below.

30. Amazingly, the NLT reads "the new bodies he has promised us," although the text says nothing whatever about "new bodies."

31. J. Christiaan Beker remarks that Paul is not referring to "a 'redemption from the body' but a redemption of the total 'body' of creation" (*Paul the Apostle: The Triumph of God in Life and Thought* [Philadelphia: Fortress, 1980], 181), although he elsewhere translates the phrase with the plural "bodies" (289).

32. Karl Barth's discussion of the glory of God offers an eloquent unpacking of this notion (*Church Dogmatics*, II/1, *The Doctrine of God* [Edinburgh: T&T Clark, 1957], 666–77).

33. See especially Peter von der Osten-Sacken, *Römer 8 als Beispiel paulinischer Soteriologie* (FRLANT 112; Göttingen: Vandenhoeck & Ruprecht, 1975), 124–28; Moo, *Romans*, 292–94.

34. Meyer, "Romans: A Commentary," in *The Word in This World: Essays in New Testament Exegesis and Theology* (ed. John T. Carroll; NTL; Louisville: Westminster John Knox, 2004), 191.

35. See especially Moo, *Romans*, 290–95, and the literature cited there.

36. Dunn characterizes 8:18–30 as "the climax of chaps. 6–8, and indeed of 1:18–8:30" (*Romans*, 467).

37. Steve Kraftchick, "Paul's Use of Creation Themes: A Test of Romans 1–8," *ExAud* 3 (1987): 72–87; quotation on 84.

38. See also B. R. Gaventa, "Interpreting the Death of Jesus Apocalyptically: Reconsidering Romans 8:32," in *Jesus and Paul Reconnected* (ed. Todd D. Still; Grand Rapids: Eerdmans, forthcoming).

39. Esler, *Conflict and Identity in Romans*, 260.

40. Ibid., 263.

41. Adams, *Constructing the World*, 181–83.

42. Leander E. Keck, *Romans* (ANTC; Nashville: Abingdon, 2005), 210.

43. Adams, *Constructing the World*, 183.

CHAPTER 5. IS PAULINE THEOLOGY JUST A "GUY THING"?

1. Howard Thurman, *Jesus and the Disinherited* (Richmond, IN: Friends United Press, 1981 [1940]), 30.

2. J. M. G. Barclay notes that Jewish women regarded this question as extremely important, because it had to do with identifying the men whom they could marry (*Jews in the Mediterranean Diaspora: From Alexander to Trajan [323 BCE–117 CE]* [Edinburgh: T&T Clark, 1996], 411–12). That concern would surely not have been shared by the Gentile women in the Galatian churches, however, who would have had little personal interest in the question of circumcision. To be sure, many other features of torah observance would have required female participation, particularly the food laws.

3. Although Paul contrasts Hagar with the "free woman," Sarah is not named.

4. J. Lieu rightly notes that the "implied readers of Galatians are undoubtedly male" ("Circumcision, Women and Salvation," *NTS* 40 [1994]: 369).

5. Brigitte Kahl, "No Longer Male: Masculinity Struggles Behind Galatians 3.28?" *JSNT* 79 (2000): 40.

6. J. M. Gundry-Volf provides a helpful review of the debate as well as a constructive analysis of the text itself in "Christ and Gender: A Study of Difference and Equality in Gal 3, 28," in *Jesus Christus als die Mitte der Schrift* (ed. C. Landmesser, H.-J. Eckstein, and H. Lichtenberger; BZNW 86; Berlin: Walter de Gruyter, 1997), 439–77. Although I concur with much of Gundry-Volf's article,

I am not convinced that Paul is self-consciously addressing questions of gender in this passage.

7. Because some Christians regard this type of anger as a symptom of insufficient faith, it is worth observing that people for whom the text prompts irritation may be those for whom it is genuinely important. Kathleen Norris recalls that, when her feminism made listening to talk about Jesus painful, a friend observed, "I don't know too many people who are so serious about religion they can't even go to church" (*Dakota: A Spiritual Geography* [New York: Ticknor & Fields, 1993], 94). Perhaps we should fret less about those Christians who have genuine questions and more about those who are utterly indifferent to the Bible or who read it through the haze of a numbing piety.

8. A vivid example of this problem appears in J. D. G. Dunn's massive volume, *The Theology of Paul the Apostle* (Grand Rapids: Eerdmans, 1998). The book largely follows categories drawn from systematic theology, with the only discussion of women falling under the heading "The Ministry and Authority of Women" (586–92).

9. Paul employs the language of calling or vocation to refer not only to himself (Rom 1:1; 1 Cor 1:1) but to believers generally (e.g., 1 Cor 1:9; 7:15; Gal 5:8, 13; 1 Thess 2:12; 4:7; 5:24).

10. The "Teachers" refers to that group usually identified as Paul's "opponents" or as the "Judaizers"; on this designation, see J. Louis Martyn, *Galatians* (AB 33A; New York: Doubleday, 1997), 117–26.

11. For a lucid introduction to the scholarly contributions compacted in this sentence, see C. B. Cousar, *The Letters of Paul* (Nashville: Abingdon, 1996), 75–86.

12. For an elaboration of this point, see chapter 7 below.

13. I refer both to J. Louis Martyn, *Galatians*, and to idem, *Theological Issues in the Letters of Paul* (Nashville: Abingdon, 1997).

14. The violence associated with language of invasion is and should be disturbing, since we have no lack of gruesome examples of the results that can follow when human beings undertake to bring about an "invasion" of the world around them. Nevertheless, 1 Cor 15:20–28 anticipates a final conflict between God and the competing powers; the redemption from the present evil age (Gal 1:4) is not achieved without real conflict.

15. See chapter 6 below and Gaventa, *From Darkness to Light: Aspects of Conversion in the New Testament* (Philadelphia: Fortress, 1986), 17–51.

16. For the argument that Paul is drawing on a traditional formula, see W. A. Meeks, "The Image of the Androgyne: Some Uses of a Symbol in Earliest Christianity," *HR* 13 (1974): 165–207; H. D. Betz, *Galatians* (Hermeneia; Philadelphia: Fortress, 1979), 181; E. Schüssler Fiorenza, *In Memory of Her: A Feminist Theological Reconstruction of Christian Origins* (New York: Crossroad, 1983), 208–18.

17. J. H. Schütz, *Paul and the Anatomy of Apostolic Authority* (SNTSMS 26; Cambridge: Cambridge University Press, 1975), 121.

18. The compromises Paul proposes regarding the eating of meat sacrificed to idols are of a different sort; on that matter he urges compromise for the sake of upbuilding the community, and in order to keep the fellow believer from stumbling (1 Cor 10:23–33; Rom 14:13–23), not because the spheres of torah and Christ are somehow compatible.

19. Paul understands that freedom and its absence always exist in relationship to one another. No one is free in any ultimate or absolute sense; the question is always whom or what one serves (see Rom 6).

20. On the theological function of this section of the letter, see below, chapter 6.

21. What happens when the media's powerful image of the attractive woman combines with entrenched racism comes to poignant expression in Ysaye M. Barnwell's song, "No Mirrors in My Grandma's House." The wise grandmother bans mirrors so that her grandchild can sing, "I never knew that my skin was too black / I never knew that my nose was too flat." Recall also the piercing clarity of Toni Morrison's early novel *The Bluest Eye*, in which a young black girl prays for the day when her eyes will become blue, so that others will find her beautiful (New York: Washington Square Press, 1970).

22. On this see H. Lerner, *The Dance of Intimacy* (New York: Harper, 1989).

23. See J. Louis Martyn, "The Apocalyptic Gospel in Galatians," *Int* 54 (2000): 257 n. 30.

24. On this point, see Gundry-Volf, "Christ and Gender," 475–76.

25. Daniel Boyarin, *A Radical Jew: Paul and the Politics of Identity* (Berkeley: University of California Press, 1994), 3.

26. The student's question bears an uncanny resemblance to Martin Buber's comment about living in an "unredeemed world":

> In the perspective of my faith, the word spoken to Jesus by Peter at Caesarea Philippi—"You are the Messiah"—was sincere but nevertheless untrue; and its repetition over the centuries has not brought it any closer to the truth. According to my faith, the Messiah has not appeared in a definite moment of history, but rather his appearance can only mark the end of history. In the perspective of my faith, the redemption of the world did not happen nineteen centuries ago. On the contrary, we still live in an unredeemed world.

Quoted in Martyn, *Theological Issues in the Letters of Paul*, 279.

27. On the power of sin, see P. W. Meyer, "The Worm at the Core of the Apple: Exegetical Reflections on Romans 7," in *The Conversation Continues: Studies in Paul and John in Honor of J. Louis Martyn* (ed. Robert T. Fortna and Beverly R. Gaventa; Nashville: Abingdon, 1990), 62–84.

28. See Martyn, "From Paul to Flannery O'Connor with the Power of Grace," in *Theological Issues in the Letters of Paul*, 279–97; "The Apocalyptic Gospel in Galatians," in ibid., 246–66.

29. One of the many contributions of Martyn's commentary is his argument that 5:14 speaks about Christ's completion (not "summing up" as in the NRSV) of

the law, and that 6:2 interprets mutual burden-bearing among believers as a repetition of Christ's act (*Galatians*, 486–91, 502–23, 547–49, 554–58).

30. Ibid., 20–26.

PART 2. MATERNAL IMAGERY IN ITS COSMIC AND APOCALYPTIC CONTEXT

1. See especially Richard Sturm, "Defining the Word 'Apocalyptic': A Problem in Biblical Criticism," in *Apocalyptic and the New Testament* (ed. Joel Marcus and Marion L. Soards; JSNTSup 24; Sheffield: Sheffield Academic Press, 1989), 17–48; M. C. de Boer, *The Defeat of Death: Apocalyptic Eschatology in 1 Corinthians 15 and Romans 5* (JSNTSup 22; Sheffield: JSOT Press, 1988); idem, "Paul and Apocalyptic Eschatology," in *The Origins of Apocalypticism in Judaism and Christianity* (ed. John J. Collins; vol. 1 of *The Encyclopedia of Apocalypticism*; New York: Continuum, 1998), 345–83; idem, "Paul, Theologian of God's Apocalypse," *Int* 56 (2002): 21–33.

2. *The Origins of Apocalypticism*, vii. The phrase "with deliberate naïveté" simply acknowledges the ongoing debate about matters of defining apocalyptic and apocalypticism.

3. M. C. de Boer notes this also ("Paul and Apocalyptic Eschatology," 355).

4. Douglas A. Campbell, *The Quest for Paul's Gospel: A Suggested Strategy* (London: T&T Clark, 2005).

5. I have had the experience of delivering lectures that were perceived as "feminist" by some in the audience, while others in the same audience, on the same occasion, declared them to be "not feminist." I suspect that this occurrence is not unusual.

6. R. Barry Matlock, *Unveiling the Apocalyptic Paul: Paul's Interpreters and the Rhetoric of Criticism* (JSNTSup 127; Sheffield: Sheffield Academic Press, 1996). The book delights in what I think is intended to be a humorous tone, but the condescension Matlock displays toward his predecessors in the field strikes me as bordering on the adolescent.

7. And in fact de Boer does do this work in *The Defeat of Death*, 39–91.

8. It is illuminating on this point to read Dale Allison's discussion, "Apocalyptic, Polemic, and Apologetics," in *Resurrecting Jesus: The Earliest Christian Tradition and Its Interpreters* (New York: T&T Clark, 2005), 111–48. Allison is discussing the debate about Jesus' own eschatological expectations, but he includes a helpful caveat about assuming that one can readily discern the motives of scholars.

9. On Paul's contrasting language about the "world," see Edward Adams, *Constructing the World: A Study in Paul's Cosmological Language* (Studies of the New Testament and Its World; Edinburgh: T&T Clark, 2000).

10. M. Eugene Boring, "The Language of Universal Salvation in Paul," *JBL* 105 (1986): 269–92.

11. The late J. Christiaan Beker made this point with urgency in *Paul's Apocalyptic Gospel: The Coming Triumph of God* (Philadelphia: Fortress, 1982), esp. 11–28.

CHAPTER 6. THE APOSTLE AND THE GOSPEL

1. A notable exception to this consensus appears in John Schütz's study, *Paul and the Anatomy of Apostolic Authority* (SNTSMS 23; Cambridge: Cambridge University Press, 1975), 128. Schütz argues that Gal 1 and 2 are to be understood as polemic rather than apologetic. Like Paul's discussion of his status in 1 Cor 15, Gal 1 and 2 are "aggressive explication rather than defensive response." Schütz further suggests that Paul may be attacking his opponents because of their attachment to tradition. Another important exception to the consensus is George Lyons, *Pauline Autobiography: Toward a New Understanding* (SBLDS 73; Atlanta: Scholars Press, 1985). Lyons surveys some major autobiographical works of the Hellenistic period and concludes that the movement in such works was away from apologetic and toward a more individual concern for one's place in history (24–73). Lyons provides a sharp critique of the practice of mirror-reading, that is, constructing the charges against Paul by reversing his own assertions (123–227).

2. Chrysostom, *In epistolam ad Galatas commentarius*, in Migne, PG 61, col. 613–614, 626; Martin Luther, *Die erste Vorlesung über den Galaterbrief* (ed. K. A. Meissinger), in *D. Martin Luthers Werke*, WA 57 (1939): 5 and 53–54; John Calvin, *In omnes Pauli apostoli epistolas commentarii* (ed. A. Tholuck; Halle: Gebauer, 1831), 532–33; J. B. Lightfoot, *The Epistle of St. Paul to the Galatians* (London: Macmillan, 1865), 65–66, 71; C. J. Ellicott, *A Critical and Grammatical Commentary on St. Paul's Epistle to the Galatians* (Boston: Draper & Halliday, 1867), xxi–xxii; W. M. Ramsay, *A Historical Commentary on St. Paul's Epistle to the Galatians* (New York: G. P. Putnam's Sons, 1900), 301; E. D. Burton, *A Critical and Exegetical Commentary on the Epistle to the Galatians* (ICC; Edinburgh: T&T Clark, 1920), lxxii, 35; George S. Duncan, *The Epistle of Paul to the Galatians* (New York: Harper, 1934), 22; Herman Ridderbos, *The Epistle of Paul to the Churches of Galatia* (Grand Rapids: Eerdmans, 1953), 58; Albrecht Oepke, *Der Brief des Paulus an die Galater* (2nd ed.; THKNT; Berlin: Evangelische Verlagsanstalt, 1960), 26; Heinrich Schlier, *Der Brief an die Galater* (5th ed.; KEK; Göttingen: Vandenhoeck & Ruprecht, 1971), 45; Hans Lietzmann, *An die Galater* (4th ed.; HNT; Tübingen: J. C. B. Mohr, 1971), 3–6; Pierre Bonnard, *L'épître de saint Paul aux Galates* (2nd ed.; Paris: Delachaux et Niestlé, 1972), 27; Franz Mussner, *Der Galaterbrief* (HTKNT 9; Freiburg: Herder, 1983), 78; F. F. Bruce, *The Epistle to the Galatians: A Commentary on the Greek Text* (Grand Rapids: Eerdmans, 1982), 87–89.

3. H. D. Betz, "The Literary Composition and Function of Paul's Letter to the Galatians," *NTS* 21 (1975): 353; idem, *Galatians: A Commentary on Paul's Letter*

to the Churches in Galatia (Hermeneia; Philadelphia: Fortress, 1979), 14–25, 58–62.

4. See the review by Wayne Meeks, *JBL* 100 (1981): 304–7, and those of W. D. Davies, Paul W. Meyer, and David Aune, *RSR* 7 (1981): 310–28. In addition, see George Kennedy's critique of Betz's analysis of the genre of Galatians in *New Testament Interpretation through Rhetorical Criticism* (Chapel Hill: University of North Carolina, 1984), 144–52; and George Lyons's critique in *Pauline Autobiography*, 170–76.

5. Betz, indeed, refers approvingly to Lightfoot's three-part analysis of Galatians, although noting that Lightfoot did not demonstrate the appropriateness of the rhetorical turns he applied to the respective parts (*Galatians,* 14). Betz apparently does not so much intend to undermine the traditional view of the structure of Galatians as to see that view informed by rhetorical analysis.

6. On this, see the comments of Paul Meyer in his review of Betz's commentary (319–20).

7. Although J. T. Sanders still looks at questions outside the text, he touches on this point when he notes that studies of Gal 1–2 regularly see the information given as a chronology of Paul's life or as proof for the claims of Gal 1:12 ("Paul's 'Autobiographical' Statements in Galatians 1–2," *JBL* 85 [1966]: 335–43).

8. Meyer, review, 319–20. See also Bruce, *Galatians,* lvi.

9. In the 26th edition of the Nestle-Aland text, 1:11–2:14 requires around 58 lines out of 280 lines for the epistle as a whole. In the third edition of the UBS text, 1:11–2:14 occupies around 55 lines out of 225 for the epistle as a whole.

10. F. F. Bruce, *Paul: Apostle of the Heart Set Free* (Grand Rapids: Eerdmans, 1977), 15–16, 69–75, 87, 188; Seyoon Kim, *The Origin of Paul's Gospel* (Grand Rapids: Eerdmans, 1981), esp. 330–35.

11. On this issue, see Brian Taylor, "Recollection and Membership: Converts' Talk and the Ratiocination of Commonality," *Sociology* 12 (1978): 316–17.

12. Schütz, *Paul and Apostolic Authority,* 123.

13. Whether or not believers should please human beings is a complicated issue in Paul's letters, as Professor William Baird has reminded me. While Paul denies here and in 1 Thess 2:4 that he strives to please other people, in Rom 15:1–3 he urges believers to please one another and not themselves.

14. On the meaning of this rare noun, see Martin Hengel, *Judaism and Hellenism* (trans. J. Bowden; 2 vols.; London: SCM, 1974), 1:1–2; and B. R. Gaventa, "Paul's Conversion: A Critical Sifting of the Epistolary Evidence" (PhD diss., Duke University, 1978), 213–15; idem, *From Darkness to Light: Aspects of Conversion in the New Testament* (OBT; Philadelphia: Fortress, 1986), 24–25.

15. First Timothy 1:12–16 ascribes guilt to Paul regarding his past but is surely not to be taken as evidence of Paul's own view.

16. Schütz, *Paul and Apostolic Authority*, 133.

17. J. P. Sampley argues that Gal 1:20 indicates that Paul has just mentioned the point at which his defense is most vulnerable ("'Before God, I Do Not Lie'

[Gal. 1:20]: Paul's Self-Defence in the Light of Roman Legal Praxis," *NTS* 23 [1976–77]: 477–82). Paul's use of ψεύδεσθαι elsewhere does not bear out this observation, however (cf. 2 Cor. 11:31 and Rom 9:1).

18. Schütz comments that "all Paul does is a reflection of what the gospel does; all that he is, is a reflection of what the gospel is" (*Paul and Apostolic Authority*, 232; see also 35). See also the comments of J. Christiaan Beker, *Paul the Apostle* (Philadelphia: Fortress, 1980), 44–47.

19. A similar reversal of expectations and values appears in Phil 3:2–11, where Paul writes of regarding as "loss" and "rubbish" all that he had previously esteemed. On this feature of Phil 3:2–11, see B. R. Gaventa, "Paul's Conversion," 276–81; idem, *From Darkness to Light*, 32.

20. For a review of the positions, see C. E. B. Cranfield, *Romans* (2 vols.; ICC; Edinburgh: T&T Clark, 1975), 1:342–47.

21. Burton, *Galatians*, 133; Bruce, *Galatians*, 143.

22. Robert Tannehill, *Dying and Rising with Christ: A Study in Pauline Theology* (Berlin: Alfred Topelmann, 1967), 57; Betz, *Galatians*, 121–22; Jan Lambrecht, "The Line of Thought in Gal. 2.14b–21," *NTS* 24 (1978): 495.

23. Note also the imitation motif in 2 Thess 3:7, 9; 2 Tim 3:10.

24. I assume the literary integrity of Philippians. On that problem see Helmut Koester, "The Purpose of the Polemic of a Pauline Fragment," *NTS* 8 (1962): 317–32; Walter Schmithals, *Paul and the Gnostics* (Nashville: Abingdon, 1972), 67–81; V. P. Furnish, "The Place and Purpose of Philippians III," *NTS* 10 (1963): 85–88; R. P. Jewett, "The Epistolary Thanksgiving and the Integrity of Philippians," *NovT* 12 (1970): 48–53; David Garland, "The Composition and Unity of Philippians: Some Neglected Literary Factors," *NovT* 27 (1985): 141–73.

25. Abraham J. Malherbe, "Exhortation in First Thessalonians," *NovT* 25 (1983): 238–56.

26. Influential here has been the article by W. Michaelis on μιμέομαι in *TDNT* 4:659–74.

27. W. P. De Boer, *The Imitation of Paul* (Kampen: J. H. Kok, 1962), 188–96.

28. On the christological grounding of Paul's ethic in Galatians, see Richard B. Hays, "The Law of Christ: Christology and Ethics in Galatians," *CBQ* 49 (1987): 268–90.

29. K. J. Weintraub, *The Value of the Individual: Self and Circumstance in Autobiography* (Chicago: University of Chicago Press, 1978), 1. On the problem of autobiography, see also James Olney, *Metaphors of Self: The Meaning of Autobiography* (Princeton, NJ: Princeton University Press, 1972).

30. Arnoldo Momigliano, *The Development of Greek Biography* (Cambridge, MA: Harvard University Press, 1971), 18; see also Lyons, *Pauline Autobiography*, 18–21.

31. Georg Misch, *A History of Autobiography in Antiquity* (trans. E. W. Dicks; 2 vols.; Cambridge, MA: Harvard University Press, 1961).

32. Lyons, *Pauline Autobiography*, 17–73.

33. Ibid., 37–42.

34. Cicero is omitted here because Lyons reconstructs Cicero's autobiographical output on the basis of his letters and Plutarch's life of Cicero (ibid., 42–46).

35. The question of the propriety of self-reference is relevant both for autobiographers and for letter writers. On this, see the material gathered in Lyons, *Pauline Autobiography*, 53–59.

36. Seneca, *Epistle 7* 6–9; *Epistle 11* 9.

37. Seneca, *Epistle 71* 7.

38. Seneca, *Epistle 32*; *Epistle 34*.

39. Seneca, *Epistle 32* 1.

40. See also Seneca, *Epistle 1* 4–5; *Epistle 2* 4–5, *Epistle 6* 1–4, *Epistle 8* 1–6, *Epistle 26* 6–7, *Epistle 54* 1–6. The function of self-reference in Seneca is discussed in Hildegard Cancik, *Untersuchungen zu Senecas Epistulae Morales* (Studien zur klassischen Philologie und ihren Grenzgebieten 18; Hildesheim: Georg Olms, 1967), 46–113. On Seneca's interest in authoritative example, see Ilsetraut Hadot, *Seneca und die griechisch-römische Tradition der Seelenleitung* (Quellen und Studien zur Geschichte der Philosophie 13; Berlin: Walter de Gruyter, 1969), 173–76.

41. Pliny the Younger, *Epistle 1* 8.4–5.

42. Cf. Crates, who describes an encounter with young men at the *palaestra* in order to encourage his correspondent to spend more time with youth and, thus, to provide them with models (*The Cynic Epistles* [ed. A. J. Malherbe; SBLSBS 12; Missoula, MT: Scholars Press, 1977], 70–71). Philo reveals the difficulties he has in his own writing in order to illustrate his teaching about the working of the soul (*Migration of Abraham* 34.35).

43. On different grounds, Lyons comes to a similar conclusion (*Pauline Autobiography*, 226–27).

CHAPTER 7. THE SINGULARITY OF THE GOSPEL

1. For discussions of the situation behind the letter, see J. B. Tyson, "Paul's Opponents in Galatia," *NovT* 4 (1968): 241–54; R. Jewett, "The Agitators and the Galatian Congregation," *NTS* 17 (1970–71):198–212; J. Eckert, *Die urchristliche Verkündigung im Streit zwischen Paulus und seinen Gegner nach dem Galaterbrief* (Biblische Untersuchungen 6; Regensburg: Pustet, 1971); W. Schmithals, *Paul and the Gnostics* (Nashville: Abingdon, 1972); G. Howard, *Paul: Crisis in Galatia* (SNTSMS 35; Cambridge: Cambridge University Press, 1979), 1–19; B. H. Brinsmead, *Galatians: Dialogical Response to Opponents* (SBLDS 65; Chico, CA: Scholars Press, 1982); J. Louis Martyn, "A Law-Observant Mission to Gentiles: The Background of Galatians," *SJT* 38 (1985): 307–24 (also available in *Theological Issues in the Letters of Paul* [Nashville: Abingdon, 1997], 7–24); T. David Gordon, "The Problem at Galatia," *Int* 41 (1987): 32–43.

2. H. D. Betz, *Galatians: A Commentary on Paul's Letter to the Churches in Galatia* (Hermeneia; Philadelphia: Fortress, 1979), 28–33.

3. J. Christiaan Beker himself acknowledges that this is the case (*Paul the Apostle: The Triumph of God in Life and Thought* [Philadelphia: Fortress, 1980], 56–58).

4. Ibid., 41.

5. Ibid., 47. In the preceding chapter I have attempted to show the problems with this conventional notion that Gal 1–2 deals entirely with matters of self-defense.

6. See the preceding chapter.

7. On the relationship between the exhortations of Gal 5–6 and the theological argument in chapters 1–4, see Richard B. Hays, "Christology and Ethics in Galatians: The Law of Christ," *CBQ* 49 (1987): 268–90.

8. I take this methodological point to be consistent with George Kennedy's comment that Paul's audience would have anticipated that the argument in the letter would develop in a linear manner (*New Testament Interpretation through Rhetorical Criticism* [Chapel Hill: University of North Carolina Press, 1984], 5, 146).

9. So also J. Louis Martyn, who writes: "And even in the parts of Galatians that are heavily concerned with the Law, it is clear that Paul's theological point of departure is not the Law, but rather the advent of Christ, and specifically Christ's faithful death" ("Paul and His Jewish-Christian Interpreters," *USQR* 42 [1988]: 4).

10. The phrase "the singularity of the gospel" comes from John Schütz's discussion of Galatians in *Paul and the Anatomy of Apostolic Authority* (SNTSMS 26; Cambridge: Cambridge University Press, 1975), 121. In my judgment students of Paul have seriously neglected that work, in part at least because Schütz was several years ahead of the discussion of Paul in the context of the social sciences. On the issue of transformation in Paul, see John T. Koenig, "The Motif of Transformation in the Pauline Epistles: A History-of-Religions/Exegetical Study" (PhD diss., Union Theological Seminary, New York, 1970); B. R. Gaventa, *From Darkness to Light: Aspects of Conversion in the New Testament* (OBT 20; Philadelphia: Fortress, 1986), 40–46.

11. This is consistent with the methodological procedure employed by Jouette Bassler in her study of Paul's use of the axiom of divine impartiality (*Divine Impartiality: Paul and a Theological Axiom* [SBLDS 59; Chico, CA: Scholars Press, 1982]). Bassler rightly contends that instead of assuming that traditional formulations reveal nothing of Paul's own thought, students of Paul need to attend to the way in which he uses those traditional affirmations.

12. I want it to be clear that I introduce this scenario entirely for heuristic purposes. It is not my intention to suggest that a "compromise party" ever existed, but I contend that the question I ascribe to such an imaginary group does logically follow from the letter itself.

13. This understanding of the παιδαγωγός image in Gal 3 is influenced by the work of David J. Lull in "'The Law Was Our Pedagogue': A Study in Galatians 3:19–25," *JBL* 105 (1986): 481–98. See also Norman H. Young, "*Paidagogos:* The Social Setting of a Pauline Metaphor," *NovT* 29 (1987): 150–76.

14. Kennedy, *Rhetorical Criticism*, 151.

15. N. T. Wright helpfully distinguishes between the way in which an individual arrives at a conclusion and the arguments that same individual may employ when demonstrating that conclusion to others ("Putting Paul Together Again," in *Thessalonians, Philippians, Galatians, Philemon* [ed. Jouette M. Bassler; vol. 1 of *Pauline Theology*; Minneapolis: Fortress, 1991], 192–94). Of course, Paul would insist that he did not choose this position; it was chosen for him (Gal 1:11–17).

16. Here I am clearly influenced by the argument of E. P. Sanders that for Paul the solution precedes the problem (*Paul and Palestinian Judaism* [Philadelphia: Fortress, 1977], 442–47). To put it as Sanders does elsewhere: "Paul's various statements about the law are not the result of theoretical thought about the law as such, but spring from and serve other convictions. The main lines of his discussions about the law are determined by christology, soteriology (especially their universal aspects), and what we may call Christian behavior" (*Paul, the Law, and the Jewish People* [Philadelphia: Fortress, 1983], 143).

17. It has, of course, been argued that νόμος Χριστοῦ (Gal 6:1) refers to just such a law, appropriate for the messianic age (C. H. Dodd, "ENNOMOS CHRISTOU," in *More New Testament Studies* [Manchester: Manchester University Press, 1968], 134–48; W. D. Davies, *Paul and Rabbinic Judaism* [4th ed.; Philadelphia: Fortress, 1980], 142–45). The expression is better understood, however, as an ironic formulation designed to counter Paul's opponents (Hays, "Christology and Ethics," 275).

18. To some this will appear to be an exaggerated statement. It may be that Paul was himself psychologically constructed such that he could not compromise, or it may be that he perceived a threat to the boundary of the community and hence would not compromise for a social reason. I do not imply that such investigations are inappropriate; however, the reasoning that Gal 3 makes available to us is theological reasoning.

19. T. L. Donaldson revives the thesis that Paul's understanding of the incompatibility between Christ and the law may be traced to the period prior to his conversion ("Zealot and Convert: The Origin of Paul's Christ Torah Antithesis," *CBQ* 51 [1989]: 655–82).

20. On the issue of the "story" of Jesus that underlies Galatians, see Richard B. Hays, *The Faith of Jesus Christ: An Investigation of the Narrative Substructure of Galatians 3:1–4:11* (SBLDS 56; Chico, CA: Scholars Press, 1983). Jouette Bassler early on drew attention to some limitations of this term ("Paul's Theology: Whence and Whither?" in *1 and 2 Corinthians* [ed. David M. Hay; vol. 2 of *Pauline Theology*; Minneapolis: Fortress, 1993], 7–9). Conversation about the use of the category of "story" or "narrative" for Paul continues; see especially

Narrative Dynamics in Paul: A Critical Assessment (ed. Bruce W. Longenecker; Louisville: Westminster John Knox, 2002).

21. So also Hays, "Christology and Ethics," 277 n. 28.

22. More extensive discussion of this reading of 1:11–17 may be found in the previous chapter.

23. So also Hays, "Christology and Ethics," 276–83, 289–90.

24. Kennedy notes that in the epilogue Paul sums up what he believes he has demonstrated with these words: "Neither circumcision counts for anything nor uncircumcision, but a new creation" (*Rhetorical Criticism,* 151).

25. On the conclusion of Galatians, I have been greatly helped by the paper Charles B. Cousar presented at the 1989 SBL meeting, "Galatians 6:11–18: Interpretive Clues to the Letter."

26. Betz, *Galatians,* 29.

27. To be sure, both 2:20 ("Christ lives in me") and the numerous references to the activity of the Spirit reflect Paul's conviction about the resurrection of Jesus, but the letter makes few explicit references to the resurrection. Beker notes "the virtual absence of the resurrection of Christ" in this letter (*Paul the Apostle,* 58).

28. G. M. Taylor, "The Function of PISTIS CHRISTOU in Galatians," *JBL* 85 (1966): 58–76; George Howard, "On the Faith of Christ," *HTR* 60 (1967): 459–84; idem, "The 'Faith of Christ,'" *ExpTim* 85 (1974): 212–15; L. T. Johnson, "Romans 3:21–26 and the Faith of Jesus," *CBQ* 44 (1982): 77–90; Hays, *Faith of Jesus Christ,* 139–76; Sam K. Williams, "Again Pistis Christou," *CBQ* 49 (1987): 431–47; Morna D. Hooker, "ΠΙΣΤΙΣ ΧΡΙΣΤΟΥ," *NTS* 35 (1989): 321–42.

29. The first-person singular here refers not only to Paul but also to believers in general.

30. Richard Hays, *Echoes of Scripture in the Letters of Paul* (New Haven, CT: Yale University Press, 1989).

31. Francis Watson, *Paul and the Hermeneutics of Faith* (London: T&T Clark, 2004), 16.

CHAPTER 8. "GOD HANDED THEM OVER"

1. See, for example, Morna Hooker, "Adam in Romans 1," *NTS* 6 (1959–60): 297–306; Jacob Jervell, *Imago Dei: Gen 1:26f im Spätjudentum, in der Gnosis und in den paulinischen Briefen* (FRLANT NS 58; Göttingen: Vandenhoeck & Ruprecht, 1950), 312–31; J. D. G. Dunn, *Romans 1–8* (WBC 38A; Dallas: Word, 1988), 53; idem, *The Theology of Paul the Apostle* (Grand Rapids: Eerdmans, 1998), 91, although Dunn here concedes that the view has not been widely endorsed. A. J. M. Wedderburn is often cited on this point, although he actually concludes that it is Gen 1, not Gen 3, that might be echoed in Rom 1:18–32; see "Adam in Paul's Letter to the Romans," StudBib *1978* (1980): 413–30, esp. 416.

2. Brendan Byrne, *Romans* (SP; Collegeville, MN: Liturgical Press, 1996), 64–65; Joseph A. Fitzmyer, *Romans* (AB 33; New York: Doubleday, 1993), 272.

3. Stanley Stowers rightly observes that God's role in this passage has been underrepresented in the discussion, although he does not address it himself in any significant way (*A Rereading of Romans: Justice, Jews, and Gentiles* [New Haven, CT: Yale University Press, 1994], 93).

4. On the expression "anti-God powers," see J. Louis Martyn, *Galatians* (AB 33A; New York: Doubleday, 1997), 370–73.

5. The verb παραδίδωμι does appear in Wis 14:15, but it refers there to the handing over of an image from father to child.

6. *Jub.* 21:22 might be regarded as an exception to this statement; however, the context is one of a general warning about sin in Abraham's farewell to Isaac and so seems quite remote from Rom 1.

7. Chrysostom, *Homilies on the Acts of the Apostles and the Epistle to the Romans* (*NPNF*[1] 11; Edinburgh: T&T Clark, 1889), 354; Ulrich Wilckens, *Der Brief an die Römer* (EKKNT 6.1; Zurich: Benziger, 1978), 108; Paul Achtemeier, *Romans* (Interpretation; Atlanta: John Knox, 1985), 40; Dunn, *Romans 1–8*, 73; Fitzmyer, *Romans*, 284; Peter Stuhlmacher, *Paul's Letter to the Romans* (Louisville: Westminster John Knox, 1994); N. T. Wright, *Romans* (*NIB* 12; Nashville: Abingdon, 2002), 433.

8. Augustine, *Augustine on Romans: Propositions from the Epistle to the Romans; Unfinished Commentary on the Epistle to the Romans* (SBLTT 23; Chico, CA: Scholars Press, 1982), 59. Luther appears to take this position, although Luther also indicates that God's withdrawal permits the activity of the devil to take control (*Lectures on Romans* [Luther's Works 25; St. Louis: Concordia Publishing House, 1972], 160–61). Calvin also combines the notion of God's withdrawal with the notion of judgment and identifies Satan as the minister of God's wrath (*The Epistles of Paul the Apostle to the Romans and to the Thessalonians* [Calvin's NT Commentaries; Grand Rapids: Eerdmans, 1960], 35). See also C. H. Dodd, *The Epistle of Paul to the Romans* [Moffatt; London: Hodder & Stoughton, 1932], 29; Ernst Käsemann, *Commentary on Romans* (Grand Rapids: Eerdmans, 1980), 47.

9. For example, C. E. B. Cranfield contends that this was "a deliberate act of judgment and mercy on the part of God who smites in order to heal" (*The Epistle to the Romans* [ICC; Edinburgh: T&T Clark, 1975], 120–21. Cranfield mentions and rejects the view that God "actually impelled men to uncleanness" (ibid., 121), although he does not give a source for it. See also the commentaries of Sanday and Headlam, Schlatter, Moule, Barrett, and Moo.

10. The connotation of handing over to the power of another person is noted by Brendan Byrne, although he does not develop it (*Romans*, 75).

11. P.Hib. 92.11, 17; P.Lille 3.59; P.Tebt. 38.6; Herodotus, *Histories* 1.45.1; 3.13.3; Xenophon, *Cyropaedia* 5.1.28; 5.4.51; Pausanias, *Description of Greece* 1.2.1. See the discussions in BDAG, LSJ, and MM.

12. See also Josh 10:32; 11:6, 8; 21:44; 24:8, 10, 11, 33.

13. Job 2:6 offers a fascinating and important exception to this generalization, since most commentators agree that, although God delivers Job to the Satan (in the LXX, ὁ διάβολος), the Satan is not an enemy but an aspect of the divine itself. Yet the *Testament of Job*, among other texts, shows that the tradition early on identifies the action of the Satan as hostile.

14. I might well bring 1 Cor 13:3 and 2 Cor 4:11 into this discussion. In addition, I deliberately set aside for now the appearance of the verb in Rom 4:25; 6:17; and 8:32, although I shall return to those texts briefly below.

15. This similarity is noted by Neil Richardson in *Paul's Language about God* (JSNTSup 99; Sheffield: Sheffield Academic Press, 1994), 108.

16. So also BDAG, 329; MM, 210; H. A. A. Kennedy, "Two Exegetical Notes on St. Paul," *ExpTim* 28 (1916–17): 322–23.

17. On the relationship between "desire" and the *yeṣer haraʿ*, see Joel Marcus, "The Evil Inclination in the Letters of Paul," *IBS* 8 (1986): 8–21; and Martyn, *Galatians*, 291–92, 528–29.

18. I am grateful to David Downs for his early suggestions to me on this point. See the discussion of impurity and the demonic in Todd Klutz, *The Exorcism Stories in Luke–Acts* (SNTSMS 129; Cambridge: Cambridge University Press, 2004), 125–37.

19. Dodd, *Romans*, 29.

20. H. C. G. Moule, *The Epistle to the Romans* (Cambridge Bible; London: Pickering & Inglis, n.d.), 49.

21. So also Douglas Moo, *Romans* (NICNT; Grand Rapids: Eerdmans, 1996), 111.

22. "Man for Paul is never just on his own. He is always a specific piece of world and therefore becomes what in the last resort he is by determination from outside, i.e., by the power which takes possession of him and the lordship to which he surrenders himself," writes Ernst Käsemann, "Primitive Christian Apocalyptic," in *New Testament Questions of Today* (Philadelphia: Fortress, 1969), 136.

23. On this point, see the important work of Martinus C. de Boer, *The Defeat of Death: Apocalyptic Eschatology in 1 Corinthians 15 and Romans 5* (JSNTSup 22; Sheffield: JSOT Press, 1988); idem, "Paul and Apocalyptic Eschatology," *The Origins of Apocalypticism in Judaism and Christianity* (ed. John J. Collins; vol. 1 of *The Encyclopedia of Apocalypticism*; New York: Continuum, 1998), 345–83.

24. I simply cannot understand Dunn's comment that Paul has little to say about the "heavenly powers" and that the references in Rom 8:38–39 and 1 Cor 15:24 "look as though they were added almost for effect," that Paul did not have "a very strong, or at least very clear, belief regarding these heavenly powers" (*Theology of Paul the Apostle*, 109). A similar position was argued by Wesley Carr

in *Angels and Principalities: The Background, Meaning, and Development of the Pauline Phrase "hai archai kai hai exousiai"* (SNTSMS 42; Cambridge; Cambridge University Press, 1981). For important arguments to the contrary, see G. H. C. MacGregor, "Principalities and Powers: The Cosmic Background of Paul's Thought," *NTS* 1 (1954–55): 17–28; and G. B. Caird, *Principalities and Powers: A Study in Pauline Theology* (Oxford: Clarendon, 1956).

25. This point is sharply made in the excellent essay by MacGregor, "Principalities and Powers."

26. Martin Dibelius, *Geisterwelt im Glauben des Paulus* (Göttingen: Vandenhoeck & Ruprecht, 1909), 119–24.

27. J. Christiaan Beker, *Paul the Apostle* (Philadelphia: Fortress, 1980), 215.

28. Heikki Räisänen, *Paul and the Law* (WUNT 29; Tübingen: J. C. B. Mohr, 1983), 97–101; E. P. Sanders, *Paul, the Law, and the Jewish People* (Philadelphia: Fortress, 1983), 125.

29. Bruce N. Kaye, *The Thought Structure of Romans with Special Reference to Chapter 6* (Austin, TX: Scholars Press, 1979), 56.

30. Günter Röhser, *Metaphorik und Personifikation der Sünde* (WUNT 2.25; Tübingen: J. C. B. Mohr, 1987).

31. Stowers, *Rereading Romans*, 176–89; Troels Engberg-Pedersen, *Paul and the Stoics* (Louisville: Westminster John Knox, 2000), 200–216. The recent volume of T. L. Carter, *Paul and the Power of Sin: Redefining 'Beyond the Pale'* (SNTSMS 115; Cambridge: Cambridge University Press, 2002), attempts to interpret Paul's treatment of Sin as a response to specific social circumstances concerning Gentile believers.

32. Richardson also notes this connection (*Paul's Language about God*, 258).

33. The connection between 1:18–32 and 11:32 is noted also by Richardson, *Paul's Language about God*, 87. Note also that "handing over" of humanity figures positively in 6:17: "Thanks be to God that you were slaves of Sin but you obeyed from the heart the type of teaching *to which you were handed over*." This statement reinforces the contention that Paul does not imagine a humanity on its own, free to make a choice with regard to the gospel. These former slaves of Sin have been "handed over," presumably again by God, to a new teaching, to which they are obedient.

34. Charles B. Cousar, *A Theology of the Cross: The Death of Jesus in the Pauline Letters* (OBT; Minneapolis: Fortress, 1990), 56–66.

35. The parallel between παρέδωκεν in 1:24, 26, 28 and 8:32 is noted also by Richardson, *Paul's Language about God*, 258.

36. The words of G. H. C. MacGregor are apposite: Paul "looked back to that defeat as having been already accomplished by God in Christ through the Cross. There the powers had been defeated once for all in what can only be thought of as an act of cosmic redemption" ("Principalities and Powers," 28).

37. Cousar, *A Theology of the Cross*; de Boer, *The Defeat of Death*.

CHAPTER 9. THE COSMIC POWER OF SIN IN ROMANS

1. The statement is from the closing paragraph in Gustaf Aulén's *Christus Victor* (London: SPCK, 1931). The context makes it clear that Aulén understands the triumph to be accomplished by God.

2. Note, however, that the word group is proportionately more pervasive in the far briefer 1 John, which employs the word *hamartia* and its cognates a combination of 27 times.

3. Stanley Stowers, *A Rereading of Romans: Justice, Jews, and Gentiles* (New Haven: Yale University Press, 1994), 184, emphasis added. The focus on Gentiles in the quotation is deliberate. Stowers largely follows a line of interpretation developed by Lloyd Gaston and John Gager, arguing that Israel continues to be related to God through the covenant and the law, while the Gentiles require salvation through the gospel. See the illuminating reviews by Richard Hays, *CRBR* 9 (1996): 27–44; and John Barclay, *JBL* 115 (1996): 365–68.

4. Troels Engberg-Pedersen, *Paul and the Stoics* (Louisville: Westminster John Knox, 2000), 207, emphasis in the original. See the important review by J. Louis Martyn in *JSNT* 86 (2002): 61–102.

5. It is necessary to read those earlier commentators with care. In Stowers (*Rereading*, 143), C. E. B. Cranfield serves as an example because Cranfield writes that Paul implies "that all contemporary Jews are guilty of the evils" described in Rom 2. Yet Cranfield's very next sentence runs as follows: "It is anyway of course quite certain that there were many Jews in Paul's day who were not guilty of theft, adultery or temple-robbing (or sacrilege), in the ordinary sense of the words" (*The Epistle to the Romans* [2 vols.; ICC; Edinburgh: T&T Clark, 1975, 1979], 1:168).

6. Stowers, *Rereading Romans*, 176.

7. On the anti-God powers and their role in Paul's thinking, see J. Louis Martyn, *Galatians* (AB 33A; New York: Doubleday, 1997), 370–73.

8. Prominent earlier advocates of an interpretation of Romans in the context of apocalyptic theology are Ernst Käsemann (*Commentary on Romans* [Grand Rapids: Eerdmans, 1980]), and J. Christiaan Beker (*Paul the Apostle* [Philadelphia: Fortress, 1980]).

9. Excellent examples of the differences between wide-screen or letterboxed versions and pan-and-scan editing can be viewed at www.widescreen.org.

10. In Rom 7:8 and 11, Paul writes that Sin seized the law as an *aphormē*, which the NRSV translates as an "opportunity." A stronger translation is needed, given that the term refers to the starting point for an expedition (BDAG, 158).

11. Note, however, that the verb *hamartanein* occurs at 2:12.

12. For a suggestive interpretation of idolatry, particularly in relationship to the Holocaust and to the sexual abuse of children, see Alistair McFadyen, *Bound to Sin: Abuse, Holocaust, and the Christian Doctrine of Sin* (Cambridge: Cambridge University Press, 2000).

13. One of the many unfortunate by-products of the various denominational wars on homosexuality is that discussion of this passage has been confined to questions of sexuality. That debate thereby obscures Paul's powerful depiction of a humankind that refuses to acknowledge God or its own status as creature. The preoccupation with a single issue also conveniently blocks out the penetrating question of how our own denial of God comes to expression.

14. The verb *paradidōmi* sometimes appears in contexts having to do with giving someone or something up to a hostile foe, as in a military context; see chapter 8 in this volume.

15. See particularly Wis 13:1–9 and 14:22–31. A good discussion of the connections between this passage and earlier Jewish attitudes toward non-Jews appears in Joseph A. Fitzmyer, *Romans* (AB 33; New York: Doubleday, 1993), 269–90.

16. Romans 16:1 recommends Phoebe to the recipients of the letter, which surely means that she is the bearer of it, the one who will read it, and thereby its first interpreter.

17. Paul W. Meyer, "Romans," in *HarperCollins Bible Commentary* (ed. James L. Mays et al.; rev. ed; New York: HarperCollins, 2000), 1045; now available also in *The Word in This World: Essays in New Testament Exegesis and Theology* (ed. John T. Carroll; NTL; Louisville: Westminster John Knox, 2004), 165.

18. On this construction and its importance, especially in Galatians, see Martyn, *Galatians*, 370–72.

19. The noun *thanatos* appears in the undisputed Pauline letters 45 times, 22 of which are in Romans.

20. On the role of death, particularly in the larger context of Paul's apocalyptic theology, see Martinus C. de Boer, *The Defeat of Death: Apocalyptic Eschatology in 1 Corinthians 15 and Romans 5* (JSNTSup 22; Sheffield: JSOT Press, 1988); idem., "Paul, Theologian of God's Apocalypse," *Int* 56 (2002): 21–33.

21. "The central protagonist in the whole of 7:7–25—not just in vv. 7–12—the adversary of that "I," is not the law at all but sin as a personified power" (Paul W. Meyer, "The Worm at the Core of the Apple: Exegetical Reflections on Romans 7," in *The Conversation Continues: Studies in Paul and John in Honor of J. Louis Martyn* (ed. R. T. Fortna and Beverly R. Gaventa; Nashville: Abingdon, 1990), 62–84, quotation on 73; now available also in *The Word in This World*, 57–77.

22. Instead of imagining that Paul employs several different connotations for the word "law" in this single passage ("torah" versus "norm" or "custom"), Meyer takes the expression "law of Sin" as a possessive referring to the law insofar as it is under Sin's control or in Sin's possession (ibid., 76–80). See the further development of this point in J. Louis Martyn, "Nomos Plus Genitive Noun in Paul: The History of God's Law," in *Early Christianity and Classical Culture: Comparative Studies in Honor of Abraham J. Malherbe* (ed. John T. Fitzgerald, Thomas H. Olbricht, and L. Michael White; NovTSup 110; Leiden: Brill, 2003), 575–87.

23. Ibid., p. 74.

24. On this much-disputed topic of God's righteousness, a helpful introduction is that of Charles B. Cousar, *The Letters of Paul* (Nashville: Abingdon, 1996), 108–12.

25. My indebtedness here in particular to the work of Ernst Käsemann, J. Christiaan Beker, and J. Louis Martyn will be evident.

26. Because the word "Satan" does not appear elsewhere in Romans, and because the letter has made no earlier reference to a group of deceivers or dissenters, it is sometimes suggested that 16:17–20 is an interpolation into the letter. There is, however, no manuscript evidence in support of that suggestion (see J. D. G. Dunn, *Romans 9–16* [WBC 38B; Dallas: Word, 1988], 901; Fitzmyer, *Romans*, 745).

27. See, for example, 1 Chron 21:1; Job 1–2; Zech 3:1–2; *1 En.* 53:3; 54:6. Paul does use the word "Satan" elsewhere; see 1 Cor 5:5; 7:5; 2 Cor 2:11; 11:14; 12:7; 1 Thess 2:18.

28. Engberg-Pedersen, *Paul and the Stoics*, 17.

29. Andrew Delbanco, *The Death of Satan: How Americans Have Lost the Sense of Evil* (New York: Farrar, Straus & Giroux, 1995), 4.

30. Ibid., 234.

CHAPTER 10. THE APOCALYPTIC COMMUNITY

1. This absence of explicit reference to *ekklēsia* was so striking to Günter Klein that he argued Paul thought there was not yet a church in Rome because no apostolic preaching had taken place there; see "Paul's Purpose in Writing the Epistle to the Romans," in *The Romans Debate* (ed. Karl P. Donfried; rev. and exp. ed.; Peabody, MA: Hendrickson, 1991), 29–43.

2. Judith Lieu, *Christian Identity in the Jewish and Graeco-Roman World* (Oxford: Oxford University Press, 2004), 62. Italics added.

3. J. Louis Martyn, *Galatians* (AB 33A; New York: Doubleday, 1997), 22.

4. John T. Dickson, "Gospel as News: εὐαγγελ-from Aristophanes to the Apostle Paul," *NTS* 51 (2005): 212–30.

5. Martinus de Boer, *The Defeat of Death: Apocalyptic Eschatology in 1 Corinthians 15 and Romans 5* (JSNTSup 22; Sheffield: JSOT Press, 1988).

6. Eugene Boring, "The Language of Universal Salvation in Paul," *JBL* 105 (1986): 283.

7. BDAG, s.v.; see also Barbara Hall, "Battle Imagery in Paul's Letters" (PhD diss., Union Theological Seminary, New York, 1973).

8. On this passage, see chapter 4 above.

9. Interestingly, Philip Esler makes this same observation about the absence of what he terms a "myth of future world transformation and deliverance," but he does so as part of an argument that the future redemption grows organically out of the present (*Conflict and Identity in Romans: The Social Setting of Paul's Gospel* [Minneapolis: Fortress, 2002], 249–67).

10. Compare Richard Bauckham's suggestive comment that the Seer of the Apocalypse and his readers are "taken up into heaven in order to see the world from the heavenly perspective. . . . The effect of John's visions, one might say, is to expand his readers' world, both spatially (into heaven) and temporally (into the eschatological future)" (*The Theology of the Book of Revelation* [Cambridge: Cambridge University Press, 1997], 7).

11. Space does not permit a fuller consideration here of the lists of Rom 8:35 and 8:38–39. Brendan Byrne suggests that the former list is the "manifestation of the hostility of super-human forces listed later on" (*Romans* [SP; Collegeville, MN: Liturgical Press, 1996], 277).

12. On the phrase "children of God" in the Septuagint, see Sylvia Keesmaat, *Paul and His Story: (Re)Interpreting the Exodus Tradition* (JSNTSup 181; Sheffield: Sheffield Academic Press, 1999), 136–43. Also see chapter 4 above.

13. J. Ross Wagner, *Heralds of the Good News: Isaiah and Paul "in Concert" in the Letter to the Romans* (NovTSup 101; Leiden: Brill, 2002), 47.

14. Eldon Jay Epp, *Junia: The First Woman Apostle* (Minneapolis: Fortress, 2005).

15. On the relationship of Rom 12 to Rom 5–7, see Thomas H. Tobin, *Paul's Rhetoric in Its Contexts: The Argument of Romans* (Peabody, MA: Hendrickson, 2004), 388.

16. See Margaret Y. MacDonald's argument that Paul's response to the world is "sectarian" and that the Pauline community is a "conversionist sect" that remains separate from the world (*The Pauline Churches: A Socio-historical Study of Institutionalization in the Pauline and Deutero-Pauline Writings* [SNTSMS 60; Cambridge: Cambridge University Press, 1988], 83).

17. Lieu, *Christian Identity in the Jewish and Graeco-Roman World*, 100.

18. Victor Paul Furnish, "Uncommon Love and the Common Good: Christians as Citizens in the Letters of Paul," in *In Search of the Common Good* (ed. Dennis P. McCann and Patrick D. Miller; New York: T&T Clark, 2005), 63.

19. Ibid., 64. See also Victor Paul Furnish, "Inside Looking Out: Some Pauline Views of the Unbelieving Public," in *Pauline Conversations in Context: Essays in Honor of Calvin J. Roetzel* (ed. Janice Capel Anderson, Philip Sellew, and Claudia Setzer; JSNTSup221; Sheffield: Sheffield Academic Press, 2002), 104–24.

20. Boring, "Language of Universal Salvation," esp. 283–85; Charles B. Cousar, "Continuity and Discontinuity: Reflections on Romans 5–8," in *Romans* (ed. David Hay and E. Elizabeth Johnson; vol. 3 of *Pauline Theology*; Minneapolis: Fortress, 1995), 203–4.

21. Two examples: Rom 2:25–29 appears to destabilize the very notion of "circumcision" and "uncircumcision." Here I am influenced by John Barclay, "Paul and Philo on Circumcision: Romans 2.25–29 in Social and Cultural Context," *NTS* 44 [1998]: 536–66. And, in 14:1–23, while exhorting the "strong" to make way for the concerns of the "weak," Paul nevertheless radically undermines the argument of the "weak" by declaring that all food is clean. Again, I am helped

by John Barclay, "'Do We Undermine the Law?' A Study of Romans 14.1–15.6," in *Paul and the Mosaic Law* (ed. James D. G. Dunn; Grand Rapids: Eerdmans, 1996), 287–308.

22. I take this to be consistent with Ernst Käsemann's observation that Paul's "ecclesiology is part of the apostle's theology of the cross and to that degree can only be understood in the light of his Christology" ("The Theological Problem Presented by the Motif of the Body of Christ," *Perspectives on Paul* [Philadelphia: Fortress, 1971], 114).

CHAPTER 11. THE GOD WHO WILL NOT BE TAKEN FOR GRANTED

1. Donald Juel, *A Master of Surprise: Mark Interpreted* (Minneapolis: Fortress, 1994), 120.

2. Ibid., 35–36.

3. Ibid., 120.

4. For a concise review of the problems involved in any such comparison, a cogent argument in favor of comparing the theologies of Mark and Paul, and an inviting example of that conversation, see C. Clifton Black, "Christ Crucified in Paul and in Mark: Reflections on an Intracanonical Conversation," in *Theology and Ethics in Paul and His Interpreters: Essays in Honor of Victor Paul Furnish* (ed. Eugene H. Lovering Jr. and Jerry L. Sumney; Nashville: Abingdon, 1995), 184–206.

5. For some orientation to the scholarly conversation, see Karl P. Donfried, ed., *The Romans Debate* (rev. and expanded; Peabody, MA: Hendrickson, 1991); James C. Miller, "The Romans Debate: 1991–2001," *Currents in Research* 9 (2001): 306–349.

6. Nils Dahl, "The Neglected Factor in New Testament Theology," in *Jesus the Christ: The Historical Origins of Christological Doctrine* (ed. Donald H. Juel; Minneapolis: Fortress, 1991),153–63. This essay originally appeared in *Reflections* 75 (1975): 5–8. An important exception to this comment about the neglect of God in the study of Romans is the work of Halvor Moxnes, *Theology in Conflict: Studies in Paul's Understanding of God in Romans* (NovTSup 53; Leiden: Brill, 1980). More recently, see Neil Richardson, *Paul's Language about God* (JSNTSup 99; Sheffield: Sheffield Academic Press, 1999), esp. 26–94 and 308–15; and Richard B. Hays, "The God of Mercy Who Rescues Us from the Present Evil Age," in *The Forgotten God: Perspectives in Biblical Theology* (ed. A. Andrew Das and Frank J. Matera; Louisville: Westminster John Knox, 2002), 123–43.

7. J. D. G. Dunn, *The Theology of Paul the Apostle* (Grand Rapids: Eerdmans, 1998). On the privileging of Romans in discussions of Pauline theology, see especially 25–26. Dunn earlier defended this methodological starting point in "In Quest of Paul's Theology: Retrospect and Prospect," in *Looking Back, Pressing On* (ed. E. Elizabeth Johnson and David M. Hay; vol. 4 of *Pauline Theology*; Symposium Series; Atlanta: Society of Biblical Literature, 1997), 95–115. See

also the trenchant critique by Steven J. Kraftchick, "An Asymptotic Response to Dunn's Retrospective and Proposals," in *Looking Back, Pressing On*, 116–39.

8. Dunn, *The Theology of Paul the Apostle*, 29.

9. Ibid., 185.

10. Ibid., 18, 713–16.

11. Ibid., 729–30.

12. Francis Watson, "The Triune Divine Identity: Reflections on Pauline God-Language, in Disagreement with J. D. G. Dunn," *JSNT* 80 (2000): 99–124. See also the review by Douglas Campbell for an account of the implied "contract" view of Christianity in Dunn's view of Paul ("The ΔΙΑΘΗΚΗ from Durham: Professor Dunn's *The Theology of Paul the Apostle*" [*JSNT* 72 (1998): 91–111]). It is, of course, a sign of the importance of Dunn's work that it generates such extended critique and conversation.

13. Dunn, *The Theology of Paul the Apostle*, 31–50.

14. To be sure, the promise to Abraham might render this move from promise to Israel to offering to the Gentiles less than startling, but it is interesting that Paul does not refer to Abraham here. The juxtaposition of Scripture's promise and the obedience of the Gentiles remains unexplained.

15. E. P. Sanders, *Paul and Palestinian Judaism: A Comparison of Patterns of Religion* (Philadelphia: Fortress, 1977), 442–47. As J. Louis Martyn has observed, Sanders's point was anticipated in Barth's *Church Dogmatics* (*Galatians* [AB 33A; New York: Doubleday, 1997], 95).

16. Leander Keck, "What Makes Romans Tick?" in *Romans* (ed. David M. Hay and E. Elizabeth Johnson; vol. 3 of *Pauline Theology*; Minneapolis: Fortress), 25. The following section owes much to Keck's analysis, although my attention is to God's actions more than to the spiral of human captivity.

17. The NRSV perpetuates the translation of *pistis Iēsou Christou* as an objective genitive, reflecting faith "about" or "in" Jesus Christ. Many contemporary scholars, myself included, favor translating the phrase here and elsewhere as a subjective genitive referring to the faithfulness or obedience of Jesus. The literature is extensive; see especially George Howard, "On the 'Faith of Christ,'" *HTR* 60 (1967): 459–65; Luke T. Johnson, "Romans 3:21–26 and the Faith of Jesus," *CBQ* 44 (1982):77–90; Morna Hooker, "PISTIS CHRISTOU," *NTS* 35 (1989): 321–42; Richard B. Hays, "ΠΙΣΤΙΣ and Pauline Christology: What Is at Stake?" in *Romans* (vol. 3 of *Pauline Theology*), 35–60; J. D. G. Dunn, "Once More, ΠΙΣΤΙΣ ΧΡΙΣΤΟΥ," in *Romans* (vol. 3 of *Pauline Theology*), 61–81. Even if the phrase is taken as a subjective genitive, however, the next phrase quite explicitly concerns "all who believe."

18. On this passage and 2 Cor 5:16–17, see J. Louis Martyn, "Epistemology at the Turn of the Ages," *Theological Issues in the Letters of Paul* (Nashville: Abingdon, 1997), 89–110.

19. An important exception to this generalization is Paul W. Meyer, who comments that "faith cannot mean some prerequisite condition to be fulfilled by

human beings before God can act" ("Romans," *HarperCollins Bible Commentary* [ed. James L. Mays et al.; rev. ed.; New York: HarperCollins, 2000], 1048). Meyer's elegant commentary on Romans is now available in Paul W. Meyer, *The Word in This World: Essays in New Testament Exegesis and Theology* (ed. John T. Carroll; NTL; Louisville: Westminster John Knox, 2004), 151–218.

20. Brendan Byrne, *Romans* (SP; Collegeville, MN: Liturgical Press, 1996), 127. For similar observations, see J. A. Fitzmyer, *Romans* (AB 33; New York: Doubleday, 1993), 342, 350; Douglas J. Moo, *The Epistle to the Romans* (NICNT; Grand Rapids: Eerdmans, 1996), 224–26.

21. Dunn, *The Theology of Paul the Apostle*, 379.

22. See especially M. Eugene Boring, "The Language of Universal Salvation in Paul," *JBL* 105 (1986): 269–92; and Richard H. Bell, "Rom 5.18–19 and Universal Salvation," *NTS* 48 (2002): 417–32. Both of these fine studies draw distinctions among various realms in Paul's discourse. Boring identifies statements regarding a limited scope of salvation as reflecting the image of God as judge and those regarding universal salvation as reflecting the image of God as king (see esp. 291). Bell understands the inclusive statements in Rom 5 as reflecting a "mythical perspective," as distinguished from the historical framework employed in Rom 11:25–32 (see esp. 430).

23. Charles B. Cousar, "Continuity and Discontinuity: Reflections on Romans 5–8," in *Romans* (vol. 3 of *Pauline Theology*), 203–4.

24. By contrast, see Stanley Stowers's claim that Rom 5–8 has to do with the way in which Gentiles "obtain obedience," not with "a scheme of sin and salvation" (*A Rereading of Romans: Justice, Jews, and Gentiles* [New Haven, CT: Yale University Press, 1994], 251).

25. The literature on Rom 9–11 is enormous. A few important recent works that address the question of God's faithfulness include Paul Meyer, "Romans," 1060–66; E. Elizabeth Johnson, "Romans 9–11: The Faithfulness and Impartiality of God," *Romans* (vol. 3 of *Pauline Theology*), 211–39; Douglas Moo, "The Theology of Romans 9–11," *Romans* (vol. 3 of *Pauline Theology*), 240–58.

26. Wayne Meeks, "On Trusting an Unpredictable God," in *In Search of the Early Christians* (ed. Allen R. Hilton and H. Gregory Snyder; New Haven, CT: Yale University Press, 2002), 213.

27. On the manifold voice of Isaiah in Rom 9–11, see the important recent work of J. Ross Wagner, *Heralds of Good News: Isaiah and Paul "in Concert" in the Letter to the Romans* (NovTSup; Leiden: Brill, 2002).

28. Confidence and certainty are not the same thing, as Wayne Meeks notes: "The reader [of Rom 9–11] is not allowed to think that confidence depends on knowing just how God will act in the future" ("On Trusting an Unpredictable God," 212).

29. Richardson, *Paul's Language about God*, 26–94.

30. See especially Wagner, *Heralds of Good News*, 126–57.

31. Meyer, "Romans," 1062.

32. To be sure, some Jewish texts anticipate not the redemption but the destruction of Gentiles as Israel's enemies. For an overview of the texts and related debates, see Terence L. Donaldson, *Paul and the Gentiles: Remapping the Apostle's Convictional World* (Minneapolis: Fortress, 1997), 69–74; E. P. Sanders, *Jesus and Judaism* (Philadelphia: Fortress, 1985), 77–119; idem, *Judaism: Practice and Belief, 63 BCE–66CE* (London: SCM, 1992), 291–92.

33. The scholarly literature on this section of the letter has given particular weight to deciphering the source of Paul's admonitions and the relationship (if any) between the content of this section and the situation at Rome. Such difficult questions necessarily lie outside the scope of this chapter.

34. Stowers, *Rereading Romans,* 318.

35. On the problem of separating Pauline theology from Pauline ethics, see especially J. Louis Martyn, "De-apocalypticizing Paul: An Essay Focused on *Paul and the Stoics* by Troels Engberg-Pedersen," *JSNT* 86 (2002): 61–102.

36. Fitzmyer, *Romans,* 640; Moo, *The Epistle to the Romans,* 750–51.

37. Ernst Käsemann, "Worship and Everyday Life," in *New Testament Questions of Today* (trans. W. J. Montague; Philadelphia: Fortress, 1969), 191.

38. Ibid., 192.

39. Paul W. Meyer, "Pauline Theology: A Proposal for a Pause in Its Pursuit," in *Looking Back, Pressing On* (vol. 4 of *Pauline Theology*), 140–60 (available also in *The Word in This World*, 95–116).

40. Ibid., 159.

Index of Ancient Sources

Index of Names

Polemo, 48
Pseudo-Ammonius, 23
Pseudo-Diogenes, 21

Quintilian, 48, 180n23

Räisänen, Heikki, 121, 197n28
Ramsay, W. M., 188n2
Rensburg, J. J. Janse van, 169n5
Reumann, John, 181n4, 182n16
Richard, Earl J., 166n8, 169n5
Richards, I. A., 25, 172nn27–28
Richardson, Neil, 155, 196n15, 197nn32–33, 35; 202n6, 204n29
Rickert, GailAnn, 182n14
Rigaux, Béda, 169n4
Ringgren, Helmer, 175n17
Robertson, Archibald, 177n2
Röhser, Günter, 121, 197n30
Rowling, J. K., 134

Sailors, Timothy B., 169n7, 170nn8, 13; 171n14
Sampley, J. P., 189n17
Sanday, William, 195n9
Sanders, E. P., 121, 152, 193n16, 197n28, 203n15, 205n32
Sanders, J. T., 189n7
Schäfer, Klaus, 179n18
Scheidel, Walter, 165n2
Schlatter, Adolf von, 195n9
Schlier, Heinrich, 173n4, 176n33, 177n2, 188n2
Schmithals, Walter, 190n24, 191n1
Schnackenburg, Rudolf, 178n4
Schneemelcher, Wilhelm, 168n29
Schrage, Wolfgang, 178n4
Schubert, Paul, 170n11
Schüssler Fiorenza, Elisabeth, 185n16
Schütz, John, 68, 185n17, 188n1, 189nn12, 16; 190n18, 192n10
Schweitzer, Albert, 83
Scott, James M., 183n28
Seneca, 97–98, 99, 191nn36–41
Shakespeare, 26
Socrates, 98
Sophocles, 172n23
Stegemann, Wolfgang, 171n20, 173n34
Stowers, Stanley, 121, 125–26, 157, 195n3, 197n31, 198nn3, 5–6; 204n24, 205n34

Stuhlmacher, Peter, 195n7
Sturm, Richard, 187n1
Sutter Rehmann, Luzia, 57, 183nn25–26

Tannehill, Robert, 190n22
Taylor, Brian, 189n11
Taylor, G. M., 194n28
Theocritus, 172n23
Theodoret, 168n32
Thurman, Howard, 63, 184n1
Thüsing, Wilhelm, 178n4
Tobin, Thomas H., 201n15
Tolkien, J. R. R., 134
Tröger, K. W., 174n16
Tulloch, Janet H., 173n1
Turner, Mark, 12, 167nn20–23
Tyson, J. B., 191n1

Venerable Bede, 168n32
Viard, A., 182n5

Wagner, J. Ross, 141, 201n13, 204nn27, 30
Walters, James C., 183n28
Ward, Ronald, 169n5
Warren, Austin, 172n31
Watson, Francis, 111, 150, 194n31, 203n12
Wedderburn, A. J. M., 194n1
Weima, Jeffrey A. D., 170n13
Weintraub, K. J., 96–97, 190n29
Wellek, Rene, 172n31
Wheelwright, Philip, 25, 172n29
Whitby, Daniel, 170n13
White, John L., 166n10
Wiedemann, Thomas, 171n22
Wilckens, Ulrich, 177n2, 181n5, 195n7
Williams, Sam K., 194n28
Williamson, Ronald, 178n5
Winkler, John J., 48, 166–67nn13–14; 180nn25–26
Wright, N. T., 52, 56, 57, 182n8, 183n24, 193n15, 195n7

Xenophon, 195n11

Yarbrough, O. Larry, 45–46, 179nn9, 19
Young, Norman H., 193n13

Zeitlin, Froma I., 167n13
Zimmer, F., 169n5, 172n24, 173n33